THE

WORLD

IS ON

FIRE

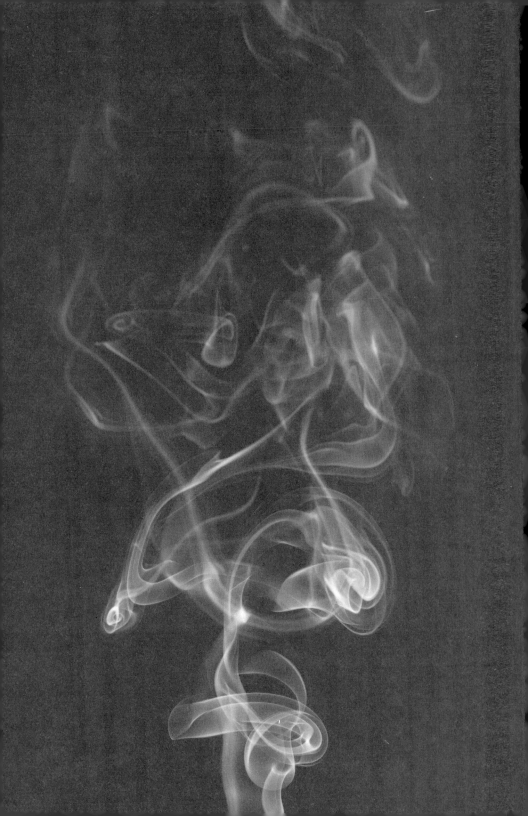

THE

WORLD

Scrap, Treasure, and Songs of the Apocalypse

IS ON

FIRE

Joni Tevis

MILKWEED EDITIONS

Published 2015 by Milkweed Editions
Printed in Canada
Cover design by Mary Austin Speaker
Cover photo by Alberto Masnovo
Author photo by David Bernardy
15 16 17 18 19 5 4 3 2 1

FIRST EDITION

Milkweed Editions, an independent nonprofit publisher, gratefully acknowledges sustaining support from the Jerome Foundation; the Lindquist & Vennum Foundation; the McKnight Foundation; the National Endowment for the Arts; the Target Foundation; and other generous contributions from foundations, corporations, and individuals. Also, this activity is made possible by the voters of Minnesota through a Minnesota State Arts Board Operating Support grant, thanks to a legislative appropriation from the arts and cultural heritage fund, and a grant from the Wells Fargo Foundation Minnesota. For a full listing of Milkweed Editions supporters, please visit www.milkweed.org.

Library of Congress Cataloging-in-Publication Data
Tevis, Joni.
[Essays. Selections]
The world is on fire : scrap, treasure, and songs of apocalypse / Joni Tevis.
-- First edition.
    pages ; cm
ISBN 978-1-57131-347-8 (softcover : acid-free paper) -- ISBN 978-1-57131-898-5 (ebook)
I. Title.
PS3620.E95A6 2015
814'.6--dc23
                                        2014038727

Milkweed Editions is committed to ecological stewardship. We strive to align our book production practices with this principle, and to reduce the impact of our operations in the environment. We are a member of the Green Press Initiative, a nonprofit coalition of publishers, manufacturers, and authors working to protect the world's endangered forests and conserve natural resources. *The World Is On Fire* was printed on acid-free 100% postconsumer-waste paper by Friesens Corporation.

For David

And for all this, nature is never spent...
There lives the dearest freshness deep down things...

GERARD MANLEY HOPKINS (1844-89)

"GOD'S GRANDEUR"

CONTENTS

If a thing is iron, then what? It rusts, you see. That's fire, too.
The world is on fire. Start your pieces in the paper that way.
Just say in big letters, "The World Is On Fire."
That will make 'em look up.

SHERWOOD ANDERSON,

"A MAN OF IDEAS," *WINESBURG, OHIO*

OVERTURE

The rust and the dust hold tales untold.
ROSS WARD, CREATOR OF
TINKERTOWN FOLK ART INSTALLATION,
SANDIA PARK, NEW MEXICO

What Looks Like Mad Disorder:
The Sarah Winchester House

San Jose, California

Midnight, she knew, tasted of bitter water but smelled good as damp dirt. The dark hours had taught her that as she'd slid from room to room. A big house creates its own sink of nighttime silence, ponderous as weather; how quiet the place back east had been. But these rooms were as noisy as she wanted, alive with the ring of dropped nails, chuffing saws. Hammers swung all night at her command.

She slept, if she slept, in a different bed every night, or else waited patiently at the little desk in the séance room. She went over accounts and sketched plans for the next day, chewing on dried apricots grown in her own orchards. Tough little suns, flat and orange—they caught in her teeth. One night she drew a spiderweb on a sheet of paper. It would become a design for a stained-glass window.

She must have seen something she recognized in the spider. How every night she spins herself a home, and every dawn destroys it. How she anchors herself in a sturdy spot, reels out a loop, and adds the weight of her body. From this triangle, everything begins.

✳

Once upon a time there lived a baby girl, the only child of parents rich beyond measure. But when she was just a few weeks old, that baby died. Some years later, her father died too, and her mother was left alone. The mother had been the hub of a small family and now was the center of nothing, drifting from room to room, eyes dimmed by grief, hands empty. Maybe she felt a curse had fallen upon her, and maybe one had.

So she went to Boston and found a soothsayer who told her to move west, begin building a house, and never stop, lest the spirits that had taken her daughter and husband come for her. There were legions of those ghosts, the medium said, all the people killed by her husband's guns. For this grieving woman had inherited the vast fortune of the Winchester Repeating Arms Company. Sarah was her name, Sarah Pardee Winchester, and this was her house.

✳

We're standing in the courtyard, my husband, David, and I, waiting for our tour to start. The fountain beside us sparkles and spurts. We hear occasional honks from the traffic outside on Winchester Boulevard, and kids squealing as they horse around in the Victorian Gardens—it's a busy place, and we squint in the sun, tickets in hand.

We're between jobs, all our things stacked in a storage unit across the country in a new state, in a town called Apex. *You have to go where the work is,* people say. Well, we've done that, following jobs from Texas to Minnesota to North Carolina. Will one of us get a steady job when the hiring season starts up again next month? If not, what then? "We'll get by," David says, but right now, I can't see how.

In the meantime, we're taking a few days off, finagling frequent-flyer miles and a spot on our friends' sofa into a California junket. When we started packing, we couldn't find our suitcases—they were buried too deep in that storage unit. So we stuffed our clothes in a box that a coffee pot had come in, taped it shut, and heaved it onto the baggage belt. An awkward fix, but it would have to do.

The intercom crackles: *Tour number seventy-one, prepare to depart from the side entrance.* Twenty of us line up, a mixed bunch: retired couples, a father with two children, a boy in a *Zapata Vive!* T-shirt. Our guide, a stony-faced college student with dark hair cut in sleek wings, lays down the law. "Keep up," she says. "Stay with the group. If you get lost, you'll have to find your own way out. Nobody will ever find you."

With that, we step inside, through what used to be a service entrance. Nothing grand, just this threshold over which Sarah used to walk, sometimes with her favorite niece, but most often alone. And entering here, I feel off-kilter—will feel off-kilter for the whole mile-long tour, through this 24,000-square-foot mishmash of a house. No time to ponder that as we shuffle up the shallow Easy Riser steps—built late in Sarah's life to help her arthritis—into the $25,000 Storeroom, as it's now called, still stocked with expensive wallpaper and stacks of stained-glass windows; along endless rubber-runnered halls, stopping here and there to hear paragraphs of the guide's spiel; and occasionally passing other groups, whose guides repeat the same anecdotes with the same scripted language. Does anybody believe this stuff?

Here's the first story they tell: workers left nails half-driven when they heard of Sarah's death. She paid them three dollars a day, in cash—double the going rate. Many

of them lived on the property, either in regular servants'
quarters or in apartments below the water tower. And she
kept them working at all hours. The Boston medium's pre-
diction included the warning that Sarah had to keep reno-
vating her new house constantly. If the hammers fell silent,
the spirits would come for her. So she made sure that never
happened. When she moved into the house, it had eight
rooms, and she was three years a widow. When she died
in 1922, thirty-eight years later, it had 160 rooms, some of
which she had remodeled six hundred times.

Right away someone asks, "Was she crazy?" The question sticks in my craw. It feels too knee-jerk, too dismissive. What can you call that level of revision but obsessive?
And yet something in it resonates with me; maybe she just
wanted to get it right. I tuck the question into my notebook
and hurry to catch up with the rest.

We don't know which eight rooms comprised the original farmhouse; we don't know where Sarah began. So start
with a nail, one end blunt and the other end sharp, ready
to bite its beam. I wonder if nails pleased her as they please
me; if she found them waiting for her on the sidewalk or
in the street; if, when she bent to pick one up, her dark
veil belled around her face. If, all day, her fingers worried
it in her pocket. Nails were newcomers here, in the Valley
of Heart's Delight, as she was. Resourceful people had
whittled pegs before. Now they prized crates apart and
hammered nails free. A good nail could be used more than
once.

How different things might have been had she married a maker of nails. But she had married a gun man,
William Wirt Winchester, and after his death she became
the weapon his family had perfected, repeating, her hammers' plosive stutter reshaping the rooms. Walking these

hot halls, past oscillating fans that don't do anything to move the air, I shift beneath the weight of the guilt Sarah chose to bear. What stories do we tell ourselves about who we are? If we repeat them often enough, we'll start to trust them.

"Recently," our tour guide says, "a psychic contacted Sarah, and do you know what she said?" She flicks her eyes over us, waiting. *"What are all these people doing in my house?"* As soon as she says the words, I know they're true.

✳

It started with a man's dress shirt: funny to remember that. Her father-in-law had found a way to make it fit better through the shoulders. From shirts he moved to guns, shot, bullets: the Winchester rifle, the Gun that Won the West. Eventually, Winchester factories would turn out products as diverse as meat grinders, scissors, fishing tackle, and roller skates—"The Skate With a Backbone"—but then as now the company was best known for its firearms. Back in 1866, the year baby Anne was born and died, the Gun that Won was underwriting Sarah's life in New Haven, Connecticut. That gun paid for roast duck, hothouse greens, down-stuffed bedticks; it kept her servants in board and uniforms; it paid for doctors, ministers, and, at the end, the sexton. That gun hired a stonecutter and paid for a small casket, lined with silk.

And a few years later, after her husband died, Sarah must have known she couldn't build the $25,000 Storeroom without the warehouses of guns, ready to be loaded into crates, into railcars, into waiting hands ready to shoot Apache and Pueblo by the thousands. Lead soldered water pipes and joined panes of glass; lead made ammunition. In the Winchester shot tower, seven stories of carefully engineered furnaces and molds terminated in the water tanks where hot shot was dropped to cool, hissing and steaming. Soothsayers used to employ lead rings to divine your future, holding the circles aloft with threads, burning through the threads, and marking where the rings fell. But Sarah asked her questions of the Boston medium, who scratched out answers with a planchette one letter at a time.

By all accounts Sarah's days in California were busy ones. The weight of her body anchored her here, on thick rugs that showed no wear and polished floors that glowed like gunstocks. Sarah became an entrepreneur, buying real estate, running her farm, selling walnuts by the barrel. She stored up spade and mattock and blade, oil and whetstone, homing pigeons and ivory leg cuffs, screws cast from solid gold. She invented a sink with a built-in washboard, and a window clasp modeled after a rifle's lock, paying homage to both cleanliness and defense. And although she set up the house to be self-sufficient, with its workshop, water tank, and gas reserves, still she answered the call of the outside world—rosewood and teak for the floors, German silver inlay for doors, pipestone for a fireplace.

In the end, she knew none of it mattered. She signed her thirteen-page will thirteen times, leaving provision for the house to be sold at auction and the furnishings to be left to Francis, her favorite niece, who took what she wanted and sold the rest. A practical way to dispose of things: leave the gaslight chandelier with thirteen jets; leave it all, with minimal instructions, so that mountain of stuff won't hold you back. Set aside a sum to hire a man to deal it all out once you're gone.

How I love a good auction, the auctioneer's chant braiding buyers, goods, price. His chant is a ballad that lasts all day, and each lot is a verse. *What will you give me,* he cries, *what'll you give?* More, always more: rugs scrolled like scripture, bareheaded lamps shorn of shades, books on orchardcraft, cobbler's tools. Sales used to be regulated by candles; bidding lasted, like a séance, until the flame guttered dry.

*

But for the kitchen, the Grand Ballroom, and the séance room, it's hard to tell what most of the rooms were used for, and that's not the only thing that gives the Winchester House a rickety, kaleidoscopic feeling. There are shallow cabinets an inch deep, and others large as generous rooms. One door opens onto a one-story drop, another onto slats instead of flooring. A staircase ends blind in a ceiling, and another forks into a Y, eleven steps up and seven steps down. Despite the fortune Sarah spent, the house feels temporary as a badly pitched tent.

Here we stand in the Hall of Fires. It's lined with hearth after hearth, strange for central California, but the guide tells us that Sarah craved the heat to ease her arthritis. I think of her sitting on this bench, listening to her house: a medium taps out a message from the dead, coins snick like knitting needles, and a gun-shaped latch snaps home. Two swings tap a trim nail true. A burning log hisses, freeing drops of old rainwater. A signal card drops into a slot: Mrs. Winchester needs assistance in the Hall of Fires, and a nurse heads toward her to help. Radiators knock, carrying waves of warmth. The rim of a plate kisses its kin, and the maid clicks the cupboard door closed.

*

By April 1906, Sarah had lived in her house twenty-two years. During that time, her workers had built, among many other rooms, the Grand Ballroom. Whereas the rest of the house follows no rules—chimneys stop shy of ceilings; an extravagant rock-crystal window receives only slantwise light—the parquet floor in the Ballroom is precise down to the hair.

"The floor builder used no nails," our guide tells us, "only glue." He would have worked a section at a time, fitting one piece of smooth wood against another in a neat herringbone. This must have been the hushed corner in a house constantly worried by sound, and even now I'd like to stand here awhile, quiet, in this sunny corner.

I wonder if he heard the remembered racket of other workers when he slept at night, as I have in my own dreams, the carnival jingles of the theater-lobby arcade, the burr and shriek of machine parts turning and dropping off the lathe.

Above the glowing floor hang two stained-glass windows with quotations from Shakespeare. From *Troilus and Cressida*: "Wide unclasp the tables of their thoughts"; from *Richard II*: "These same thoughts people this little world." According to legend, only three people ever entered the house through the richly carved front door: Sarah, the man who delivered it, and the door-hanger. When Theodore Roosevelt dropped by one afternoon to express his admiration for Winchester rifles, servants sent him around back.

But on April 18, 1906, just after sunrise, the earth shook. In San Francisco, the ground liquefied and houses crumbled, their fronts peeling off and their walls buckling and kneeling. There must have been screams and silence—people shaken from sleep and too surprised to speak. When the gas lines ruptured, walls of flame pushed up the city's hillsides; pictures taken just after the disaster show buildings planed open, whole city blocks of blackened rubble where houses had stood, rifts carved in the countryside, oaks riven, fences fallen, barns sucked flat.

Later, some witnesses told of hearing "an approaching roar" at dawn, or feeling a cold touch upon the cheek. Others said dogs pawed at doors and birds flew strangely; earthworms wriggled to the surface and tied themselves in knots. In the Daisy Bedroom, a fireplace shook loose and collapsed, and Sarah was trapped alone.

"Sarah believed she caused the quake," our guide says. "She thought the spirits were rebuking her for spending too much time on the front part of the house." So, the guide goes on, she ordered those rooms to be boarded shut and never went there again. No one danced across the Grand Ballroom's smooth parquetry, no chamber orchestra warmed the walls with music, and no friend paused in front of the Shakespeare windows and asked Sarah what she meant in choosing them.

But the guide hustles us away too quickly from the earthquake-wrecked rooms, with their crumbling plaster and naked studding, lengths of ship-lathe and dusty little cobwebs. Light bends from a curved window. Torn wallpaper and scrawls of glue stain the walls, and I think of that old line from Pliny the Elder: "Hence also walls are covered with prayers to ward off fires." The floor creaks companionably, and there's no armchair to distract, just the bones of the tired old house. I'd stay here all day if I could.

*

A telling detail hides in the house's thirteenth bathroom: a spiderweb window Sarah designed. The artisan rendered the web's arcs in balanced curving sections of glass, but this is shorthand; in any real web, something more pleasing than symmetry develops. After all, symmetry leaves gaps, and if prey escapes, the spider starves.

Jean-Henri Fabre, a French naturalist writing during Sarah's lifetime, noted that the orb-weaver spider works in a method that might seem, to the untrained observer, "like mad disorder." After the initial triangle, spokes, and spiral, she rips out the preliminary threads, whose remnants appear as specks on the finished web. (In one added room of the Winchester House, you can make out the slope of a previous roof, a vestige of what the house used to be.) The spider fills out the web, testing its tension as she goes, finally building up the "sheeted hub," a pad near the web's middle where she rests and waits. Fabre calls this area "the post of interminable waiting." When night fades, the spider destroys the web, eating the silk as she goes. Says Fabre: "The work finishes with the swallowing."

The spider carries within her belly a store of this strong, pearly stuff, which nobody has yet been able to replicate. She dashes along an invisible line to bind a fly with bights of silk; she bluffs her foes by "whirling" or "shuttling" her web at them. Naturalists used to carry scraps of velvet to the field, so they could have a better backdrop for examining the webs they found. An entrepreneur once made wee cork-padded cuffs and fitted them to a spider's legs, then wound skein after skein of silk from her spinnerets until the creature ran dry. He repeated the process with thousands of spiders until he had enough material to weave a gray gown of spider silk, which he then presented to Queen Victoria. During World War II, British gun manufacturers used black widow silk to make crosshairs for rifle sights.

As for me, when spring comes, I keep a lookout for the "sea of gossamer," as it's been called, when spiderlings take flight. In summer I have spied many a tight purse or reticule in which a swaddled grasshopper still struggles, staining the silk with dark bubbles of tobacco juice. And in fall I watch big garden spiders move from holly bush to camellia, spooling out guy lines and waiting under the streetlight for miller moths. With articulate legs, they pluck strands of silk and load them with gum. When dawn comes they finish hunting and tear down their webs, swallowing the golems a line at a time.

✳

The Winchester House was once a living thing, Sarah's shadow self, breathing in and swelling out, tough as twice-used nails. There are many threads to this story; many entrances, but only one safe exit. Not the door that opens onto a one-story drop, or the one that opens onto slats above the yellow kitchen. Sarah knew the way out; she designed it. After she died, movers needed maps of the house to empty it.

The house's largest cabinet is the size of a generous apartment. A cabinet is a container, a room with single-minded purpose. Pliny tells of a house built of salt blocks mortared with water; how the sun shining through those walls must have glowed red at sunset. A fitting shelter for ghosts: crimson, translucent, walled with tears.

Sarah knew her house to be founded on blood, invocations written on the walls, looping script of glue holding the heavy wallpaper tight. Such a house, built for the dead, turns itself inside out, night after night. Windows mutter curses, drains align with Saturn rising, nails turn from gold to lead. She moved veiled through her nights, knowing what others did not, and placing a coin on every tongue her guns had stopped. Some jaws opened easily, others she wrenched apart, still others (blown away) she could not find: for these she placed gold on the breastbone, flat as a plectrum. The hum of voices grew. Sarah heard them all.

Step through a little door. "Welcome to the séance room," the guide says, and something about the room does feel mysterious. Not just because of the thirteen hooks in the closet, or the three entrances and one exit (two doors only open one way). Here was where Sarah moved the flat planchette across the divining board, spelling out messages from the dead. The room feels like a sheeted hub, a knot.

Samson spoke false when he said, *Weave my hair into the web of your loom, and I will become weak as any man*, but it would have been natural for Delilah to believe him; superstitions about weaving have been around as long as knots themselves. Part a bride's hair with the bloodied point of a spear. Forbid pregnant women from spinning, lest the roots of the growing child tangle. To treat infections of the groin, tie the afflicted person's hair to the warp of a loom, and speak a widow's name (*Sarah, Sarah, Sarah*) with every knot.

Move from legend to artifact and find hair jewelry, a practice that reached its obsessive height during the Victorian era, a way to keep a scrap of an absent loved one close. Women wove locks of hair into watch chains, button covers, and forest scenes, or braided ribbons from forty sections of hair, weighting them with bobbins to pull them flat as they worked. In Boston, a man had two hundred rings inset with locks of his hair and had them distributed at his funeral; their inscriptions read "PREPARE TO FOLLOW ME."

When Sarah searched for the center of her life she found her child, quick breath in her ear, warm weight on her heart. She remembered the slight rise and fall, remembered counting the breaths, standing in the dark nursery past midnight, holding her own breath to better mark her infant's.

She tucked a simple lock of baby's hair in a safe and knitted a house around it. Whose grief could be more lavish than hers? She wove a row of rooms—hummed calls toward the dead, boxes made of music, measure upon measure. Began, like a spider, with three: herself, her husband, their child. Or herself, the rifles, those slain. The séance room has three entrances, but only one exit. The Fates hold three lengths of line and a keen edge to cut them.

From three points, she moved outside of language, opening the priceless front door, stepping over the threshold and bolting the door behind her. Spoke notes and rhythm and commerce (per box of dried apricots, less the cost to grow them). In her youth, she had spoken four tongues, but now she spoke the language of nails, to which no one could reply. While her carpenters built, she spoke through them, though they remembered nothing beyond *Worked on the kitchen today*. They cracked jokes about ghosts while they worked, but that wasn't what made them uneasy; it was the way she used them to get outside speech. A good enough reason for paying them double—once for building, twice for hiding her secrets. Her army of men, working day and night, could drive a nail for every bullet sown and not feel the debt of guilt she had to bear. No wonder she kept them working throughout the dark hours.

✳

In a gravel-floored aviary, Sarah kept tropical birds. To understand the speech of sparrows, touch a marigold to your bare foot on the appointed day. Tuck a bittern's claw into your lapel for luck. The blood of a pelican can restore murdered children to life.

I read Aesop's little-known fable, "The Lark Burying Her Father." The lark lived before the beginning of the world. Water stretched out before her; she hollowed a home in the mist. When her father died, she was forced to let him lie unburied six days, because there was no earth to cover him. Finally she split open her head and buried her father inside. To this day, her head is crested like a burial mound.

Spared the problems of the birds who would come after her—the myrtle tree to ensnare, the gems to distract from food—the lark's difficulty was elemental. Just the primary problem of grief, and not a bit of dust to hand to help. Later, Aesop relates, she would tell her children, "Self-help is the best help."

The problem of what to do with the dead was one Sarah also confronted. She buried her bodies in the usual way, then moved across the country and built a living house in which she buried herself, again and again. Pliny records that magpies, if fed on acorns, can be taught to speak. Going further, he claims that they develop favorite words, "which they not only learn but are fond of and ponder carefully. . . . They do not conceal their obsession." Did any of Sarah's tropical birds possess the power of speech? If so, what did she long to hear them say? *Help* or *home* or *Mama*, a name no one had ever called her? We don't know if they were toucans or macaws or quetzals, whether they screamed or croaked, only that they were tropical and that they came, like Sarah, from far away.

*

After a quick pass through the basement with its ancient furnace and rust-stained cement floor, the tour ends and we're escorted out a low door. Our guide takes her leave, and we're free to wander the grounds, crunching along gravel paths between the carefully clipped boxwoods, the thirteen palm trees, and the bronze sculpture of Chief Little Fawn. Press a button by the fountain and listen to the talking box tell its story. A boy of twenty, probably a guide-in-training, studies a stapled script underneath an ancient grapefruit tree. It's a lot to remember.

You can see anything you want in Sarah Winchester. Craft a story from what bits and scraps you know. Her house is the primary document left to show us who she was, and it's so easy to read it wrong. What was she trying to say? Was the house a letter to herself, or a cryptic message to the outside world?

Whatever the place is, it makes people uneasy. I heard it in the nervous banter of the other visitors. ("I think we should visit the firearms museum," a man said to his son. "I think *that* would be interesting.") ("She might have been *too* educated," a woman said to our guide, who ignored her.) I can't say whether the house is haunted or not, but it got under my skin.

Her naked display of long-term grief makes me flinch. Could I do any better? Could any of us? When her husband and child died, she mourned them the rest of her life. All that buying and selling couldn't distract her. She did not hope for heaven—*what will it profit a man if he gains the whole world and loses his soul?*—but let the world pass through her fingers: imported stone, brass smelted in faraway furnaces. Cared for none of it except as material bulk, something to make the house more than what it had been. Ordered the gardener to put in a new bed of daisies and hawthorn; paged through a catalog offering English yew and monkey puzzle, catalpa and persimmon, whose bitter fruit she craved.

For me, the stories about Sarah are the worst of it. All the easy myths, free of real life's half-measures; the tour guide's flip answers, and the dismissive chorus: *She must have been crazy.* In fact, in Sarah's constant rebuilding of the house—an occupation with roots in the daily and domestic, but which she was able to take to new lengths because of her tremendous wealth—she looks a lot like an artist at work. If she'd been like her father-in-law, perfecting one object and mass-producing it, we'd remember her for her innovation and engineering. If she'd been like most upper-class women of her time, creating House Beautiful around her and then living out her life there, we wouldn't remember her at all.

But Sarah Winchester did a bit of both when she created her house. Because she didn't leave explanatory documents behind, all we have is the coded message of the house itself. Linger over its crabbed lines, fish-scale shingles, and old-growth redwood painted over to look like birch, and you'll see she was doing what an artist does—leaving her mark and seeing what happened; working through an idea via metal, wood, and space; expanding the notion of what life is all about.

✳

After we left the Winchester House, we stopped at an Army Navy store and bought a duffel bag to replace the battered coffee-pot box for the trip home—a step in the right direction. But long after I dragged the duffel through the door of our new place and started unpacking, I couldn't let Sarah go. Dangerous, maybe, to take a big trip like that, when you're between stages of your life, looking for work, unsure of who you are. I kept coming back to a postcard we bought in the Winchester House gift shop, a reproduction of the one extant photo of Sarah. She's seated in a carriage behind a driver, and even though she's at some distance, there's a smile on her small, expressive face. She looks content, someone with work that needs doing. In that moment, she's far away from the morning she buried her child, farther still from her husband's rattling sickbed, and just like that she passes through the one safe exit into the realm where time shunts away and hours, days, thirty-eight years pass and she follows the unspooling line of her thought to its ragged end and looks up to see the marks she's made. Floor, ceiling, wall; this covers me; this crowns me; this pushes me forward. *Self-help is the best help*: perhaps she believed it. But Sarah's story ends not with a tidy moral but a dashed-off map. The movers, at least, would find that useful.

She could have filled scores of rooms with visitors. But in the end, the memory of her lost ones was enough for her. We are the crowd she never invited. (*What are all these people doing in my house?*) Now every day is filled with the tread of feet, the whisper of hands sliding along her banisters, the hum of conversations she can't quite make out.

*

We signed a year's lease on a brick cottage outside Apex. I spent my days running among libraries: an elegant domed one with a smooth marble floor, barrister's tables, and an echo; the main one, eight stories and two sub-basements crammed with no-nonsense metal shelves; the zoology one, where I read Fabre in a cozy little carrel; the geology one, with maps of historic earthquake activity and potted succulents growing in deep-silled windows. I read an article about scientists feeding LSD to spiders to see how it affected their webs. I read that earthquakes leave coded messages in the earth around them, and that San Francisco politicians tried to deny the 1906 quake after it happened. That an old Roman myth tells of a gown made of moonbeams, and of the pages, with eyes sore and blood-shot, who carried it to Hera. That barbed wire used to be called "the devil's rope," and that you can tell the construction date of a house by the nails that bind it together.

At the time, it didn't occur to me that I was obsessing over the details of someone else's house even as I craved a place of my own. When our year's lease was up, we moved to yet another state, where we've been ever since. Now we live in a tidy little bungalow with green shutters and a tight roof we paid for ourselves, with gleanings from those steady jobs we scoured the country to find. From this place of greater stability I see the Winchester House in another light: maybe an art installation, as I initially believed, or maybe just something to fill Sarah's time.

Still, nights when I can't sleep, I walk the halls of a darkened library, a place Sarah bequeathed to me. Her ramshackle house provided me plenty of work, paragraphs to draft and revise again and again, dry little suns to gnaw on, morsels sweet and tough by turns. Even now, telling these secrets, slick pages whisper beneath my fingertips and I smell marvelous old dust and glue. I breathe in air that carries with it words tucked between heavy covers, tales spelled out one letter at a time.

ACT ONE

Remove this sheet and keep it with you
until you've memorized it.

SURVIVAL UNDER ATOMIC ATTACK,

OFFICE OF CIVIL DEFENSE, 1950

Damn Cold in February:
Buddy Holly, View-Master, and the A-Bomb

OK. So then when you get sent out to the test site,
first of all I'm curious what your impressions of that
were, because you are now in the middle of a desert
compared to a—
It's damn cold.
Yes, the desert's cold in the winter.
In February, it's damn cold.
First impression: cold.
And it's dry, except when it rains.
—Robert Martin Campbell Jr.,
atomic veteran (Navy), describing his initial
impression of the Nevada Proving Grounds, 1952

Click through the images, one at a time. VIEW-MASTER
ATOMIC TESTS IN 3-D: YOU ARE THERE! reads the package.
The set's reels show the preparations for the 1955 Apple-2
shot, its detonation, and the Nevada Test Site today. Three
reels, seven images each.

Of the hundreds of atomic devices exploded at the
Nevada Test Site from 1951 until 1992, the ones that stand
out are those featuring Doom Town, a row of houses,
businesses, and utility poles. It makes sense: the flash, the
wall of dust, and the burning yuccas are impressive on
their own, but without something familiar in the frame,

the explosion can seem abstract. Doom Town—also called Survival City, or Terror Town—makes the bomb anything but theoretical. These are the images I can't forget.

Click. Here's Doom Town's iconic two-story house, a classic Colonial with shuttered windows balancing a front door. Neat and tidy, with white-painted siding and a sturdy red-brick chimney: if this were your house, you'd probably feel pretty good about yourself. But something's wrong. The vehicle parked in the drive isn't a Dodge or a Packard but an Army jeep; on the chimney's edge, a bloom of spray paint shows the siding was painted in a hurry. This is a house nobody will ever live in. Its only inhabitants are mannequins with eyes like apple seeds.

All part of the plan, and the planning took far longer than the event itself. A crew unloaded telephone poles, jockeyed them upright, and drilled them into the alluvium. Down in Vegas, men bargained for cars and stood in line for sets of keys. Imagine the hitch and roar of a '46 Ford, '51 Hudson, '48 Buick, and '47 Olds as they pull onto the highway, headed for the proving grounds. Click. Here's one of the cars now, a pale-blue '49 Cadillac with 46 painted on its trunk in numbers two feet tall, marked like an entrant in a demolition derby.

You could say the whole country pitches in. Fenders pressed from Bethlehem steel, lumber skidded out of south Georgia piney woods, glass insulators molded in West Virginia, slacks loomed and pieced and serged in Carolina mills. And mannequins made in Long Island, crated and stacked and loaded onto railcars.

Click. In an upstairs bedroom, a soldier tucks a mannequin woman into a narrow bed, the mattress's navy ticking visible beneath the white sheet. Outside the open window, the white blare of the desert at noon. Downstairs, another soldier arranges a family, seating adults around a table and positioning children on the floor, checking the dog tags around each of their necks.

What's a plan but a story, set not in the past but the future? Someone in the Civil Defense Administration already decided how many mannequins this house will hold, what they'll wear, whether they'll sit or stand. But surely this soldier can allow himself the freedom to choose, say, which game the children on the floor will play. For Brother and Little Sister, how about jacks? A good indoor game. And Big Sister, let's set her off from the rest, next to her portable record player, its cord lying on the floor like a limp snake. Father leans toward the television, one hand on his knee and the other on the pipe resting in the hole drilled in his lip. The blank television reflects his face; he could be watching the news.

*

The tremendous monetary and other outlays involved (in testing far away) have at times been publicly justified by stressing radiological hazards. I submit that this pattern has already become too firmly fixed in the public mind and its continuation can contribute to an unhealthy, dangerous, and unjustified fear of atomic detonations. . . . It is high time to lay the ghost of an all-pervading lethal radioactive cloud (to rest). . . . While there may be short-term public relations difficulties caused by testing atomic bombs within the continental limits, these are more than offset by the fundamental gain from increased realism in the attitude of the public.
—Rear Admiral William S. "Deak" Parsons, 1948

In 1945, Manhattan Project physicists exploded the first atomic device, Trinity, in the desert outside Alamogordo; a little more than two weeks later, the *Enola Gay* dropped Little Boy on Hiroshima, and three days after that, *Bockscar* dropped Fat Man on Nagasaki. Scientists predicted that the United States' monopoly on atomic weapons would hold for at least twenty years, but in 1949, the Soviets proved them wrong, exploding a bomb named First Lightning. In response, Harry Truman authorized the building of Mike, the first hydrogen bomb, tested in the South Pacific. The logistics of testing so far away made the process costly, so a public relations campaign was conducted in order to convince Americans that testing closer to home—at the Nevada Test Site, an hour or so north of Las Vegas—was desirable and safe. By and large, the public got on board with this campaign, and although much of the evidence generated by the tests was kept classified for decades, the Department of Defense and the Atomic Energy Commission made it a priority to publicize some of the information. Broadcasts of the tests were shown on television, newspaper reporters and photographers documented them, and civilians were encouraged to witness the explosions.

In the summer of 1957, an article in the *New York Times* explained how to plan one's summer vacation around the "non-ancient but none the less honorable pastime of atom-bomb watching." Reporter Gladwin Hill wrote that "for the first time, the Atomic Energy Commission's Nevada test program will extend through the summer tourist season, into November. It will be the most extensive test series ever held, with upward of fifteen detonations. And for the first time, the A.E.C. has released a partial schedule, so that tourists interested in seeing a nuclear explosion can adjust itineraries accordingly."

Hill's article suggests routes, vantage points, and film speeds, so that the atomic tourist can capture the spectacle. But is there anything to fear from watching an atomic explosion? Rest assured, he says, that "there is virtually no danger from radioactive fall-out." A car crash is the bigger threat, possibly caused by the bomb's blinding flash or by "the excitement of the moment, [when] people get careless in their driving."

In the article's last paragraph, Hill writes, "A perennial question from people who do not like pre-dawn expeditions is whether the explosions can be seen from Las Vegas, sixty-five miles away. The answer is that sometimes enough of a flash is visible to permit a person to say he has 'seen an atomic bomb.' But it is not the same as viewing one from relatively close range, which generally is a breath-taking experience.".

That summer, after winning the title of Miss Atomic Bomb, a local woman poses for photos with a cauliflower-shaped cloud basted to the front of her bathing suit. Thanks to trick photography, she seems to tower over the salt flats on endless legs, power lines brushing her ankles. With her arms held high above her head, the very shape of her body echoes the mushroom cloud, and her smile looks even wider because of the dark lipstick outlining her mouth, a ragged circle like a blast radius. Not only do Americans want to see the bomb, we want to become it, shaping our bodies to fit its form.

A studious-looking young man who totes his electric guitar like a sawn-off shot-gun.
—Review of a Buddy Holly performance in
Birmingham, England; March 11, 1958

There's a lot going on during that atomic summer. Buddy
Holly, for instance. His career's taken off by 1957, thanks to
hits like "That'll Be the Day," "Peggy Sue," and "Everyday,"
songs that combine country inflections with rock's insistent rhythm. He looks ordinary, like someone you went to
high school with; in fact, you were born knowing him, the
bird-chested guy, sexless and safe. But look more closely: at
the story of how he gets into a "scuffle" with his buddy Joe
B., the bass player, before a show, and Joe B. accidentally
knocks off Buddy's two front caps. Buddy solves the problem by smearing a wad of chewing gum across the space,
sticking the caps back on, and playing the gig. Or at the
story of how he met dark-haired Maria Elena in a music
publishing office and that same day asked her to marry
him—and she said yes. Or look at this, a clip from a TV
show he played in December of '57.

"Now if you haven't heard of these young men," the
hostess says, "then you must be the wrong age, because
they're rock and roll specialists." The camera's trained on
Buddy, and he doesn't waste time: *If you knew Peggy Sue, then
you'd know why I feel blue,* giving it everything he's got, and as
he moves into the second verse, the camera on stage right
goes live, and he pivots smoothly, keeping up. I'm staring back from better than fifty years out, watching as he
follows the camera with a studied intensity magnified by
the frenetic speed of his strumming. His fingers are a blur,
but he doesn't make mistakes, and as I watch the clip, I'm
startled by the distinctly handsy look in his eye. This is not
what I expected.

The whole song's a revelation, from the rapid-fire
drumming, to the stuttering *Pretty pretty pretty pretty Peggy
Sue,* to the way his falsetto warps the words of the last
verse. *With a love so rare and true*—you know he doesn't mean

a word of it. He's just telling you what you want to hear, and that tamped-down sex—how had I missed it?—burns in his eyes. And there's something about the way he stares at the camera that sets him apart from his contemporaries. Elvis, the Big Bopper, Johnny Cash all play to the audiences they have at the time, mugging for the camera and making the kids squeal. Jerry Allison, the drummer for the Crickets, said later that playing on TV made him nervous: "That was something different," he said, "an audience that wasn't there." But watching Buddy, you'd never know it. He's playing to the fans of the future—to the camera, to now.

> First floor, living room. First floor, dining room.
> Children at play, unaware of approaching disaster.
> —"Declassified US Nuclear Test Film #33"
> (Apple-2/"Cue"), 1955

Ever since I watched *La Bamba* as a kid, I've known about the plane crash that killed Buddy Holly, Ritchie Valens, and J.P. "Big Bopper" Richardson. It happened before my time; it was a foregone conclusion, verifiably historical. Knowing that, I couldn't see Buddy Holly as anything other than a dead man walking, doomed to die young, tragic. But of course there's more to him than that.

He was a writer, for one thing. The year before that TV appearance, he'd gone to the movies with his friends and seen a John Wayne picture. *That'll be the day*, Wayne kept saying. Well, that was a nice line, and he wrote it down, to see if he could put it to use.

Not long ago, I watched *The Searchers* myself, trying to figure out what about that line had compelled Buddy Holly. The movie follows Ethan Edwards, played by

John Wayne, over the course of five years spent tracking a band of Comanche across the desert Southwest. He's trying to find his niece Debbie, kidnapped as a child during a raid on her family's ranch. Along the way, other riders join Ethan, but you wouldn't call them his partners. He's the one calling the shots, and he's vengeful, cruel, and all the more dangerous because he has enough cultural know-how to really hurt his enemy. This image stays with me: when the group finds a Comanche warrior buried under a stone, Ethan opens the grave and shoots out the corpse's eyes. "Now he'll have to wander forever between the Spirit Lands," he says, leaving the twice-blinded body behind.

For me, the movie's most compelling moments are the early ones leading up to the raid on the ranch. In a low-ceilinged adobe room, Debbie's mother scolds her older daughter for lighting a lamp and revealing their presence. "Let's just enjoy the dusk," she shrills, trying to hide how frightened she is. Outside the half-timbered window, the desert glows white-orange, sunlight pouring in like fear made visible. Her voice cracking, she orders Debbie to run away to the family's burial plot and hide there: "Don't come back," she says, "no matter what you hear."

That light, brilliant and threatening, stays with me. No matter what Mother tries to pretend, this is no ordinary sunset. We don't see the war party attacking the ranch; it's enough to see the helpless family anticipating disaster, and the aftermath, in which nobody's left standing. When Ethan and the rest of the men return to the ranch, they find it a smoking ruin, the death inside so grisly they can only allude to it. "Don't let him look in there," Ethan commands one of the men. "It won't do him any good to see it." The people killed had been Ethan's brother and his family, but he doesn't show signs of sorrow or surprise when he finds them. You can't catch him off guard. He's an icon, not a real man, and he says "That'll be the day" four times.

ALERT TODAY

ALIVE TOMORROW.

—Poster, Mr. Civil Defense, 1956

Seems like nothing goes according to plan. The date for Apple-2 had been set well in advance, but after weather conditions force several delays, some of the would-be watchers pack up and head home; surely some of them regret missing the chance to see the bomb up close. Finally, conditions are right, and the countdown begins. Just past 5:00 a.m., full dark over the desert, photographers brace on boulders overlooking Frenchman Flat, and soldiers hunch in trenches. The speakers crackle, and the announcement goes out for observers to put on their dark goggles; those without goggles must face away from the blast. A transmitter broadcasts canned music that pours from the radios in the houses of Doom Town. It plays in the dark rooms as of a house asleep, but only one resident is in her bed. In the dim living room still smelling of sawdust and damp cement, Sister reclines on the floor beside her record player, and Father leans toward the dark television, pipe clamped in his mouth.

Not far away, a reporter embedded with a group of soldiers takes notes from inside a fifty-ton Patton tank. "'Sugar [shot] minus fifteen minutes,'" he writes. "Then it was 'sugar minus ten' and 'sugar minus five.' Someone tossed me a helmet and I huddled on the floor."

> We just hoped somebody would buy our records so we
> could go on the road and play.
> —Niki Sullivan, rhythm guitarist for The Crickets

Sometimes it must seem he's never known anything but
life on this bus, its engine groaning up the grade of every
back road in the Upper Midwest, his clothes wrinkled and
ripe in the bags overhead, his hands tucked under his arm-
pits for warmth. When the bus breaks down again and the
heater conks out, they burn newspapers in the gritty aisle
between the seats to try and stay warm. Carl, the drummer, gets frostbite and has to go to the hospital. He's a fill-
in; Joe B. and Jerry are back in Lubbock. But Buddy needs
the money. On cloudy days after snow falls, you can't tell
where the fields end and the sky begins, and the fences
down the section lines must be a comfort to him. Iowa's a
long way from Texas, but at least the barbed wire tells you
what's solid and what's not.

They all play the show in Clear Lake and gear up for
Moorhead, nearly four hundred miles away, a full night's
ride in that freezing bus, and probably another breakdown
on the side of the road. Why not charter a plane instead?
Then he'll get to the next gig in plenty of time, have a hot
shower, do everyone's laundry. The Beechcraft seats three
plus the pilot. He's in for sure, and J.P., sick with a cold.
Ritchie and the guitar player flip for the last seat, and
Ritchie wins. See you when we see you.

*

> And I'm not married yet and I haven't got sense
> enough to realize the magnitude. You see it visually
> but it's *beautiful*. It's *beautiful*. Just *gorgeous*, the col-
> ors that are emitted out of this ball of mass, and the

higher it goes into the air, it becomes an ice cap on top
of it because it's getting so high, and it's just a beautiful ice cap.
—Robert Martin Campbell Jr., describing test
George, the thermonuclear detonation he witnessed
in the Marshall Islands on May 9, 1951

The plane's thin door clicks shut. Past midnight, and
Buddy's beat. The pilot turns the knobs and checks the
instruments, and the engine roars its deafening burr.
When he looks out the windshield, there's nothing to see
but snow, swirling in the lit cone thrown by the hangar
lights. Slowly at first, then faster, the plane rolls down the
runway and lifts off. Up, and bouncing in the air pockets,
the roar of the engines, no way to talk and be heard but
he's too tired to talk anyway. Three miles out, then four,
then five.

When do they realize something's wrong? Does the
pilot panic, trying to read the dials and not understanding
what they say? The windshield's a scrum of snow, white-
swirled black, no way to tell up from down and headed
for the ground at 170 miles an hour, the plane shaking
hard, going fast, and this gyroscope measures direction in
exactly the opposite way from the instruments the pilot had
known before. What does it feel like? You can't trust your
senses when you're this beat, this far from home, and all
you know for sure is that your bones hurt from hunching
into the cold. One day you're playing the opening of a car
dealership outside town; the next you're leaving the movies with your friends; the next you're on *The Arthur Murray
Party*, standing in front of a girl in a strapless ball gown the
color of winter wheat. She'll stand there the whole time,
swaying gently, looking over your shoulder at America and

wearing a little smile that says there is nothing better than this, to be here in this place, young, feeling this song in your body, warm inside the theater while outside the wind blows, louder and louder, sneaking its way in through any crack it can find and shrieking now in your ear, higher and colder and harder and harder until finally it stops.

Amen! There's no more time for prayin'! Amen!
—*The Searchers,* 1956

The second hand on the watch's round face ticks toward vertical: three, two, one. A great flash, then peals of thunder, and a wall of sand radiates out from ground zero. When the heat hits the house, its paint smokes but doesn't have time to catch fire. The shock wave rolls over it, the roof lifts off, and the whole thing collapses. Two and one-third seconds since detonation.

There's a lot of atomic film out there; you can watch the bomb explode as many times as you can stand. But although the different cameras and jump cuts can make the clips hard to follow, the View-Master parcels out a single image at a time. Push the reel home with a click, and put the eyepieces to your face. All of the images on this second reel are colored yellow, everything lit not by the sun, but by the bomb. A bomb with a twenty-nine-kiloton yield, about twice as powerful as the one dropped on Hiroshima. "Observers are silhouetted by the Atomic Flash," reads this caption. I stare at the dark shapes of the people, the bleachers, and the telephone poles behind them, everything outlined in a gleaming yellow that could almost be mistaken for a very bright sunrise, but the color's all wrong. Like many other shots, Apple-2 was detonated before dawn specifically so that the photographs taken of it would be better. And I have to admit, this is an image I can't forget.

Next slide. Here's our house, the one with Father and Big Sister in the living room. As "the heat burns the surface of a two story house," smoke issues from the roof and from the car in the driveway, a '48 Plymouth. The house's front windows, blank and white, reflect the fireball. Click. By the next image, when "the shockwave slams into the two story house," the window glass is gone, the roof canting back as the siding dissolves in granular smoke. Support beams fly up as the trunk shears from the Plymouth, and already the light has changed to a pallid yellow, the black sky less absolute, greasy with smoke and sand, carpet, copper wire.

Click. On this house, a one-story rambler, the roof goes first. Smoke rises from the gravel drive, the portico, the power lines. "The house is blown to pieces from the shockwave," says the caption; I click back to the previous slide and can't find anything I recognize. Click. When "an aluminum shed is crushed by the shockwave," the roof and sides crumple inward in a swirl of dust. Click. The last slide shows a stand of fir trees, brought in from the Siskiyou Forest in Oregon, maybe, or the Willamette. Soldiers implanted them in a strip of concrete, a fake forest built of real trees. There's a rim of low mountains in the background; in the middle distance, this strange forest, bending in an unnatural wind; and in the foreground, no seedlings or fallen logs, just the flat expanse of desert, covered over by what might be choppy water, or snow. And if any stowaways were hiding in the trees, bagworms in the needles or termite colonies under the bark, they're vaporized like everything else, flat gone.

Live a bucolic life in the country, far from a potential target of atomic blasts. For destruction is everywhere. Houses destroyed, mannequins, representing
humans, torn apart, and lacerated by flying glass.
—*Las Vegas Review-Journal*, May 6, 1955

It could be any cornfield, any stretch of snow. What's left
isn't recognizable as a plane, and the dark shapes on the
ground don't look like bodies, although they must be.
The coroner's broad back is dark against the white as he
leans over to take their measure. The thin snow crusting
the ground makes everything look even colder. There's a
shape a few yards distant that looks like someone trying to
crawl away. You know it's a lie. They didn't have a prayer.

Time to clean up. Down in Las Vegas, employees at
car dealerships sweep up window glass that had been shattered by the blast, sixty-five miles away. Someone dumps
the pieces in a barrel and starts charging for them: atomic
souvenirs. They sell out by day's end. In Doom Town, cars
lie flipped onto their tops or burned where they stand.
Telephone poles are snapped in half, their lines a snarled
mass.

I watch a clip from "Test Film #33." A camera pans
down a line of mannequins staked to poles in the open
desert. Their clothes wave in the breeze. "Do you remember this young lady?" the narrator asks. "This tattoo mark
was left beneath the dark pattern." As she speaks, the hand
of an unseen worker lifts the skirt a modest few inches,
smoothing the slip to show how the heat seared a design
onto the fabric beneath. "And this young man? This is how
the blast charred and faded the outer layer of his new dark
suit." The same worker's hand, a wedding band gleaming
on one broad finger, pushes the cloth back to reveal the

lapel shadow seared on the mannequin's chest. Then he smoothes the lapel back in place. For a brief moment, he presses his ungloved palm to the mannequin's shoulder, as if to say, *There you go. You did your best.* Such a slight gesture, here and gone—he probably didn't give it any thought. But it moves me, his moment of pity for even this mute copy of a man.

> He never said hardly a word but "thank you."
> —Daniel Dougherty, of Buddy Holly's banter during
> the Winter Dance Party at the Surf Ballroom in
> Clear Lake, Iowa; February 2, 1959

Corn or soybeans, the field gets replanted every year. A beaten path runs along the fence, and at the site, there's a memorial, metal records and a cutout guitar with BUDDY HOLLY RITCHIE VALENS BIG BOPPER 2-3-59 etched on the aluminum. People leave things: flowers, quarters, a red model Corvette, guitar picks, pairs of glasses, ticket stubs from the State Fair, a CD with WE LOVE YOU and RIP written on it, a WAYLON tour button, a small American flag. In winter, snow covers the offerings, and the metal records look like pie pans left out to scare the crows.

He died young and far from home, and snow drifted around his body all that long dark night. Damn cold in February, but at least it was over quick. At least you can say what caused it and nobody will argue with you. The reporter who wrote about the "honorable pastime of atom-bomb watching" wrote another article that scoffed at the threat of fallout, writing that "some of the scare talk is simply a matter of individuals' basking in the limelight of public attention for the first time." The woman who crouched in the trenches thirty-five hundred yards from ground

zero—"the closest any Caucasian women have ever been
to an atomic blast"—told of "the normal feminine excitement" in the air, but insisted that "I didn't feel that my life
was in any danger." The leukemia clusters in downwind
towns would emerge over the next three to ten years, but
the government would fight the link between testing and
disease for far longer. "Hysterical," the reporter called a
letter writer who claimed cause and effect.

I can't stop thinking about the bare-handed worker
showing the mannequin to the camera. About the news-
paperman in the tank they nicknamed Baby, and about
the soldier driving the tank, who was twenty years old,
and from Bellefontaine, Ohio, the town where I was born.
About the workers serving lunch at the test site the day
after the shot. "I particularly remember some roast beef,"
says the narrator in "Test Film #33." "It was done to perfection and roasted in cans which could have been salvaged
from demolished buildings." The camera lingers over a
woman spooning stew into her mouth, the cafeteria tray
before her holding an opened can, an apple, and a carton
of milk. What she took inside her that day, carried home to
bed with her that night.

> Today, there is no second-best for family's civil defense.
> The urgent need to prepare now against the threat of
> atomic warfare. Or will you, like a mannequin, just sit
> and wait?
> —"Declassified US Nuclear Test Film #33"
> (Apple-2/"Cue"), 1955

When you see the explosion, even from a distance, you
might be stunned into repeating inanities: *Pretty pretty pretty
pretty*. (You see it visually but it's *beautiful*. It's *beautiful*, just

gorgeous.) The song gets caught in your head and you run through it again and again without realizing it; the song enters your life like a new reality. One quart of water per day. Food in bare rations. In the film about fallout shelters, the narrator advises you calmly to make your way to the shelter, unpack, and "take your bearings." Someone chose actors; someone directed them. But you don't think about that when you watch the film. Instead, you unconsciously select one person on screen to identify with, the woman with the child in her arms, taking neat steps downstairs and finding a place in the damp room, setting up the smaller cot beside her own and spreading a plaid blanket smooth.

> There's no other product that gives me as much fear and respect for the power of mass culture as the Hula-Hoop. It has a life of its own.
> —Dan Roddick, director of marketing at Wham-O, 1988

The Hula-Hoop demands a lot of space. It has no place in a fallout shelter, the domain of compact games that pass time until the radioactive isotopes decay enough for a family to return to normal life. (Two weeks, says the narrator in the film.) Checkers, dominoes, or pickup sticks would all make better choices, or marbles or cards, or View-Master, "The World at Your Fingertips." The hard-shell box is packed with reels in paper envelopes: The Grand Canyon, Beautiful Rock City Gardens, Petrified Forest, The Islands of Hawaii, Disneyland. Little Sister savors the quiet satisfaction of pulling the Yosemite reel from the Yosemite envelope. *Summer vacation without the headaches,* Father might say, the box of reels shelved between the powdered milk and the canned beef. *Just about better than fresh.*

And View-Master's images are sharper than life, more

saturated with color, Spider Rock's crisp shadow a deep black on the desert valley, the polished spume of Old Faithful standing tall above a crowd of tourists leaning in to get a better look. Little Sister presses the viewer to her face and clicks through the shots, and when she gets up from the floor, Mother looks at her strangely; the viewer has left a mark. *Time to go outside*, she says. *Get some fresh air.*

Click, click, goes the hoop against the button of her jumper. Click, swish, go the button and the breeze. She can keep it going. The plane crash in Iowa behind her, the fallout shelter before her, but here she is, now, feet planted firmly on the ground, eyes on the horizon. Click swish, click swish, and when the hoop worries downward she kicks it back to the right place with a little jab of her hip. The drumbeat of "Peggy Sue" goes faster than her heart ever has, *tacka tacka tacka tacka*, like gumballs dumped onto a corrugated roof. The singer had been twenty-two, exactly twice her age. Impossibly old.

The Hula-Hoop fad begins in '58 and peaks by '59. I want my Hula-Hooping girl to be the same girl who pressed the View-Master to her face, the same girl who listened to records in the living room, but that's impossible. The girl with the View-Master waits in a dark room underground; the girl with the record player lies buried inside the ruined house. But as long as the machine in the mannequin factory pours plaster into a mold, as long as a conveyor belt sends the shape through the oven to cure, as long as a worker's there to stretch a sleeve over the arm and pull the torso upright and snap it to a pair of legs, I can have my girl, standing in a silent room full of dozens of her kind. You'd never mistake her for the real thing. Leave her in the house; make her your substitute. Send her through hell and see how she holds up.

Someday this country's gonna be a fine, good place
to be. Maybe it needs our bones in the ground before
that time can come.
—*The Searchers,* 1956

One night in Vegas, I stood under the neon in Fremont
Street and watched as a crowd of strangers linked arms,
swayed, and sang along with the chorus *This'll be the day that
I die,* smiling like it was a lullaby. Then I read about the
phenomenon of nostalgia for the A-bomb as a symbol of
a "simpler time." For me, these iconic images of the late
1950s—Buddy Holly's grinning face, the exploding Cape
Cod house, and the mushroom cloud—all signify the same
thing, death. And they all demand that we grapple with
them.

Despite all the documentation of Apple-2 and tests like
it, there is something fundamentally unknowable about an
atomic explosion. Physicists can explain how it happens
and why. Historians can place it into the larger context of
time and place. Eyewitnesses can tell the story of how it
felt to watch it rise from the desert, unfold into the sky, and
veer off toward the mountains. But for me, the atom bomb
represents the breakdown of certainty. Here is a weapon
that enacts hell in three ways: fire brighter than the sun,
wind stronger than a cyclone, and fine particles that imbue
the air with death. Only myth can explain it. This is the
salamander that lives in the fire and eats of the fire. This is
the basilisk that binds you, once you look. And this is the
hammer that fractures time: the house is gone in the space
of a moment, but the radioactivity of the fallout, what the
house becomes, will be deadly for millennia, longer than
our languages will last.

Let's be honest. To really imagine what happened, you

have to put yourself in her place. So make me the girl with
the View-Master. Me with the Hula-Hoop, staring at the
horizon, watching for something terrible. Me on the living-
room floor, listening to the song with its bridge like baby-
doll music. And on the television, light fills the screen, and
thunder pours from the speakers. (*Should the girls be watching
this?* Mother says. To which Father replies, *You can't shelter
them forever.*) Man, woman, and child, millions of them,
exposed to these tests, whether or not they drove out into
the desert to watch. According to the *Bulletin of the Atomic
Scientists,* "the National Cancer Institute estimates that
around 160 million people—virtually everyone living in the
U.S. at that time (mid-1950s)—received some iodine dose
from fallout." All water exposed to the upper air since 1945
contains radioactive signatures. The A-bomb is in us all, its
isotopes in all our blood: the tests, all 1,021 of them, live on
through us.

> Well, I'm either going to go to the top—or else I'm
> going to fall. But I think you're going to see me in the
> big time.
> —Buddy Holly, to concert promoter Carroll
> Anderson, before the show at the Surf Ballroom,
> February 2, 1959

How we paw over these old relics, a picture of his overnight bag stuffed with Ban, a half-used roll of adhesive
tape, a Stanley hairbrush exactly like mine, all these ordinary things freighted with disaster. Twelve years after
the crash, a man wrote a song about it. Thirty years after
Apple-2, moviemakers repurposed its footage for *The Day
After*'s depiction of atomic devastation. To simulate fallout,
they used cornflakes, painted white. The man who flipped

Ritchie Valens for a seat on the plane bought a bar and named it Tommy's Heads Up Saloon. In the gift shop at the Buddy Holly Center in Lubbock, you can buy a Buddy Holly Spinning Snowflake Ornament.

"This is the way we get our word out," said the atomic veteran. "This is the way we get the word out. It's the only way." At the National Atomic Testing Museum in Las Vegas, you can turn a thumb reel and watch a school bus burning, smoking, tipping, and being swept away, or you can turn the reel the other way, and put it all back together. In the gift shop, you can buy a T-shirt of Miss A-Bomb wearing her rictus of a grin. Or sterling silver earrings, one of Fat Man and the other of Little Boy.

> Well, that's my life to the present date, and even though it may seem awful and full of calamities, I'd sure be in a bad shape without it.
> FINIS
> FINALE
> In other words,
> THE END.
> —From "My Autobiography," written by Buddy Holly for his sophomore English class, 1953

The year *The Searchers* was released, John Wayne filmed another movie, *The Conqueror,* in St. George, Utah, downwind of the Nevada Test Site. Before the filming, shot Harry, later called Dirty Harry, was exploded. The movie's action, set in Mongolia, required several scenes with blowing sand, and maybe nobody thought much of it when they brushed the dust from their hair and eyes, shook it from their shirtsleeves, wiped it from their feet. They had work to do. Years later, when John Wayne died of cancer, he blamed his smoking habit, and maybe he was right. But ninety other actors and crew from *The Conqueror* were also diagnosed with cancer, over 40 percent of those who worked on the movie, along with uncounted extras, most of them local people.

In the last scene of *The Searchers*, Ethan Edwards returns the kidnapped girl, now a woman, to her neighbors, the closest thing to kin she has left. The movie's theme song rises—*Ride away, ride away*—and Ethan turns his back on the camera. As he walks slowly out of frame, the white rectangle of sun in the door grows brighter and brighter, until finally the door closes. By the time *The Searchers* was playing in movie theaters from Lubbock to Clear Lake, John Wayne was in Utah, fighting through swirls of dust to finish that day's scene. He just wanted to get a good take. Buddy just wanted to wash his clothes and take a shower.

Hardly worth dying over, but then what is? One of Apple-2's objectives was to determine blast effects on different types of clothing. Today, historians list Apple-2 as one of the dirtiest atomic tests; its fallout made its way into children's bodies in disproportionate numbers. No matter how many times you click through these images, they don't change.

When asked what "American Pie" meant, McLean replied, "It means I don't ever have to work again." —Alan Howard, *The Don McLean Story: Killing Us Softly With His Songs*

Does Buddy go on the road to sell records, or does he sell records to go on the road? Does he savor these giddy minutes of getting ready in a strange place, cement-floored dressing rooms with chipped green paint, hand-me-down dressers, and mirrors fastened to the wall with daisy-shaped rivets? He carries with him what he needs: guitar strings, fuses, handkerchiefs, nail file, pencil stub. Safety pins. Nobody ever has one. He could make a fortune if he started a new safety-pin factory; the world desperately needs more. And outside, the scurf of people talking, waiting for the show. Waiting for him.

Waiting for him, Maria Elena, back in their little apartment, lighting the pilot on the stove and talking to her mother in a warm haze of gas fumes and soup. Blue feathers of flame under the pot, telephone on the wall, push button to light the kitchen: all of these cost money. The honeymoon in Acapulco. The property in Bobalet Heights; he's signed his real name on the deed, Charles "Buddy" Holley, with an *e*. The stage manager says it's time, high time. He finds his mark, waits for the curtain, and when the stagehand hauls it up he can't hear the creaking of the rope for the screams, and he's playing the first chords of "Peggy Sue" without even realizing it, diving deep into a pool. Feeling the crowd stomping through the soles of his feet, shaking with the bass like he's hooked to it, and between songs he has to take off his glasses and wipe the sweat from his eyes. *Hey*, he says, *we sure are glad to be here.* The crowd's a blur but he can see the mike, its woven mesh familiar as his own fingerprint. *Whew! That's better.* Slides the glasses on. Looks back. *"Oh Boy," do you think?* When you're with me, the world can see. That you were meant for me.

Every day
It's a-getting closer
Going faster
Than a roller coaster.
—Buddy Holly, "Everyday," 1957

Southern Paiute and Western Shoshone lived, once, on the land that became the Nevada Test Site. But by now, clicking through this third reel, "The Test Site Today," it's hard to believe anyone ever lived under this acid sun at noon. Here's one of the few Doom Town houses still standing, its siding burned brown, windows empty. Here's a bank vault, slung the length of two football fields. Here's a shot tower, never used, abandoned after the moratorium in '92. Tumbleweeds rest on the broken tarmac against the guardhouse. It all looks so ordinary, the orange plastic webbing seen in countless construction zones, the ground bristling with rusty rebar. If you stare at these things, even from this remove, you carry something of them with you. Brilliant blue sky; the dust the photographer breathed, close now as the tongue in your mouth. Turn the knob of your own front door and observe how it smokes in the heat's first blast. Stand at the kitchen sink and watch the window bow inward and break, the eyelet curtain tumbling out and tearing free. Wake suddenly from your last dream to the fireball's flash and realize the shock wave is coming, will be here in a single second's tick.

Click. The guitar case snaps shut. Click. He opens a stiff new pair of glasses. Click. Dog tags rattle in the soldier's hand. Click. A photographer documents the crash scene. Click. The arm of the record player drops a 45 on the turntable. Click. A soldier stacks cans in the pantry, bottom to rim. What's still there, in that dark, silent room? A stray jug of water; an empty coffee cup. In a crack in the floor, a safety pin.

All I got here is a bunch of dead man's clothes to wear.
—*The Searchers*, 1956

That'll be the day. When Ethan Edwards says it, it's cynical; he's seen it all, and none of it's good. But in Buddy's voice, the words change. *Baby, I got your heart,* he's saying; *you ain't gonna leave me. It'd kill me if you did, you know that.* He's brave, but vulnerable, too, and maybe that's his gift, turning bitterness into hope, an alchemy possible only because he's so young, clean-cut, the favorite son. Will you say goodbye; will I cease to be? Not a chance.

Close your eyes. They're in the studio in Clovis, in rooms close in summer and drafty in winter; a studio that was formerly a grocery store, smelling of paint and mice. He sits in a corner, threading a fresh string onto the guitar and tightening it, adjusting, tightening again. Meanwhile, Jerry's working on the drum part. Norman Petty, the producer, says, "That cha-cha isn't going to work," and he's right. He charges not by the hour, but by the song, and they like that; gives you time to get it right. They try different things until they hit on the idea of paradiddles, *tacka tacka tacka tacka,* a rhythm that rolls like breakers, and when they try a take they have to wait because a passing truck makes the windows rattle. Outside, it's a hundred dark miles back to Lubbock, and nobody's in the mood to quit. Grab dinner, come back, and work some more, and later they'll stretch out on the narrow beds in back and sleep.

Maybe sometime during the night one of those big old thunderstorms rolls up out of the west, and maybe they stand outside the studio and watch it come. Forks of cloud-to-ground lightning silhouette long reefs of cloud, flashing on eighteen-wheelers barreling toward Vegas with a ways yet to go. Arc, crack, boom. Moist wind presses the boys against the wall, the smoke from their cigarettes swirling around their heads and shunting up into the downdraft. Time stops cold in moments like this, everything sharper in the strange light, the ambient electricity strong enough to raise the hair on your arms. Rain on gravel, hot smoke in your throat. When they say, *We better go in*, you say, *Give me a minute*. Lean against the still-warm cinderblock and feel the storm coming. If it's got your number, ain't nothing you can do. It's late by now, the night almost gone, but you're swinging with caffeine and nicotine and a head full of notions. Inside, your friends are waiting, and there's a seat with your name on it. Soon you'll walk through that door, an explosion now from close by and closer still, not yet, not yet, now. *Does it really happen like that?* You bet your life it does.

Beautiful Beyond Belief:
Rock City and Other Fairy Tales
of the Atomic Age

THIS WAY NEXT
–Trailside sign, Rock City

Frieda Carter was an entrepreneur's wife, and all she wanted was a garden. But it grew. In 1930, she walked through the woods with a string in her hand, letting it trail behind. Across the big flat stone, down a vale and through a narrow cleft, up a hill and out to the edge of the mountain, where the sandstone fell sharply away. Lookout Mountain was Georgia, but the valley was Tennessee, close enough to spit. This is a place where many boundary lines touch.

Do as she did and head down the narrow path through the boulders, winding past hemlocks and bluebells, each plant neatly labeled. Autumn fern, Florida azalea, leatherleaf mahonia, Lenten rose, sourwood, buttonbush. The Enchanted Trail doubles back on itself; you can't see where you're going, but you know where you've been. The brochure in your hand notes each location of interest.

Which came first, paving the way or planting the specimens? Laying stone for bridges or saying the names? Fat Man's Squeeze, Needle's Eye, Tortoise Rock. Who claimed (a stretch) that you could see seven states; who sent money overseas for the fallow deer? These deer, entirely white, bleached as old negatives, recline on granite slabs. *Are they statues?* people whisper. Not until one of the creatures flicks away an insect with its ear do we move on, spell broken.

Standing here at the lookout, lean against the guard-rail and sweep your eyes over the rim of the curving Earth. Alabama, Georgia, Kentucky, North Carolina, South Carolina, Tennessee, Virginia. But these faraway border distinctions must be taken on faith. What you're sure of are the new subdivisions spreading over the grassy fields below, the pines' dull green, a barn roof painted SEE ROCK CITY. Closer now: drop a quarter into the slot and fix your eyes to the peepholes. The cold metal hugs the bridge of your nose as you swivel the viewer toward various sights of interest: the nearby waterfall, ice rimming its edges; Stone Face, Missionary Ridge, Lover's Leap; the freeway.

High atop Lookout Mountain, overlooking Chattanooga, sits Rock City—garden, grotto, moneymaker. It opened in 1932, and if you've heard of it you can thank Garnet Carter; he started it, started, too, the marketing campaign that made the place famous, paying to have SEE ROCK CITY painted on barn roofs all over the Southeast. Today, thanks to stricter billboard laws, the barns have become relics. The Rock City gift shop offers birdhouses, coffee mugs, and ball caps shaped like those old barns.

I haven't been since I was a little girl and am not expecting much. At first, Rock City seems like any other walk through the woods. But see the circles cut in plywood? Look carefully through these round portals at all the dark dreams on display.

*

The iron handrails sweat cold drops on this chilly day. Next up: Fairyland Caverns, a partially man-made cave lined with dioramas of fairy-tale scenes, lit with ultraviolet light. It's a strange adjunct to an otherwise conventional rock garden, and the black light is what makes it unusual. To get there, you follow the trail to this entrance, Diamond Corridor.

Step into the shadowy portico and let your eyes adjust. Sparkling minerals cover the walls: crystals of dogtooth quartz, rough blossoms of calcite, glassy chunks of smoky and rose quartz. The gems gleam in the poor light. Coral lines the ceiling, some bleached white, some dyed pink, all of it from somewhere else. Yes, I remember this from my childhood visit—this entrance room, covered in glittering rocks. Back then, I'd always kept one eye on the ground, searching for treasure. During the day I pored over field guides and begged my parents to take me on rockhounding trips; at night, I dreamed of stumbling upon caches of rare specimens. I must have coveted the quartz lining this room, would have been tempted to worry a piece loose, like a tooth, knowing that even the impulse was wrong. I would have longed to sit in this niche for hours, hoarding this sharp beauty.

Not long ago, I uncovered my old rock collection, its specimens packed away in newspaper. There were tiny garnets I had sieved from mud at a North Carolina mine; quartz, still stained from the red clay it had been buried in; fluorite crystals, purple and white, safe in their old pharmacy bottle. Other specimens were glued to cardstock that provided bits of information: galena, heavy for its size and shiny, used in the manufacture of batteries; spotty bauxite, from which aluminum is made. There was the lavender muscovite from Canada, and the yellow knob of sulfur, still smelling as sour as it ever had. Best of all, there was a polished slab of agate, small as a baby's fist, whose every wrinkle and stripe I remembered immediately. The band of rich red with a stutter of white floating above! It looked like the horizon of a desert landscape I hoped even then to someday see.

I loved the world, believed its every inch paved with treasure, but knew it could be ripped away at any moment. Death was real; the preaching we heard every Sunday underscored that. A farm accident instantly killed my grandfather. A girl my own age, eight or nine, lost her mother one Friday night when her mother's car was forced off a bridge. *You're no different*, the preachers said, and I had to admit their logic. They'd start in on the scary parts of the Bible: Ezekiel, Daniel, Revelation, the moon turning red on that great and fearsome day. *The Battle of Armageddon could start at any moment*, the preachers would say, *even now, while we're sitting here in this big beautiful sanctuary, and are you right with God?* Well, who could be? *There will be a blast of wind, the rivers will turn to blood*, the preachers said. *Matthew 24:29, The stars shall fall from heaven, and the powers of the heavens shall be shaken.* What a relief when we could all file out of the barn-like church, shaking the preacher's hand on the way into the bright sun, past the blooming crepe myrtles and the old crabapple tree. How could we go out for fried chicken after that? How could I lie on the living-room floor and read the funnies or look at the paper's pictures of boring debutantes? I asked my parents about the end of the world, and they said, *Try not to worry about it too much.* Sometimes, after that, when my mind wandered during the sermons, I let it go—down the path my own feet had made through the pines; later, to dresses, always red, that would fit only me. I gazed at the fake stones set in the little rings I loved to wear, saw the lights of the sanctuary reflected in them, and let my eyes go out of focus, staring at my earthbound vision.

TO ESCAPE TEMPORARY BLINDNESS
BURY YOUR FACE IN YOUR ARMS
—*Survival Under Atomic Attack*,
Office of Civil Defence; 1950

Fairyland Caverns is a grotto, of course, and a grotto is a place with a long history. The ancient Greeks worshipped caves, the water flowing through them, and the nymphs associated with that water. The first grottoes were naturally occurring caves, but in time people dug caves out of rock, expanded existing caves, and heightened the effect of water sources by installing pipes that spurted liquid on the unwary. The practice of building grottoes was revived in Italy during the Renaissance, when wonderful things such as water organs—pipe organs played by falling water—were invented. Artists embellished cave walls with bas-relief; they arranged shells, mineral specimens, and chips of glass in swirling mosaics. If there were no natural stalagmites, they made their own, dripping cement into elaborate towers. If there were no nearby beachcombing sites, they imported shells from the West Indies. Those with enough money created spaces where the natural world was represented in abundance. They entered, perhaps, through the carven mouth of an ogre, his forehead inscribed OGNI PENSIERO VOLA: *"Every thought flies."* These were places to dawdle, shilly-shally; places to dream.

As in a traditional grotto, part of Fairyland Caverns is natural, and part is man-made. There are mechanical elements: piped music, rotating water wheels, animatronic

sailors gone to sea in a yawing washtub. And, as traditionally, water is a key feature from the first fountain to the
final room, where a stream tumbles over quartz in a four-
stepped water stair, *catena d'acqua*. Minerals line the walls,
the ceiling bristles with coral, and the pool glitters with
wishing pennies.

Leaving Diamond Corridor, make your slow way
through the caverns, pausing here and there for a look at
dioramas through those round portals cut in plywood. The
artist, Jessie Sanders, had been expert at creating the look of
real surprise. Had sculpted dozens of figures for Fairyland:
miners, Santa's helpers, bootleggers, skaters floating on a
flannel-rimmed pond. Bears chase Goldilocks, but their
hearts aren't in it. Dwarfs cluster with squirrels and rabbits,
Snow White poses in a pretty glen, and the faint strains of
"Rock-A-Bye Baby" filter in from somewhere. Hansel and
Gretel approach a sad-looking Witch too tired to be sinister, just an old woman getting home after a long shift. Her
cottage's peppermint-stick pillars tilt out-of-true. *Not much,
but it's paid for,* she seems to say, trudging heavily toward the
kids, their hands already out.

I'd remembered Diamond Corridor but forgotten the
dioramas inside, how they fiddle with dimension, tautly
foreshortening or stretching out into delirious long shots;
how the gnomes' jaws and cheekbones jut sharply, shiny
with lacquer. How their beards gleam in the ultraviolet
light, and how their tights shimmer. Fairyland Caverns
opened in 1947, and the ultraviolet light there carries a
hint of radioactive threat. Everyday things—teeth, white
T-shirts—glow under it.

In July 1945, as I've mentioned, scientists exploded the
first atomic bomb in remote New Mexico. I imagine Jessie
Sanders working on her sculptures during the Trinity test,

dipping her brush in pots of fluorescent paint as scientists half a continent away calculated what the fallout might be, the half-life of plutonium, where the winds might carry the particles. Some of those particles rained down on a rancher—nobody knew he lived where he did. Of the fallout he said, *It smelled funny.*

Here's a scene from "Rip Van Winkle," Washington Irving's version of an ancient story. Unhappy at home, Rip escapes to the woods with his rifle and his dog. High in the mountains he meets a group of strange, silent men, bowling and boozing. *They stared at him with such fixed, statue-like gaze, that his heart turned within him and his knees smote together.* When they look away he sneaks draughts of their powerful wine, waking in the morning to find his rifle rusty and his dog vanished, twenty years lost. He returns to his town, a place gone strange. When he insists, *I was myself last night, but I fell asleep on the mountain,* folks just laugh.

Rip leans on his rifle for support. Two men stand nearby, jubilant, leering. One clenches a pipe in his teeth, and the other carries a basket of glowing coals. But the look on Rip's face strikes me; despite his long sleep, he's exhausted, eyes dark with worry, and if he could speak he'd say, *What have I done?*

Well, he's survived his own mortality, nothing less. And so he's rewarded with the rare chance to see his place—family, home, community—after his death, for so his twenty years' disappearance had seemed to be. How would he be remembered? For his kindnesses to strangers, for his gentle playfulness with children? Psalm 31:12, *Forgotten as a dead man, out of mind.* To fall asleep under the mountain is to be erased as though you had not been. If not for the tired welcome of his long-lost daughter, Rip would not be remembered at all.

What draughts do we drink to make us forget so much? The world shifts around us; like an old man said to me once, *Used to joke you could lie down in the middle of Highway 123 on a Saturday night and go to sleep. Look at it now.* You can't see where you're going, but you know where you've been. Rip awoke old, safely doddering, ignored. They'd cut down the oak tree and planted a flagpole in its place. He'd slept through the revolution.

DIAL: 4
OBJECTIVE: CHICKAMAUGA BATTLEFIELD
—View scenic points through these Bausch & Lomb binoculars. 25 Cents.

We aren't the first to visit this mountain, not by a long shot. Consider the Battle of Lookout Mountain, also known as the Battle Above (or Within) the Clouds. See *Mission Ridge and Lookout Mountain, with Pictures of Life in Camp and Field,* B. F. Taylor, 1872. "And here we are pleasantly walking where sleeps an earthquake; making each other hear where slumbers a voice that could shake these everlasting hills," wrote Taylor, musing in the munitions tent of the Army of the Cumberland, 1863. After the battle, he wrote, "Mission Ridge has been swept with fire and steel as with a broom."

Taylor's camp imagery, vital and immediate, lets the reader in on a world that war movies skip. He notes the tents' "genuine home-like air. The bit of a looking-glass hangs against the cotton wall; a handkerchief of a carpet before the bunk marks the stepping-off place to the land of dreams; a violin case is strung to a convenient hook. . . . The business of living has fairly begun again." Can't you see the place, clear as a stage set? So with a few strokes here and there, we make a resting place, as if to stay awhile.

But things change quickly when the order comes to strike camp. Overnight, "the canvas city has vanished like a vision. On such a morning and amid such a scene I have loitered till it seemed as if a busy city had been passing out of sight, leaving nothing behind for all that light and life but empty desolation." Broken branches in a smoldering heap; trampled fields of stubble. Give it a few years and you'll never know anything out of the ordinary had happened here, though decades from now some keen-eyed person might turn up a bullet casing or a coin crusted with verdigris.

Of the soldiers, Taylor wrote, "If there is a curious cave, a queer tree, a strange rock, anywhere about, they know it. . . . Home they come with specimens that would enrich a cabinet. The most exquisite fossil buds just ready to open, beautiful shells, rare minerals, are collected by these rough and dashing naturalists. If you think the rank and file have no taste and no love for the beautiful, it is time you remembered of what material they are made." So they might have loved the grotto of Fairyland; they might have created their own cabinets of wonder, protomuseums, in the lidded boxes of peacetime life.

If there is nothing new under the sun, neither is there anything new beneath the earth. Grottoes functioned as early theaters; caves have interesting backdrops and good acoustics, and their shape lingers still in the arch over the stage in modern theaters. So, too, Fairyland Caverns is stuffed with scenes from childhood stories, frozen and stiff. And that light! Ultraviolet light is a way for humans to see the world as some other creatures do; it translates their vision into our own language of sight. Honeybees see patterns on flowers that direct them to pollen and nectar. Because these patterns show up at shorter wavelengths, they are visible to bees, but not to humans. In a rock shop I visited once, a curtained corner hid a display case containing mineral samples. When you pressed a button, an ultraviolet light switched on, and certain samples glowed green and purple. Once the timer ran out, you saw the same specimens, dull and unremarkable. Ultraviolet light let you in on their secret.

The light in Fairyland Caverns points toward something larger than itself; like an anxious friend, it pokes you in the side, whispering, *This isn't right.* Things have changed, and it feels wrong to repeat the same old stories. Although it's a comfort to know what comes next—*Yankee Doodle went to town / Riding on a pony*—there's a disconnect, a break: Trinity. If you want to see something of Trinity, go to New Mexico, where the nuclear age began. Face the explosion, the original light that Fairyland slantwise reflects. Yes, you could trace it further: say the bomb started with the Curies' radium research, or with Jewish physicists on the run from Hitler; say it started under the old squash court at the University of Chicago; say the seeds of apocalypse were sown at the Earth's very beginning. But for argument's sake, start in New Mexico.

Drive the wide freeway to Albuquerque, past adobe houses and mitt-shaped buttes, anvil clouds and remnants of Route 66, and pull over at the National Museum of Nuclear Science and History. The exhibits there explain the preparations involved in the making of the first atomic bomb, with thumbnail biographies of the scientists working on the Manhattan Project. One of the most interesting things on display is an old copy of the Los Alamos newspaper. Dated June 25, 1945, the *Bulletin* lists the movies to be shown at the compound's theater;

it scolds the mystery person who's been pocketing the knives from the mess hall and promises that no new ones will replace those stolen.

None of this would be all that noteworthy were it not for the fact that the Trinity test is less than a month away. There will be a blinding flash and rolling thunder, hot wind and shock waves, but in the meantime someone on the base has lost a "long-haired black Persian cat with yellow eyes, wearing a collar with bell"; someone else misses "a Buick hub cap," offering a reward for its return. The list of items FOR SALE includes a "Large, strong, varnished clothes basket. Used 1 month as bassinet. $3.50." This bears out what I've read about the growing Los Alamos maternity ward, as does the WANTED TO BUY list, which includes a request for a "Good baby buggy. Call 496." Trinity's plutonium core will arrive at the test site three days early; someone will drive it down from Los Alamos to Jornada del Muerto in the back seat of a '42 Plymouth. A good family car.

AND WE ARE IN A STRANGE NEW LAND
—"The Atomic Age," *Life*, August 20, 1945

Does Rock City show our past or our future? Without the ultraviolet light, it's the past—nursery rhymes, fairy tales, a garden static as blooms preserved under glass. But the ultraviolet light shows the future, a place radiant with garish color. The familiar fairy tales are transformed by this luminous color scheme into something peculiarly atomic-age. I read about the workers, mostly women, who painted the glowing tips of alarm-clock hands. They licked their paintbrushes to get a fine point; at night, their skin, clothes, and hair glowed. The radium in the paint gave them bone cancer, and they filed suit in 1927. By court day, they were too weak to raise their right hands. This strange light makes innocent stories sinister, recognizable but changed. The atomic calves who grazed in the desert during Trinity look normal but for their dusting of white. *Swept with fire and steel as with a broom.* Seared everywhere the fallout touched.

Before Trinity, the scientists at Los Alamos made a wager. Would the bomb set the Earth's atmosphere on fire, and if it did, would the consequences be local or global? They liked betting, those physicists; in another pool, each of them guessed how much power the bomb would have, as compared to tons of TNT. The man who won happened to come in late, after all the reasonable figures had been taken. Out of politeness, he guessed what seemed like a ridiculously high figure, and it turned out he was the closest. (Twenty thousand.)

At the moment of detonation—July 16, 1945, 5:29:45 a.m.—a passenger was on her way to morning music class. She saw the bright flash of light and thought it was the sunrise. *What was that?* she asked her brother. She saw the explosion, this woman—even though she was stone blind. Hadn't it seemed like any other morning? Maybe the brother drove a little too fast through town, running late, past the still-dark filling station, radio dimly on. Suddenly a blast of light, unlike anything ever seen, and what must he have thought, the brother?—blind too, at that moment, and too stunned to steady the car. No word for thought, not at first, silence then thunder and hot wind as not far away, the physicists lifted their faces from the ground, and Oppenheimer thought of a line from the *Bhagavad Gita: I am become Death, the destroyer of worlds.*

It smelled funny, the rancher said, standing in the desert as the fallout rained down. Was that the vaporized jackrabbits, kangaroo rats, greasewood, killed at the moment of detonation, falling on him? Rip woke from his long sleep and staggered out from under the mountain to a world scrubbed bare, glowing gray in dull light. *Slept through the revolution.* What if he were the only one left? Even Wolf long gone; every dog gone.

THE FUTURE BELONGS
TO THOSE WHO PREPARE FOR IT
—Advertisement, Prudential Life Insurance, *Life*,
September 24, 1945

After Trinity, Hiroshima, Nagasaki, it makes perfect sense: you go underground, a place of safety, but also a place of ancient, subconscious threat. Go where the dead go and make your home there. Where ants and blind worms tunnel, where moles stroke smoothly through the clay. *You will beg the mountain to cover you, and the rocks to hide you.* It will not be enough. By August of 1945, the bomb no longer secret, an editorial in *Life* read, "For if there is no defense, then perhaps man must either abolish international warfare or move his whole urban civilization underground." Fallout shelters (suburbia below ground) are grottoes lined with hoarded goods. Hollow out a place and fill it with the stories you used to know, but even the light is changed here, and things shine as they once did not, setting your glowing teeth on edge. Continued *Life*, "Constructing beautiful urban palaces and galleries, many ants have long lived underground in entire satisfaction."

Paging through these old magazines, you want to shake the people in the ads for Packards, frozen peas, Campbell's Soup. Wake up! But the draught's been drained; done is done. What can follow the photos of the Trinity crater?

An article about the new Miss America, flutist, a tall New
Yorker. Ads for underwear and Arrow dress shirts. *Mamma,
use Swan soap. Free cake of soap to any baby born in 1945;
write away for coupon. The business of living has fairly begun
again*, wrote Taylor; said Mom and Dad, *Try not to worry about
it too much.* Good advice, if you can take it. At breakfast, just
after Trinity, physicist George Kistiakowsky sat in the din-
ing room at the Los Alamos Lodge and said, "That was the
nearest to doomsday one can possibly imagine. . . . I am
sure that at the end of the world—in the last millisecond of
the earth's existence—the last man—will see something very
similar to what we have seen."

Who knows how Jessie Sanders felt about the bomb?
She was busy in her studio, pouring Hydrocal; a survi-
vor, building a new world. How do we live with this new
knowledge of how the Earth will end? Set it aside. Keep
on working. Said journalist William Laurence, witness-
ing Nagasaki—of which Trinity had been a test—"We
removed our glasses after the first flash but the light still
lingered, a bluish-green light that illuminated the entire
sky. . . . As the first mushroom floated off into the blue it
changed its shape into a flowerlike form, its giant petals
curving downward, creamy-white outside, rose-colored
inside." It's an artist's description, filled with color and
comparison, and yet this is light unwholesome, strong-
armed into something never before seen. If Fairyland
Caverns is a memento mori, it is unlike the Renaissance
ones, where sculpted skeletons reach from caskets to claw
the air. Here there are no bones—vaporized instantly—just
the glowing circles of Baa Baa Black Sheep's wool, hanging in the darkness like an afterimage. What made me
think of Trinity as I walked through Fairyland? Light
spoken in a new tongue; a cave peopled by children with

glowing faces. But the truth is you find what you look for. Maybe not the exact specimen, but once the scales fall from your eyes you must see the world, strange and dark. A red moon floated above a stadium on a noisy Friday night. I could have read there a sign of doom, or atmospheric dust, or both. Just the same, once I saw Trinity I would see it always, everywhere.

Imagine the world deserted. The raven did not return to the ark, but lit on the bodies of the floating dead. Under a photo of the Trinity crater, the caption reads, "The first atomic bomb's crater is a great green blossom in the desert near Alamogordo." The heat from the blast fused desert sand into a greenish glass, trinitite; how I would, as a child, have loved to find a piece of that poison glass. Imagine a desert rasped clean of every living thing. The bomb's crater, shallow to start with, fills in a little more every sundown when the wind kicks up. Now, sixty years out, you wouldn't know anything had happened there if not for the plaque, though there's rarely anyone around to read it. Bits of trinitite pocketed years ago, ground to powder, or buried. A waste place. Neither stubble nor crumb. *Till it seemed as if a busy city had been passing out of sight.* So it has been. Will be.

Outside the caverns, safe in the half-empty parking lot, come back to yourself. Unlock your car and drive slowly down the mountain road, careful on the switchbacks. Turn on the radio. Pass the first barn: GOOD BYE TELL YOUR FRIENDS ABOUT ROCK CITY. Yes, that's right; these barns are how you heard about the place to start with. SEE SEVEN STATES. WORLD'S 8TH WONDER, BRING YOUR CAMERA. BEAUTIFUL BEYOND BELIEF.

THE LORD'S WILL SHALL BE DONE
NOT YOURS OR MINE
—Roadside sign outside Chattanooga

The barns were new once. Bright boards wept sap. There
was that one roofed with hand-rived shakes cut from the
great felled oak. The old men said, *You got to do it at the right
time of the light of the moon lest the shingles curl.* Shakes nailed
down tight.

Clark Byers didn't need stencils; understood the different iterations of barn, varying shapes in the same family.
Painted SEE ROCK CITY on roofs with a wide brush. That
dry wood drank paint, didn't it. Hot work, sweat running
down his spine, paint spattering his forearms, pulling his
hair as it dried. Carolina grasshoppers leaping from yellow
straw to light on tall pokeweed. Pokeweed juice a dye the
Cherokee used. Had used.

Made his own paint from linseed oil and lampblack.
"There were no such things as rollers," he said. "Used a
four-inch brush, never had to measure letters and always
worked freehand. Once that paint got on, there was no getting it off." He carried paint, rope, chalk, brushes. Dying
barns deflate like lungs. Inside them it is dusty, with a different kind of darkness, and in the rafters you might see
wasps swarming, or old swallows' nests. Termites chew
the planking, piling gray dust on the floor of pounded red
clay. TO MISS ROCK CITY WOULD BE A PITY read the John
Molyneux barn. That was from the 1930s. It's torn down
now.

Traditionally, it took forty days and forty nights to cure
tobacco in the barns. In early spring, you weighted seeds
with ash to sow; come midsummer, cut green leaves, working slowly down the line. Bundled stems together in hands

and set a slow fire. The leaves cured to brown, supple as skin on a wrist. Smoke wriggled out through gaps in the walls. You'd see it wafting over the fields, smell it on a still night, dusty and sweet, like grass in August but darker. Most people have forgotten all this by now, or never knew. One day won't anyone remember.

Ten Years You Own It

Salton Sea, California

Smears of heat rise from the car, the pavement, my sister's head. I step out of the car and onto a dead fish, crushing its skull under my heel. The air's so dry it shivers, the sun's so strong that freckles pop like paint across my arms, and the stink—from tons of decaying fish—is making us all sputter and choke. The Salton Sea is the kind of place most people go out of their way to avoid. Not me. I've talked my family into coming here, all because of a photograph I've seen.

Tilapia can stand bad treatment—hotter water, higher salinity, more pollution—better than most fish, but sometimes the Salton Sea gets to be too much even for them. When that happens, they die off in huge numbers, sometimes as many as eight million a day. I walk down the beach with my family, all of us crunching tilapia underfoot. The fishes' eyes go first, pecked out by ravenous shorebirds, but eventually all the fish transform from curled-up wholes to neat ladders of vertebrae to, finally, pearly piles of loose scales that lie scattered across the beach like bingo chips.

I lean over the water's edge but don't step in. The water itself is tea-dark, but its surface is as bright as tinfoil. Broken slabs of concrete and stubs of rebar jut underwater. We walk slowly past a row of abandoned house trailers, wrecked during the last of the big storms. Here's a planed-open shower stall, a rusty oven with its door wrenched off, a shank bone from a big dog, probably a Lab. Here, washed up on the water's edge, lies an empty pack of Skydancer cigarettes, a warrior in a headdress lifting his open palm to the pale-blue sky.

We were joking in the car, but that's all evaporated now as we squint at the water, a little confused, a little sweaty. It's eerie here, even at high noon, and I'm not sure why. This feels like a place located outside the bounds of normal time, like an amusement park, but we're missing something. Calliopes and tin whistles: this beach is silent.

MIRAGE: 1958

Cue the music, coming to you live from an unseen band. *Somewhere*, some fellow sings, *beyond the sea / Somewhere, waiting for me.* The trumpets, nasally muted, swing along in the background, counterpointing the melody, propping it up. A drummer brushes the skins, and despite the terrific heat, everything is very, very cool. And you're here to see it all: the sleek cigarette boats peeling the water open; the gulls flying past crinkled mountains; the platinum sun. The ice in your drink goes to water and you swallow it. When a breath of wind passes over your face you're immediately grateful, as if heaven sent it particularly to you, just to see if you'd notice.

For thousands of years, Desert Cahuilla Indians lived here, watching the water come and go, and farming on these banks. But the Salton Sea's current incarnation began as a mistake. In 1905, the Colorado River, which had been diverted to irrigate local agriculture, overcame its banks and poured full bore into the desert for two years, when engineers from the Southern Pacific Railroad finally blocked it with tons of riprap. The Alamo and New Rivers continue to drain into the Salton Sea, as does agricultural runoff from the Imperial Valley. Since 1909, the Torres Martinez band of Desert Cahuilla has held the title to ten thousand acres of land that lie on the bottom of the Sea.

In the mid-1980s, Richard Misrach shot a series of large-format photographs of the Salton Sea. These images, collected in *Desert Cantos*, are dangerous viewing for those with a certain bent: they'll put a spell on you. Take this one, *Diving Board, Salton Sea,* of an empty swimming pool with a diving board and a flooded horizon receding to the vanishing point. The floodwater surrounding the pool is a strange, limpid blue, with a depth impossible to divine. I've gone back to the image again and again, trying to figure out why it haunts me. Partly it's the story that the empty pool contains; what turned a resort into a ghost town?

But more than that, it's something in the water. This is no ordinary sea, no ordinary sunset, and despite its calm surface, the water reminds me somehow of solvent, mercury thinned with gasoline. This is water with an opinion.

MIRAGE: 1902
The sun doesn't do all the work, but it does what you can't. You pour barrels of water into pools you've dug, then go round to tend the ones you set out yesterday and the day before. The sun licks the pools dry, like the fire of the Lord on Elijah's offering, licking up the water on the altar and the water in the trough and the water soaking the wood, then the wood itself and the pieces of the sacrifice and the stones of the altar, cracked open in the flames. Sweat crawls down your neck as you rake these things over, turning the

damp spread of new salt into neat piles. Pinch the stuff between your fingers and taste of it. Precious dust, come to you free, waiting in the desert like manna. Bow down in the sand, eyes shut from gratitude or knifelike sun. Nobody here to see you or ask why.

After World War II, speculators promoted the Salton Sea as a resort destination. At just fifty miles south of Palm Springs it seemed like a sure bet. Agents brought investors by the busload from Los Angeles to put their money down on tidy lots lining the curving residential roads. Boomtowns like Salton Sea Beach, Desert Shores, and Bombay Beach—where we're standing now—grew up along the water's edge, near boaters who raced across the water, setting world records. The salinity (saltier than the Pacific) and elevation (more than two hundred feet below sea level) combined to make this very "fast water." Frank Sinatra and Guy Lombardo played shows at the Yacht Club just down the way.

But over the next twenty years, the boom faded, and then the storms hit. Hurricane Kathleen in 1976, Doreen in 1977—the second "hundred-year storm" in two years' time— followed by seven years of heavy rains, which reduced the trailers we're walking past to support beams and twists of insulation. A few people still hang on in town, but nobody lives on this beach anymore. The flooding patterns are too unpredictable, and most of the time the whole area stinks to high heaven. A few years ago, the state tore the Yacht Club down.

I can see why Richard Misrach shot his photographs in the mellow, rosy light of sunset. Noon is grimmer than I'd expected, and the scene is stark and sad in the eye-watering sun. Scalded, scabbed. There's a woman in a bikini doing a fashion shoot on the water's edge. She vamps and poses on the broken concrete, the Sea shimmering behind her. A car whips into the parking lot, the woman at the wheel scanning the area for someone she doesn't find. (Vanity plate: KANNABA.) She cuts the wheel hard, and as she streaks away, we can hear the Bon Jovi she's cranked up. *Who says you can't go home?*

Wasn't this what I'd wanted to see? Evidence of a practice apocalypse, terrible but local: if you're lucky, you can leave it behind. We stopped to see the disaster, but which one? Several bird species depend on the Salton Sea, and these beaches can teem with egrets, herons, gannets, terns. Yet there are massive bird die-offs, too; during the worst one, in 1996, park rangers worked day and night and still couldn't keep up, stuffing dead pelican after pelican into the blazing maw of the same incinerator model favored by undertakers.

I head for the car. Buttons of salt on nail heads, rusty radio stuffed with sand: if you go looking for a portent, everything you find will seem like one. I know that on the bottom of the Sea there's an old salt works, a locomotive, a railroad track. When the river flooded in 1905, it covered everything, double lines of track leading down and vanishing into the water. On a slab of broken concrete, someone's written MEMENTO MORI, MEMENTO VIVERE in neat Sharpie letters. What looks like lime Jell-O bubbles in a pair of footprints on the water's edge. It would be so easy to float in the Sea, the muscular water holding me up, but I can't bring myself to do it.

We drive away, passing a truck loaded with gleaming fists of garlic and a tidy trailer park named for St. Anthony, patron saint of lost things. Past a billboard that reads $99.80 DOWN, $99.80 A MONTH, TEN YEARS YOU OWN IT.

EVERYONE QUALIFIES. And even though I know the Salton Sea is an old-time swindle, even though the car still reeks from dead fish and iodine, I'm tempted. You can get it for a song. Said Bon Jovi, *Who says you can't go back?*

But you can get more than you bargained for. What did I come here to see—aftermath or prophecy? *It's not a tourist trap*, my sister says, *because there's nothing to buy.* But this isn't the worst of it.

*

A pleasure ground needs to be crowded or it feels strange. Waiting in line is part of the ritual; someone else must want what you want. It helps to have something to crunch between your teeth—popcorn, fish scales—and a pocket full of quarters. Drop a coin in the slot, and nine brown Skee-Balls come rocketing down the chute. This is the game's sweetest moment, anticipation made tangible by spheres of hard, sweat-oiled wood. Take one in your hand, lean back, and let it fly, rolling up the ramp and onto the rim; it drops into the hole marked one hundred and vanishes from sight. And here's your next chance, right at hand. You could do this all day, waxed cup of cola sweating a ring on the floor. Time passes without your noticing, your back to the open arcade door, eyes on the prize. In the background, a pneumatic hiss and thump as the heavy zinc ball exits the air gun and knocks down the clown. The alarm-bell *ding ding ding* from another player's high score, sweet fumes of cotton candy and hair spray and WD-40, a clink as a red plastic ring bounces off a milk bottle. By the time you turn to go, it's dark outside. You shake your head to clear it.

A pleasure ground's natural features, if there are any, must in fact be engineered in order to create a particular effect. Its river becomes a flume upon which people ride in fiberglass boats shaped like dugout canoes. Its trees are oases of shade under which children sit and eat fried dough. And the sun at a pleasure ground always seems to shine more brightly. You'll get the worst burn of your life and won't even feel it until you leave, spiriting the heat away under your skin.

The Salton Sea feels like a pleasure ground that people abandoned years ago. But don't be fooled by the burned-out trailers on the edge of the water that say this story's been told. Look more closely. At the water the color of beef broth, so full of salt and herbicides—atrazine, bentazon, diquat, metribuzin—it's two steps from solidifying, like aspic. I've eaten my share of spinach and grapes and strawberries from the Imperial Valley; their runoff is here now, reducing every minute under the powerful summer sun. Look around. This is what happens when the money runs out and nobody's left to clean up the mess. This is what's next.

*

We're back on the road now, making good time. Wendover Air Force Base sits a ways to our north, but it would have been an easy hop for the pilots flying their Silverplate B-29s. God, how they blinded you to look at them.

But all of that came later. Before they built the hangar, before they painted ENOLA GAY on the forward fuselage, the men needed a water source, a barracks, and a target range. When they built the range on the Bonneville Salt Flats in '42, they used what they had. They built a city of salt.

MIRAGE: 1942

It's hell on a blade. The salt eats the steel and the sand nicks the edge, but you fight that with the whetstone you keep wrapped in old shirt flannel. You have to

feed the stone with oil or it gets squirrelly, dry climate
like this. Only shade here is what you make yourself.
Everything here is temporary, and the brass are planning something big, keeping it quiet. Salt City hurts
to look at, once it's done, blinding white during the
day, and at night, you can't help but dream about it, its
silence, how it glows softly on the Flats. When dawn
comes, you'll bomb the dickens out of it, practicing for
the real thing.

When Paul Tibbets arrived at Wendover, in September
of '44, he was almost thirty years old and considered the
best pilot in the United States. And even though his mission
was top secret, people all over the country were involved in
his work. He flew a Nebraska-built B-29, from which he
would drop a new kind of bomb, if the boys in Los Alamos
could finish in time. SAFETY STARTS BETWEEN THE EARS,
read the sign on the wall in Oak Ridge, Tennessee, where a
boomtown had grown overnight to support the enrichment
of the uranium that would power Little Boy. Wormholes in
the Arizona desert showed where Navajo yellowcake miners had been. And in Washington State, the new town of
Hanford, charged with collecting plutonium for Trinity
and Fat Man, sat just up the bluff from the old Hanford,
abandoned because of contamination. Hurricane fencing
separated the shuttered high school from the toxic trees
surrounding it.

From October 1944 through August 1945, Tibbets flew
practice runs from Wendover to the California desert. On
August 6, 1945, he would pilot *Enola Gay* over Hiroshima.
But he couldn't have known that then, not really, as he
sped over the sand and the cholla, dropping fake A-bombs
into the Salton Sea.

Inert bombs are called "pumpkins" or "shapes." They aren't real, exactly, but they show you how the real thing is likely to behave. They're weighted like the real thing, dull bulbous metal like the real thing, and when they crashed to the Sea floor, they raised clouds of silt in the dark water. They must still be down there, dozens of them, resting on acreage to which the Desert Cahuilla still hold title. Just like anything else, you have to get a feel for it, practice until you get it right.

I think I get it now. The Salton Sea pulled me in as a haunted place—anyone could see that—but once I stood on its edge I knew in my bones that it was more. When you need to try out a new kind of bomb, come to this uncanny Sea, a place caught between ground zero and a city of salt. The Salton Sea's surface at midday is bright as Mylar but its waters are dark, oily, forced to contain everything we hide.

"The only trips we ever made were to funerals," I read in an old letter to Ann Landers. So when you visit the Salton Sea, wear closed-toe shoes. Carry water and a camera. Don't approach the birds, or scribble down the real-estate agent's phone number. This water keeps its own counsel, claiming salt miner, soldier, burnout, pulling them near. Resist the urge to jump. Look past the rust-eaten bus out onto the open desert, marked by signs but no streets, twists of black plastic, a go-cup that skitters and skips in the wind. This is as good a place as any to watch and wait. For a rain of fire to lick up the windrows of salted fish. For a crooner and a band. For a long-forgotten bomb to explode.

Backstage with John the Beloved Disciple

James the Less is looking mighty rough. Half of his face might have gotten the worst of a bar fight—creases and bruises around the eye sockets, maroon-blue smears on his right cheek, jawline seamed, neck sore and stippled.

The makeup artist holds a Styrofoam head in one hand and a dripping brush in the other. She paints James's right side pretty thick, but because he'll have his face turned toward Christ, the left stays almost bare. She checks his face against the Styrofoam reference, touches up his shadows. "I'm gonna rob a Chick-fil-A after I leave," he says. "Police report'll say, 'He got away with two number ones and eight dollars.'" Simon, Peter, and Andrew laugh. James is a mess.

Good Friday a year ago, I found myself sitting in this auditorium with my mouth open, unable to tell which figures were painted and which were real people. I didn't know anyone still did *tableau vivant* anymore—I'd only read about it in Victorian-era novels—and I didn't know it could be done so well. Years ago, *tableau vivant* used to be an evening's entertainment, akin to putting on a play, but static. The goal is to come as close in real life as you can to an original piece of art.

I had to know the trick, so I called the director, who invited me to go backstage before the show. He explained how he sources images from the ceilings of European cathedrals, and showed me the lighting secrets that make a body look flat from a distance. He's had to cast men as women in order to make the forced perspective work. Think Mary Magdalene washing Christ's feet with her hair; you just can't find a woman tall enough. And in the stained-glass tableau, the makeup artists paint eyeballs on the actors' closed lids lest the whites of their eyes ruin the effect.

✳

IT'S A SIN TO DO LESS THAN YOUR BEST, says the sign on the wall. Well, I've always believed that myself. We're standing in the sewing department, a sunny room on the theater's top floor stocked with bolts of gorgeous fabric, spools of brilliant thread, plastic-zipped capes and ball gowns and robes from past productions. Potted philodendrons send out green vines along the windowsills.

The wig-maker demonstrates technique, her graceful hand flicking strands of invisible hair and securing them to the lace's open weave with a curved needle, a few strands at a time. Nobody knows how to do it the old-fashioned way anymore. Once a woman came from Hollywood to give a workshop on the finer points of wig-making and offered this artist a job on the spot; she didn't take it, but it's nice to have options. The sign outside the door says BUT THE VERY HAIRS OF YOUR HEAD ARE ALL NUMBERED.

✳

In spite of his ghoulish makeup and paint-matted wig, John the Beloved Disciple is a knockout, in an all-American, Bible-Drill-Champion kind of way. The director needed someone tall, the only way to make the perspective work, and he's six feet three. (The bodysuits are prepared in a downstairs room called the Body Shop, which I can't visit. Just as well.) But it's more than that. There's a sweetness about him; I can tell that he wants to get it right. During the actual tableau, it's very hard to stand perfectly still, but he lets me in on his secret. "I focus on the emergency exit sign in the back," he says. He counts the letters, reading them over and over again, trying not to waver.

I walk around backstage, staring up into the fly space where old sets dangle from chains three stories above. Velcro stripes the current sets where costumes will attach. Here's a hole cut through plywood where Pilate pushes his shoulder, or where Christ kneels. A block for a footrest, padding for a bended knee.

Golgotha's ground is paved with Styrofoam pebbles, beanbag fill. The centurion's life-sized horse is Styrofoam too, roughed out with a chain saw, carved with a hot wire, and coated with Elmer's for a smooth finish. But the cross that dominates the scene is made of yellow pine, pressure-treated and kiln-cured. Midway up, Jesus has a bike seat and a woven belt to keep him from falling. It will hold him invisibly, buckled under his robe.

*

Showtime. The disciples file out of the greenroom, onto the stage, and take their places: Thaddeus, Peter, John, James, Judas Iscariot. Little hooks screwed to the underside of the table hold watches and eyeglasses. Christ sits in the middle, and though the audience can't see it, he's wearing Nikes.

When the curtain rises, the disciples sway slightly and blink, but they're as motionless as they can be, until the chorus of the song plays—"In Remembrance of Me." Then they start to move, their lips forming silent words, silently laughing, silently gesturing. "We don't animate the Christ figure," the director whispers to me. And suddenly I realize—how had I missed it?—that it's Leonardo da Vinci's famous *Last Supper* they're portraying, the one in Milan. As many times as I've seen reproductions of it, I hadn't recognized it here. It's a gift, to see this familiar painting with fresh eyes, to get a real sense of the sorrowing Christ, unmoving as the rest of the group celebrates. He knows what's coming; the rest, for now, are just sharing a meal.

Usually when you look at a work of art you can trust your senses. They are a given, as little investigated as the parquet floor beneath your feet. The painting in the frame is two-dimensional; lean close and you can see the brush-strokes. But *tableau vivant* obscures the boundary between inside and outside the work. You attend wanting to be tricked, to flirt with your own basically trustworthy (yet fallible!) senses. To push the translation between seeing and understanding what you see. This man seems to be part of the painting, and for a time he can pretend to be, fitting himself to the shoulder-shaped hole cut to hold him. Then the shifting stage lights reveal the truth. When the music ends, he drops his eyes and steps offstage.

I wait in the wings, staring, with John the Beloved Disciple, at the lighted sign in back that says EMERGENCY EXIT, holding very still and fixing on those black letters as the reality of what's about to happen dawns on the men and the sky grows dark beyond the window of the upper room. When the curtain drops, they climb down slowly, each one waiting for his brother at the bottom of the step-ladder. Ready, should he stumble, to break his fall.

Something Like the Fire

NEVADA TEST SITE, 1953
Put yourself in his shoes: cold, Army-issue, treads packed
with sand. Rise before dawn, climb into the truck and
bump down the road to the work site, and as the convoy
tops the last ridge, narrow your eyes at the rising sun's brilliant seam. Showtime. Up the ladder you go, sun already
warm on your neck, roof shingles softening underfoot, nail
heads gleaming silver.

The day wears on in pounding and shouts as you move
down the line, lapping layers tight enough to turn any
water, although this roof will never see rain. Down below,
masons raise the chimney a row at a time, scraping the
excess mortar free. Next to them, painters spray the siding,
not bothering to tape the windows. Saltbush shivers on the
ridge as you ride back to Base Camp Mercury, day's work
done, clothes heavy with sweat and tar, paint and dirt,
tacky with sap from lumber that six months ago was a tree.
A world away.

OPERATION DOORSTEP-SHOT ANNIE, 1953
See how easy it is to make a family, twins sprawled on
the floor, Baby in his high chair, Mother bending near, a
spoonful of pear in her shapely hand. J. C. Penney provided mannequins and wardrobe for publicity: rompers for

81

the twins, footed sleeper for Baby, and for Mother, a sensible skirt, button-front blouse, clip earrings. (Father's at work, offstage.) Just before dawn. The bomb will detonate in a minute's time.

See the desert, scraped bare, hash-marked with distances.

Abandoned tanks wait in arrow formation. Testing instruments nestle in the cold sand. Standing on a little hill, journalists press dark goggles to their faces, to give their hands something to do.

There must be sound, but it's been edited out. So all of this unspools in silence, Mother's face lighting up, bleaching white, catching fire. Then the blast wave punches in the wall, shattering the window and knocking Mother off her stool. There must be the sound of glass splintering, a noise lost in the roaring wind that snuffs the blazing bodies, shreds the curtains, shears the door from its hinges. Then the house collapses in a raw hex of timber. Two seconds all told, the roof blown straight to hell.

"THE RIVIERA: A NEW HIGH IN THE LAS VEGAS SKY," 1955

Sixty-five miles south of the test site, in Las Vegas. The audience waits in the darkness, new chandeliers glowing pink on their dimmest setting. A man unwraps a peppermint, and taffeta rustles as someone crosses her ankles, high heel scrubbing an arc in the floor. But quiet for being so many; the Clover Room seats one thousand, every cough muffled by layers of gray and green, drapes the colors of new money.

A click as the mike goes live, and a spotlight snaps on. *Ladies and gentlemen.* Cut left; drumroll. *The Riviera is proud to present.* And he strides on from the wings, this man in his prime, smile bright as his gleaming jacket. Waving to acknowledge the applause, he seats himself at the piano and flips his coattails free. He starts with something serious—the opening fanfare of Tchaikovsky's Piano Concerto no. 1, maybe, a few commanding chords—and slides from there into the "Beer Barrel Polka," sweeping that famous grin over the crowd. Undercut the highbrow, that's his game, native son of West Allis, Wisconsin. His long fingers trill and flutter, and the piano's mirrored fallboard makes it look like two sets of hands playing. If he misses a note you can't hear it for the thicket of others, the melody's narrow path winding and weaving through the embellishments. (How would he play if nobody was listening?) His brother leads the backing orchestra, parrying the between-song banter. *Does he make that stuff up on the spot?* The songs unreel, one after the other, and when the audience stands for the final ovation they're exhausted, stuffed full. *Well, we saw it,* they say, shuffling out the door. *What a show.* They don't know the half of it.

✳

Operation Doorstep-Shot Annie was one of a hundred or so nuclear weapons that exploded in the sky above Nevada from 1952 until 1962. I'm mesmerized by their names' blunt cadences: Ranger-Able, Ranger-Baker, Ranger-Easy. Tumbler-Snapper; Greenhouse-Dog. Fox shot rose in three ice-capped steps. Climax made a narrow stem, a wide-beamed cap, and a batch of skinny tracers. Buster-Jangle-Charlie was a textbook cloud, opening in classic mushroom shape. Upshot-Knothole, in motion: a tidal wave of dust pushing across Frenchman Flat, strewing tires, twisted chassis, and an upended tank in its wake, track lying on the ground like a zipper. (After Operation Hot Rod, the Federal Civil Defense Administration warned citizens not to think of their cars as "rolling foxholes" that would save them.) I watch the old clips, listening as the narrator calls this landscape "the desert," or the "dusty precursor-forming surface." Bombs exploded, sometimes once a day, and tourists visited Vegas—the "Up and Atom City"—to watch the shots, as I've said. As one observer pointed out, the "visual show" proved to be "very spectacular."

I wonder about those tourists. What would she have thought of, she who might have—as I would have—talked her husband into rising early from a rented bed to stand in the cold desert dark, waiting? Did she say, *Drive faster; I don't want to miss it*? Or *I brought my sunglasses; you wear yours too.*

We don't have much time. What's a minute worth? Ten seconds? Counting down, *nine, eight, seven.* Did she squeeze his hand and think of unbalanced bank statements, piles of stale bedsheets, relics of another age? Moments long past, safe now in the warm light of memory. Nothing like this stark, blinding flash.

Standing there on the hill, did she gasp, or shout? Did it thrill her, the searing blaze, the weird shadows the greasewood threw, just like she'd seen in the news clips? Rumbling. Wall of dust racing across the flats toward her, howling in her ears and crusting her lips with powder. Her sunglasses hung at her throat; a kerchief covered her hair.

Afterward she was tired, windburned, sick of the Geiger counter's staccato clicks. Now everything was tainted: stones, the newspapermen's laced-up shoes crushing gypsum to powder, cars, cactus, road, bird. Even her husband. Even herself, empty face reflected in the smudged windshield. A sheet of notebook paper jumped across the desert, whirled high on air currents, and caught on a yucca, some forgotten detail or maybe still just a blank sheet, an open mouth with nothing to say.

✳

The idea was that we'd learn from it. Will a fresh coat of white paint reflect the bomb's flash, protecting your house? What about a clean-swept yard? Is it safer to build walls of brick or cinder block? If you keep things tidy inside—end tables unburdened by magazines, sofa cushions tamped firmly in place—will your living room be less likely to catch fire? If you know what to do, you can save yourself. Your family too. And the unstated corollary: *Do as we say, or you'll have only yourself to blame.* But what do we really learn? The house with the bare yard catches fire a few seconds later than the other, but still burns to the ground, sofa cushions and all. Said Val Peterson, Eisenhower's civil defense chief: "The best way to be alive when an atomic bomb goes off in your neighborhood is not to be there."

"I expected to see something like the fire that consumed the world," atomic witness Patricia Jackson told a reporter. What had she hoped for—obliteration? She sounded disappointed to be spared.

✳

Down in Vegas, the show went on. As one year melted into the next, Liberace's trills and flourishes and between-song banter lengthened until they threatened to squeeze out the tunes themselves, and his gold lamé jacket grew into costumes ever more embroidered and embellished. Christmas, Stars and Stripes, King Neptune: what awed an audience last year bores them now. How can you top a two-hundred-pound outfit? The days of the $15 junk-store candelabra were a joke from the nostalgic past, reheated for his memoirs. Money wasn't the limiting factor, creativity was. So: the double cape of pink-dyed turkey feathers, the ostrich ruff, the billowing ermine robe. Sooner or later, the joke wears thin. He must have felt it menacing him from around the corner. Which did he fear more—getting stale, or being found out? He never let an inch go to waste. So the folks in back could see it too.

As I watch old film clips of the atomic tests and Liberace's shows, I start to think they're cut somehow from the same cloth. The bright gleam of the desert at noon, what you shade your eyes against; the floodlit stage, what we still call the "theater of war." *I'm telling you the truth, and you won't believe me.*

Laughter from his last joke still hanging in the air, he ducks backstage for a costume change. An assistant hefts the cape onto Liberace's body and the folds fall true, weighted with cabs and bugles, rhinestones and foil, satin rippled with embroidery and pimpled with seed beads. Heavy as a lead apron. He pushes back his shoulders, straightens his spine, and steps into the light.

*

What happened after the cameras stopped filming, and the journalists and the tourists packed up and drove away? The fallout drifted and spread and sifted silently to the ground, soaked into the soil and was absorbed by grasses, which were eaten by cows, whose milk children drank. When the children grew ill, their mothers wrapped their baby teeth in kraft paper and mailed them to scientists at Washington University, in St. Louis, who found that the teeth of the sick children held surprising amounts of cesium and strontium, which settle in the bones.

So in 1962, the bombs went underground, and over the next three decades, more than eight hundred bombs exploded beneath the Nevada desert. One of them stands out: Baneberry. Baneberry was a test that went wrong. On

December 18, 1970, Baneberry was exploded about nine hundred feet underground; shortly after detonation, it broke through the desert, venting smoke and vapor and sand and dust ten thousand feet in the air. The radioactive cloud drifted high, far, wide. Just a matter of time, really: one tore through. Where do we go from here?

*

Fast-forward to a decade after Baneberry, smack in the middle of testing's underground years. As the familiar strains of Tchaikovsky's Piano Concerto no. 1 play, a man rises theatrically from bed, dons a thick robe, and pretends to play along on a grand piano he has in his bedroom. As he walks through his house, performing his morning ritual—a dip in a swimming pool whose edges are tiled with piano keys; a mouthful of a piano-shaped chocolate cake—he continues to mock-play the concerto, grinning and tilting his head as if to say, *It's so nice to be in on this with you.* Leaving the house, he drapes a floor-length ermine coat over his shoulders, steps onto a wide portico, and tucks himself into a rhinestone-encrusted Rolls-Royce. A handsome chauffeur closes the door with a click. Cut to an auditorium; timpani roll: "Ladies and Gentlemen." "Proud to present." "Famous for his piano" (brassy flourish!). "His candelabra" (!!). "MIST-er Showmanship" (!!!). "LIB . . . erace!"

The Rolls pulls up onstage, rhinestones winking in the glare, and the chauffeur opens the door to crashing applause. "Well, look me over," Liberace says. "I didn't dress like this to go unnoticed." He's a looker, all right, from his bouffant hair to his crystal-encrusted collar, a jabot of lace at his throat peeking out from under a bejeweled vest, hands brass-knuckled with amethysts and emeralds, sparkling oxfords on his feet. "Do you like it?" he asks.

"You do? Wonderful, great. Sure," he says, "there's enough for all of you. Go ahead, help yourself. Oh yeah." And the crowd eats it up. Stage right, the chauffeur tips his cap and eases the car offstage, tires squeaking on the polished floor.

Of course, it's way too much. And yet there's something about the glitter that feels exactly right. For me, glitz and apocalypse go together; I blame it on a childhood steeped in fire, brimstone, and *Lifestyles of the Rich and Famous*. In the early 1980s, when Liberace's show was at its most baroque, I watched his TV specials on Friday nights, and on Sunday mornings, I sat on the church's left side so that I could see the pianist play. Her hair in a neat bob, her body obscured by a shapeless choir robe, she kept her eyes fixed on the music director as her small hands marched up and down the keyboard.

I knew I shouldn't stare at her while she played. That made it too much like a show, and she performed for the glory of God. But why, then, did the choir stand onstage at the front of the sanctuary, even in front of the baptismal tank, where I had once floated buoyant in the water and afterward, sitting in the pew, pictured angels seated on the narrow ledges up by the ceiling? For that matter, why did we all applaud when the choir special was done? There had to be a little pride in that, a thing done well. God gives you the talent, but you don't hide it under a bushel either.

My parents signed me up for lessons with the church pianist. "If you're serious, you'll keep your nails short," she said. "Don't let me hear them clicking when you play." I did as she said, but noticed how Liberace performed with small stones bound to his fingers. (*How do you play with all those rings on your fingers?* "Very well, thank you.") She taught me to read music and to practice every day, to count out loud to keep the timing straight, to respect the dynamics and tempo the composer had written. But from Liberace I learned that sometimes "too much of a good thing is *wonderful.*" And that people believe what they want to believe.

A diamond may be forever, but the rhinestones he wore were brazenly temporary, beautiful fakes. And the costumes required that he be sturdy. Never slight, never shy, or the suit wears you. He built his career on welcoming the audience into his life, yet there was this secret in plain sight, this lie they came together to create. Lee to his friends, Liberace on stage. You will not know me.

There's something collusive about any performance: silently, the audience and the performer ask each other, *Deceive me.* Let's make believe we're friends, that the only exchange we're making is of each other's attention; don't mention money. (But as Liberace said of his critics: "I cried all the way to the bank.") Let's pretend that this night isn't like all the others; *you know, there's something special about you.* When the spotlight focuses on the man in the glittering suit, little gleams multiply in the darkened auditorium. With a flash, the bomb detonates and the fireball expands. What would he play if nobody were listening? What would they detonate without a witness?

I have been too fascinated by bright surfaces, have stared too long at zinc nail heads blinding as sunspots. As a child of green shade, the desert out west has ever been a fantastic place for me, and I expected it to be paved with knobs of agate and slabs of quartz, not dead antelope and wild horses and burned cattle. (Richard Misrach finds them in the vast expanse of the Nevada Test Site by following the crows who feed on the carcasses' eyes.) Some official numbers: from 1952 through 1992, the year of the last official atomic test, 1,021 nuclear weapons were exploded at the Nevada Test Site. The first hundred or so were atmospheric, and the rest were underground, except for Baneberry, which was a little of both. A secret will always break through.

Since 1992, the Nevada Test Site's Base Camp Mercury has become the region's newest ghost town, something like the earlier incarnation of St. George, Utah, downwind of the tests and poisoned now for longer than anyone cares to say. Atomic detonations create radioactive fallout composed of (among other things) cesium 137, strontium 90, iodine 131, carbon 14, with half-lives of thirty, twenty-eight, five thousand six hundred years. Diamonds are forever, and these tests will always be with us. In Las Vegas, you can sign up for a bus tour of the Nevada Test Site. You can visit the abandoned control tower at Base Camp Mercury; you can see the only Doom Town house still standing, now a historical landmark, and eligible for federal preservation funds. You can see the crater that Sedan shot dug in the sand, the warped wooden bleachers where spectators sat, and shiny bits of metal and glass thrown out by the bombs, glittering now on that "dusty precursor-forming surface." I've seen the day I would have visited the Test Site on a whim. Not anymore. Not for anything.

*

In 1987, not long after his fabulous specials featuring the sparkling Rolls and whipped-cream medleys, Liberace died of AIDS. It was a shock; the public hadn't known he was sick, and even in his last interviews, he looks pretty good. Tanned, fit, a little thin, sure, but who wouldn't look smaller, without those bulky show clothes? I grieved when he died, and so did everyone I knew. As for *those rumors about his personal life*, people said, *Well, you can't believe everything you hear.*

You can't take it with you. Not the mirrored piano or

the world's largest rhinestone; not the chunky jewelry or the gold-leaf ormolu desk that once belonged to Czar Nicholas II. But of all the things Liberace left behind, I love his clothes the best. One hot summer day not long ago, I visited the Liberace Museum in Las Vegas. I stood in the Costume Gallery a long time, staring at the mannequins and thinking of the man who had worn those gorgeous outfits and of the people who had labored to make them. Someone's eyes burned under a bright task lamp as she knotted score after score of salt-grain beads to the pink-and-pearl King Neptune costume. Her palm took a bruise from the scissors handle, blade keening through inky satin; her foot pressed the sewing-machine pedal in her sleep. The finished product erased the chalk marks that preceded it, stray threads swept into the trash, misshapen beads cast aside, flourishes stretched longer and trills repeated until the ring fingers (always the weakest) gained strength like the rest.

It's the furthest thing from a fallout shelter, this windowless room. No stolid cans of beans or Spam, no barrels of purified water. Just mannequin after mannequin dressed in sapphire or crimson, jet or rose, madder or lime, double-dyed, dusted with silver, crusted with cabochons. For the Stars and Stripes show, he wore a silk tailcoat in red and white, a platinum-beaded vest, and a pair of royal-blue shorts; in the Gallery, those clothes hung on a plastic figure over hairless thighs. On a shelf nearby sat a gift a fan had sent, a toy piano made of glued-together matchsticks. Any one of which could have burned the place to the ground.

*

It all gets back to the piano, doesn't it? As an object, it demands space, a room free of drafts and direct sun, a sturdy foundation. In return it bears within its body the tension of tightened steel strings. Felt pads ritually pierced with a three-part needle. Its plate is bell-quality iron, dipped in shiny brass alloy for appearance's sake.

I watch a factory film that shows how pianos are made. You start with lumber, hard rock maple; someone's spray-painted a smiley face on the side of the lumber, but once it's sawn into veneers, nobody will ever know it was there. A worker pours thin glue from a bucket. Another tightens a clamp around a form. Twenty-four hours later, they will remove the clamps and wheel the rim into a conditioning room stacked with empty pianos, their shoulders chalked with dates.

I keep noticing the workers' hands. A woman tests the action by weighting each key with a lead cube. Her hands, small and strong and practiced, make notes with a gnawed pencil, its point whittled by a pocketknife. She is ensuring that the piano has the "proper depth of touch." The man who installs the soundboard has knuckles whitened by fine sawdust. I can almost smell it as I watch him, as I watch another man plane the wood, as another man chisels a pattern on the rim with a keen blade. Table fans whir, and a locker is decorated with a newspaper photo of a man dunking a basketball and a bumper sticker that reads I LOVE MY UNION. The man who sets the pins and threads the strings (three for each note) wears fingerless gloves, his thumbs and index fingers taped for protection. "And now for the voicing," says the narrator.

As an object, the piano draws you to itself. It sings and you resonate. A practiced hand plies a brush loaded with glue. Someone tightens a tuning peg with a socket. DON'T TOUCH, someone writes in red crayon on the piano's fallboard. Its time has not yet come.

*

You can spend too long inside. I left the Liberace Museum, walked down the Strip to the Bellagio, and waited beside a wide, shallow pool whose turquoise floor was mined with hundreds of dark nozzles. People lined up along the wrought-iron railing, smelling of new T-shirts, their arms and necks beaded with sweat. The Bellagio gleamed white against an aquamarine sky; it hurt to look at it, hurt, too, to watch the duck paddling in the brilliant, chlorine-smelling water, washing desert dust from her wings.

At the stroke of noon, the jets clicked to life. *DUM da da*, three confident steps down to signal the beginning of "The Star-Spangled Banner." The water sprayed in time with the music in a carefully choreographed display, with some jets circling and others blasting water hundreds of feet into the air. As the nozzles twirled and the music blared, we gasped with pleasure.

After about ten minutes, the show's finale started: "Con te partirò." You didn't have to understand the Italian, warped from the amplification system and the background traffic on the Strip, to know this song was the best kind of sad, show sad. The melody found and built on itself, knitted sixteenth notes climbing gently to a plateau. A breath. Then the chorus, *Con te . . . partirò*, slower now, simple and steady, a hesitant walk away, and with a backward glance the melody leapt high into a sob. It was a strange scene—the desert afternoon, hundreds of bystanders, a shimmering pool pouring forth music and light. And even though the show was completely manufactured, it still moved me.

I stood there thinking, *Liberace would have loved this.* Years before, his stage show had incorporated colored jets of water that arced and swirled to complement what

he played—the exact precursor to this. And "Con te partirò" would have been just his kind of tune, sweeping and
grand, a real tearjerker. The song satisfies our yearning to
feel a version of sorrow in a group. We want to share this
with other people, even if they're strangers, even if it's only
for a moment.

Sure, Liberace seems like a phony. Sometimes I pity
him—for the way he craved the audience's applause, for
how he tried to guess what they wanted, how he had to
hide from them who he was. But as I watch the old clips,
I see something more. After telling a joke for what must
be the thousandth time about the enormous ermine coat
he's wearing, he strides across the stage, strikes a pose, and
flings his arms wide as a prizefighter. In that moment, he's
triumphant; he's not in his first or even his second youth,
but he's still the man of the hour, the one they're all paying
to see. And when he plays, I can't take my eyes off him.
Between the jokes, riffs, and "Chopsticks" played with two
fingers, sometimes his grin fades, and in those moments,
he's not showboating. Just playing, and playing well. No,
stores don't stock Liberace albums anymore, but it doesn't
matter. The record, scored with its rings of iridescent
sound, is as empty as the gorgeous robe without a body
animating it. There was something alive when he played,
and he buried it as best he could, protecting it.

He was Liberace to his fans, Lee to his friends, and
when the world first met him, he called himself Walter
Busterkeys. It's a Vegas litany—Busterkeys, Buster-Jangle,
Tumbler-Snapper, Upshot-Knothole. Maybe the Bellagio
stole Liberace's "dancing waters" and raised them an
order of magnitude, or maybe Liberace stole them from
Baneberry—at ten thousand feet, that jet was still higher
than any New High in the Las Vegas Sky. It's all a show,

and we participate in it every time we gather together and wait for something to happen. And at the end of "Con te partirò"—"Time to Say Goodbye"—the booming water cannons detonate with a sound undeniably martial, quoting Baneberry even if in a language we don't realize we understand. When the explosion sets off the nearby car alarms, nobody notices. That ricochet of sound is just part of modern life. We take it in with the air we breathe; we hear it in our dreams.

$$*$$

Sometimes the performer and the audience want the same thing: to break the bonds of daily life by losing themselves in a shared experience. And sometimes they don't want the same thing at all. The performer needs to be listened to, and the audience wants to be invited in. *Let me see something different from the other shows. Make tonight special, even as I am special.*

But in a show, there's also the implicit promise of safety, which is why it's so unsettling when Evel Knievel crashes his motorcycle trying to jump the pool at Caesars Palace. (*Were we supposed to see that?*) That makes the atmospheric tests uncanny: although they purport to be mere performances, at least to the tourists lining the road, they're actually planned disasters. Call it a test, but it's a real atomic bomb. The clips I'm watching are snuff films, even though the ones killed are off camera, soldiers in their foxholes, downwinders asleep in St. George or Bountiful.

It must have been alluring to think that going to see the bomb explode would be a lark. But in reality, it's a flash-picture of how the world is likely to end. Why did the tourists go to see it? So they'd recognize the "real thing" when it came? (*The one you've all been waiting for.*) Now I think that disappointed witness—who wanted to see "something like the fire that consumed the world"—sensed the truth. She faced the test for what it was, a vision of destruction, and was disappointed, maybe in herself, for needing it to be more than what it seemed.

And that other woman standing on News Nob, sunglasses fallen around her neck, what did she think? Did it comfort her that she wasn't watching this alone? Maybe she caught the hands on either side of her; other fingers laced through hers, slender bones. And the soldier who set the stage when he nailed shingles to the Doom Town house. If he saw that house explode, did he think *I did my part*? Or *What does it matter? Nobody lives there anyway.*

✳

In an interview he gave *Good Morning America* in 1985, about six months before his death, Liberace meets Ron Reagan—the son of the president—and walks him backstage, through his dressing room at Caesars Palace in Las Vegas. "Someone famous once said never criticize a man," Reagan jokes, "until you've walked a mile in his rhinestone cape," staggering beneath the sequined platinum-and-ebony cape's weight. Then Liberace gives him a tour of his house on Shirley Street. It's the same place from the TV specials I've watched, from the pool with the piano keys to the sunken bathtub with a special faucet just for bubble bath. From a mural overhead, Liberace's disembodied face beams down at the bather. I think it's terrific. Liberace leads Reagan through the house—really two ranch houses joined together by a Hall of Mirrors sort of like the one at Versailles, stuffed with antiques and froufrou and dogs—and as they sit across from each other on low sofas, Reagan says something to Liberace that I think gets at the heart of it all.

Leaning forward, he says, "You know, I get the feeling that all of this that we see around us—the crystal, the porcelain and everything, your costumes—is really, to a large extent, a calculated effect. It's not really you. You're almost making fun of it at the same time—"

And then Liberace interrupts him. "That's right," he says. "I discovered that you have to draw the line between the performer and the person." Looking back, knowing now how close he was to the end of his life, I see something moving in this admission—as though, finally, he could admit that he'd been telling the truth but telling it slant, protecting himself ever since he put on that first shiny dinner jacket. "By now, my costumes have become a very expensive joke," he says, looking away. In another interview, he said "I'm a product that I've created." Does the show become reality, if repeated enough times? Hundreds of atomic devices exploded outside the city, most of them many times larger than the bombs dropped on Hiroshima and Nagasaki. Poison impregnated the air, and the sand, and the water deep below the desert floor. The excesses of Vegas come to seem like the perfect reaction to the destruction that bloomed on the northern horizon before dawn.

✳

Not long after I visited, the Liberace Museum closed. Some of its items have been showing up in online auctions: framed gold records, a sculpture of a sheep, even one of the Stars and Stripes costumes, hot pants and all. And recently I saw a video that a Vegas resident, an Elvis impersonator, had taken of the house on Shirley Street. The house sits empty, its iron gates bent and broken, and although the cameraman can't get inside, when he places the lens up close to the window, it's almost like you're there. Through the glass, you can see the dim outline of the door to the master bedroom; over there is where the Hall of Mirrors must be. And in the foreground there's the living room. In the 1985 interview it's crammed with furniture, soft rugs, lamps on the fireplace hearth; in the middle of the shot, Liberace sits on the sofa. Without even trying, he's the center of attention, pulling in everything in the room—furnishings, interviewer, camera crew; the audience at home; me, now, watching from years later and leaning in to hear him better.

Then the interview ends. The house is in foreclosure. The empty living room looks cold even on the August afternoon of the video, the floor shiny as a stage, clean as a hospital.

The audience expected something particular, and he gave it to them. But how it must have chafed. What if Liberace watched the test shots? I don't have any evidence that he did—in his memoirs, he spends time describing his possessions, not reflecting on his inner life. But he spent a lot of time in Las Vegas during the atmospheric testing years, and it's possible. Later he was known as a night owl, so maybe after one of his evenings at the Riviera, too wired to sleep, he drove out to the desert to watch the show. Put yourself in his shoes. Picture him standing there in the chill dark before dawn. Wrapped in a plain jacket, waiting, nobody watching, longing for something like the fire that consumed the world. Something to wipe all this clean, all the props borne along in a cloud of dust on the precursor-forming surface. They say it's the most gorgeous thing you can imagine. You have to see it to believe it.

The Measure of My Days
(Buddy Holly Reprise)

SOMEWHERE IN CERRO GORDO COUNTY, IOWA

It was an old upright piano heavy enough to bow the floor where it sat. At one time it had been fronted with mahogany, but that was long gone, and you could see the guts clearly: hammers coated with dusty felt, wire-wrapped strings, tuning pegs marching down the soundboard of glued-together maple. I pressed a key and the hammer struck a flat, slow note. To be expected. Outside it was a hot afternoon in late July, but as far as I could tell, the power hadn't been on in here since '92. That's a lot of winter nights cold enough to etch frost across the drafty old windows, make the maple pull tight and the pins contract. Now, midsummer, the old glue relaxes; gives up might be a better term.

I was standing in an abandoned one-room schoolhouse with my friends, and we were lost. We'd been hunting for the field where Buddy Holly's plane crashed and we'd gotten confused after one too many ROAD CLOSED signs. Backtracking down gravel roads, scaring up red-winged blackbirds and rooster tails of dust, passing farmhouses and NO HUNTING signs painted on old tractor tires, we happened upon this little white gable-roofed school at a crossroads and pulled over on a whim. Weeds grew through the steps but someone had broken down the door, and we stepped inside.

There's something about an old schoolhouse. Cooped-up kids, the necessary grind of times tables, pair alliances formed and severed. That would be enough. But this room held even more. Posters tacked to the walls said things like KEEP THE HEART OF LIBERTY BEATING: REGISTER & VOTE. The slips of paper on the floor were some kind of voter verification tickets. Hymnals were stacked on flip-top student desks. WE LOVE OUR MOMS AND DADS, someone had chalked on the board. Education, civics, God, family. A narrow box atop the piano held nails someone had set aside to save, and a ruler tucked inside a drawer said LORD MAKE ME TO KNOW THE MEASURE OF MY DAYS.

We turned to go, and I picked up a copy of *Sing Sociability Songs* (1943, price 20¢) to steal away with me. Someone had written the singer's name, Erwin P., on the top right corner in tidy, new-teacher hand. Together the chorus had learned, maybe, the words to all four verses of "The American Farm Bureau Spirit."

And even though I knew it was junk, I hated to leave that old piano behind. Someone needed to make it jump. "Brighten the corner where you are," one of the Sociability Songs read. "Someone far from harbor you may guide across the bar." Said the preface, "Some who cannot sing may make a definite contribution by whistling." All the songs that piano had played sunk traceless inside it now, stones dropped in a well.

SURF BALLROOM, CLEAR LAKE

I parted the heavy curtains and stepped onstage. The place was set up for a wedding reception, and the bride and groom's table looked out over the dance floor, the blue-painted ceiling, the peonies floating in glass bowls. Buddy would have stood in this very spot that night, and the dance floor would have been packed with fans. I jumped down on the floor, nobody looking, and did a little twist. It felt good, the narrow-gauge maple springy beneath my sandals, even with "Rebel Rouser" on the speakers, and then "The Wanderer," *Yeah the wanderer, I roam around around around around.*

Relics lined the lobby. There was a copy of the lyrics to "La Bamba," handwritten by Ritchie's aunt; he wasn't fluent in Spanish and needed her help. There was the pay phone where Buddy called Maria Elena for the last time, a framed note confirming his use. There was an invoice written in slanting ballpoint, revealing that it cost one hundred dollars for the "care, embalming, treatment, and delivery of body of Jiles P. Richardson to Mason City Airport. Paid in full February 4, 1959, Ward Funeral Home." There was a pair of shiny black pilot's headphones salvaged from the wreckage of the plane.

All too much, and I headed backstage. Signatures covered the walls, all of them more recent than the crash. ZZ Top, Little Feat, the Kentucky HeadHunters. People left notes like "I'm humbled" and "It's an honor to play here." Three little steps led up to the stage door. Buddy would have stood here, checked his hair in the mirror, maybe hopped a little bit on the balls of his feet to get the blood moving. Then, on cue, he would have run up the steps without thinking much about it.

Before leaving, I bought a piece of Original Maple Flooring (1948) in a clear plastic treasure box. The top of the wood was thickly waxed but the bottom was splintered where the sander didn't reach. The cut edge smelled good, and you could see the tight parallel banding of the year rings. I counted seventeen, the same age as Ritchie.

The four of them—Ritchie, Buddy, J.P., and the pilot, Roger Peterson—will always step up into the little plane, brush sleety snow from their shoulders, and pull the doors shut. The plane will always crank up, taxi down the runway, and disappear into the snow. That cannot change. What can change is what you make of it.

It keeps pulling me back, that spot onstage where Buddy stood. The dance floor was full of unseen others, maple polished for them and tables laid, napkins pressed and folded, saltshakers close at hand. Booths lined the perimeter of the dance floor. Empty then, but later that night people would slide inside, set glasses on the linen-print Formica tabletops, laugh at the toast the best man would give. Then they would walk past the Buddy Holly telephone, disconnected years ago, and push through the double doors into the summer wind, rich with the smell of algae, that still blows in off Clear Lake. They'd make for the highway, driving past the convenience store sign spelling out REDEMPTION in tall red capitals.

CRASH SITE

Standing there in the soybeans, I couldn't bring myself to feel much of anything. There was the fence, just like in the photographs. There was the memorial marker with the names and the dates. But most of the leavings looked like people had dug in their pockets and dumped what they didn't need. Swipe-card room keys, bottle caps, pennies. A purple latex glove, guitar picks, a disintegrating plush monkey. And glasses, lots of them: sunglasses, half-moon reading glasses, 3-D glasses, knockoff Buddy Hollies they sell at the Surf for five bucks a pair.

I'd wanted to leave an offering myself—a pinch of dusty dirt from Lubbock, a uranium crumb, an irradiated dime (circa 1959) from the lab at Oak Ridge, a hammer from that old schoolhouse piano. Nothing felt right. What we abandon, someone else must face. I stood beside the fence with my friends, whistling. *That'll be the day, ooh ooh, that'll be the day.* Little purple butterflies swarmed the path. After deer pee, I bet. They shivered and trembled, going about their business, consumed with the stuff of life.

I turned the felted hammer over in my hands—a dropped tooth, useless on its own—and remembered a night from years before, in a city on the other side of the world. Dresden, shortly after reunification, a city marked even then by the firebombings of '45. I had just finished college, and was working on a translation project with a group of people I'd never met before and haven't seen since. We were staying in a Soviet-style apartment block with a basement common room and a heavy old upright in the corner. Like most things in that town the piano had seen hard use, and like the piano in the old schoolhouse its faceplate had been taken off. Something in us wants to watch the music happen, as if that might help make sense of the mystery.

My friend drank too much; I knew it even then. He was a graduate student in musicology, and he played piano and destroyed bottles of cheap red like the tanks were coming for him. I remember tottering around the city one night, searching for the grave of Carl Maria von Weber; it eluded us, and it's not like it moved.

But on this night, my friend made his way over to the old upright and started playing. The basement was packed with people, and he played quietly at first. Chopin, messy, and then he played louder, pounding it out, big hands

spread in chords that muscled up and down the keyboard. And even as he mumbled, *I'm getting this all wrong*,
he kept going, skidding over fumbles to hit his mark, plastic cup of wine shivering on the piano's top. Outside, the
sausage man sold brats and Radeberger Pilsner, and all
around us the room swirled with laughing people, but his
playing carried over everything, the slurry conversations
I barely understood, the street noise that came in when
people opened the door for a welcome breath of air, the
little Trabants careening down the boulevard as the long,
bleached-out evening slid toward night.

I used to pray for perfection; how flat that seems to me
after watching him, his eyes fixed somewhere far away. I
pushed my way through the crowd to the back of the piano
and stared at his hands as they leapt and fell and stretched,
knowing that the keys beneath his fingertips, cool at first,
had warmed as he played, yielding and resisting and playing along with him on a song someone had written long
ago, when the Frauenkirche still raised its dome beside
the river and the Semper Gallery still sheltered Titian's
The Tribute Money and Liotard's *The Chocolate Girl* inside its
cool rooms. After all those stones were pulled down so
that one was not left atop the other; after Chopin, the man
who wrote this song, died far from home; after someone
tucked a jar of dirt from Chopin's homeland inside the
coffin before sealing it—it must be there still, that soil he
knew, mixed now with the dust he became—after all that,
this song, still, this song. And someone liking the way it
sounded and losing himself in playing it and hauling me
along, gripping the back of the piano and willing time to
stop as I listened clear through to the end.

ACT TWO

If we can't fix it
Nobody can!
Destroy it.

BUSINESS CARD,
AUTOMOTIVE REPAIR SHOP,
GREENVILLE, SOUTH CAROLINA

The Lay of the Land

Pickens County, South Carolina

Head north out of town, veer right at the fork, and take it slow. No sense in rushing. The road's gullied and steep, so tight there's no centerline. As the grade climbs you'll see little towns on the right and mountains on the left, but keep your eyes on the road. There at the summit you'll find the fire tower. Park the car and make sure you lock it.

And enter this memory with me. Of climbing the chain-link fence (sneaker toehold in each little diamond), holding down the barbed wire with one hand, pushing up and over, and landing down on the grizzled grasses on the other side. Dead rats, spray-painted pentagrams on the cinderblock toolshed. The tower's steel struts burned cold but I held tight and swung my legs underneath me, soles of my Keds slipping on slick frost. I balanced on the V of the strut and edged up higher to where the steps started, flight after flight, dry-rot wood greasy with ice. Walked on the edges where it was stable. The trapdoor opened with a cry and I boosted myself up and into the cabin.

Stand here with me and feel cold wind on your face through the busted windows. Floor crunchy with a wicked little crush of shattered bottles. Rusty bolts worked loose by time.

See mountains upon mountains, crumpled and old and

quietly themselves, catching my heart, bumps and waves
of green close by and in the distance purple and blue.
Walnut Cove, Mount Chapman, Grassy Knob, Potato
Hill. Country worked over time and again. Down in the
pasture, braces of tied-up hound dogs moan.

What if we could see further, see more? Rhododendron
growing on the mountainsides, sourwood, laurel, a trillium
that gives off a smell like rotting meat to lure pollinating
flies. Under gneiss shelves live spiders that knit lampshade-
shaped webs, black rat snakes excellent at tree-climbing,
groundsel that sparks like tinder, the click beetle some say
foretells death if you hear it ticking in the walls.

Like in the walls of the house sitting empty beside a
hook in the road. Silent oak tree and grass high as your
pockets. In summer, moss turns the shingle edges to velvet
and paper wasps nest in the windows. Iris corms push up
neat blades, still obedient to the old woman who planted
them shallow, remembering warm sun and the press of her
fingertips on their papery sides.

And as the years pass, wild grapevines tug the roofline
slumped. Gelatinous light in green rooms. Kitchen cabinets lined with home-canned quarts of tomatoes, corn,
chowchow. Nailed to the wall a calendar only a few years
out of date. Sometimes a puddle of old blankets where
someone slept or sleeps. Beside the back stoop, wild rose
pushes crumpled silk from canes stubbed with thorns.
Carpenter bee drills his perfect circle and dry dust sifts
down. When frost comes, the pokeweed goes to slime.
But the pile of sawdust still sits where the bee left it, tidy
mound piled on the floor someone long ago painted white.

Summer will swoon you but these winter roadsides
hold a grudge, ash gray and brown, lichen splatter, shiny
holly tree. From high up here you can see plenty, but

not the indigo reservoir that cools the nuclear turbines nor the sunfish that swim in that warm bathwater, nipping the freckles on your thighs. Not the gashes in the red clay where someone ran off the road nor the junked cars arranged in curving ranks by the river that marks the county line. Not Easley High School, not the stadium nor the auditorium the Works Progress Administration built in '39. Not the shadowy seats bolted to the floor, their green velvet crushed by generations of rumps in slacks and skirts, the fabric's weave pressed into the nap—grosgrain, twill, dimity, denim, lace overlay. Fabric we once wove here.

We should go. The sheriff could drive up the road any minute, and the wind's cold; your palms burn when you touch the rail. But before we leave, look over your shoulder and see one thing more: the town, my town, its white-painted churches gleaming in the valley and its tin water towers like old spoons. The towers fed the mills. IPA SOUTHERN, the painted letters say, ALICE MANUFACTURING, PLATT SACO LOWELL. Fragments of a dead language now but I stretch my mouth to speak them.

✳

I wait at the red light in town and watch cars stream past. I don't know any of these faces now, not those, not those, not yours. The sign outside the carpet outlet reads DISCOUNT HARDWOOD $2.99 SQUARE FOOT / REV. 6:1-17. That's the part about the four horsemen of the apocalypse. Pale horse, pale rider.

If the fabric that separates earth and eternity is so threadbare, a chute to hell yawing open beneath your feet at any moment, then it makes sense to name your roads Gethsemane or Golgotha, Sinai or Calvary. Set aside even common land as hallowed. There is no bright line between

now and forever. MAY YOU TAKE A LIKING TO THE GOOD
LORD, that old sign on Highway 8 said, HE LOVES YOU.
And the one beside 183, IT IS APPOINTED UNTO MAN
ONCE TO DIE AND THEN THE JUDGMENT. YE MUST BE
BORN AGAIN. If I painted a sign and planted it, what
would it say? (*What thou hast seen, write.*)

Sometimes of a Sunday, I remember, a deacon would
stand in the pulpit and give his testimony—the tale of
where he came from, how he'd gone wrong, and how he'd
found God. Even as a kid, I had heard enough of these to
know what was coming, the genre conventions both a comfort and a bore. Still I had to respect the fact of his doing
it, standing up in front of everyone. Not easy to know what
to say. And I knew I would never have to. Back then it was
only men who were called. Times have changed.

Say, the little children demand after asking a question.
Say. Listen well and I will.

Warp and Weft

Tell me a story you know by heart.

All anybody could talk about that summer was the rain. Tomatoes split, pole beans molded, muskmelons turned to rot. Roadbeds gullied and the jockey lot washed out. Boughs exploded off oak trees. Mountainsides slid downslope in a crush of mud. The sign at the Baptist church said WHOEVER IS PRAYING FOR RAIN / PLEASE STOP.

And the song I couldn't shake was "When the Levee Breaks." Memphis Minnie Douglas and her husband, Kansas Joe, wrote it about the devastating 1927 flood that killed nearly three hundred people and wiped out tens of thousands of acres of the Mississippi delta. Refugees from inundated towns waited in tent cities above another, bigger levee while they figured out their next move. Thousands of them left the delta forever, setting off for cities like Chicago in what became known as the Great Migration.

The version of the song that most people know is Led Zeppelin's, and the classic-rock stations around here play it plenty. John Bonham's drum line—fleshy, thumping, heavy as a millstone—sounds like dread made physical, and yet somehow it's tempting. It catches your ear and you sidle over, lean against it. Down on the river's edge, weeds grow in the clay. Surely there's no harm in letting your toes play in the water, in the bodied current, thick with silt.

*

Little tunnel, dark as a culvert. I crawled inside on hands and knees until I reached the middle of the smokestack and could stand, cool walls around me, circle of sky high above. Steel rungs mortared into the brick ran to the top; it would have been somebody's job to climb the ladder, now and then, and check on things. I knew I shouldn't be there.

It was a muggy July morning twenty-three years after the mill closed for good. Thickets of blackberry canes fortified the fence and scribbles of green creeper fluttered against the walls; the overall effect was that of a castle left to wrack and ruin while its inhabitants slept off a potent curse. I jumped the fence with my husband, David, and my friend Brad. I've known Brad since we were kids, a time when hundreds of people—our classmates' parents—made their living here. But over time cheaper imports flooded the market and this mill went the way of most upstate factories. A scab-dark work glove, swollen with rubber warts, lay bloated in the weeds.

A hundred and fifty feet tall, made from clay very like the stuff beneath our feet, the stack was visible for miles, and like all of these old stacks it had little trees growing from its top.

Standing inside, I was at the center of something, and felt it. Behind me, the cleaning tunnel; in front, a dark mouth leading to the boiler. Something in me said *Leave*. It's dangerous to treat with the past, and you can't stay as long as you'd like. The place smelled deliciously of cool earth but there was no ash left in the pit, only brick powder, crushed-flat beer cans, and a dirty sign reading KEEP OUT.

*

Why do the mills pull me? I never worked in one, didn't grow up on the mill hill. I moved here with my family when I was small, and left at eighteen for college in another state. I didn't expect to move back; there weren't jobs. Over the next dozen or so years, I lived and worked in six other states. When I finally landed, I ended up just down the road from where I'd started. It seemed there was something important to understand about that, about here.

Boosters used to call this part of South Carolina the Textile Capital of the World, and it wasn't idle talk. You could sleep all night on our sheets and in the morning wash your face with our ring-spun cotton. Drink your coffee at a table spread with Dacron, slice sausage loose from local stockinette, press a shirt pieced here with an iron insulated by woven cotton electrical cording. These mills made twill and sateen, T-shirts and cardigans and lace and fiberfill. They made the diaphanous curtains with which Christo fenced the hills of northern California; they made space suits and parachutes for the Apollo astronauts. Braid, yarn, griege cloth, carpet. Webbing, florist wire, fiberglass. To keep a child's idle hands from the devil's business, you could buy a bag stuffed with the loops of many-colored stocking remnants. We had a handloom on which you stretched the loops over little teeth (warp) and a steel hook with which you could pull a second loop over and under (weft) and make a pot holder.

But by the time I started high school just down the hill, the mill had shut down and somehow I missed it. Brad and I were in the marching band together, and when we played our home games, our music would have bounced off these very walls. Yet in my memories of those Friday nights, where the mill ought to be there's blank space.

If you could get a better perspective, say by climbing the rungs hidden inside the smokestack, here's what you would see: the roof's wide expanse, dimpled with stale rain; crackerbox houses in neat rows; the funeral home; the Hotel Easley (now condemned); the railroad tracks gleaming in the morning sun. If you stood at the top of that stack, high above the ground, leaves would brush your face from the little sumac trees that grow in the rim's worn-down clay. Of the sumac, my field guide says, "a dear child has many names": sumach, summaque, shumac, shoe-make. The stack was once the life of the mill, breathing out black smoke. Cold now as a copperhead's mouth. What does it mean to lose who you are?

In the fall, sumac blazes red and orange; you can use its wood to make picture frames, napkin rings, or darners, or you can boil its leaves to make black ink, with which you can write all this down to help you remember.

✳

Listening to Memphis Minnie and Kansas Joe singing, your ears play tricks on you. For a blues song "When the Levee Breaks" is almost upbeat. But Memphis Minnie knew hardship. What hadn't she seen? Playing Beale Street corners for dimes by day, entertaining hungry men for rent money by night. In her early teens she toured with a cir-cus—ribby tiger, milky-eyed monkey, a steer whose horns she padded with rags. We all know sawdust but she knew chalk, splintered tent peg, a dancer pressing spangles in riverbank mud.

Did she see her childhood farmhouse lapped with waves? Did she see the river sixty miles wide and black with the topsoil of Kansas, Missouri, Oklahoma? Did she see fence posts and sodden quilts float past; did she see a hair bonnet, drowned children? The levees broke in 145 places. Water filled cellar, kitchen, haymow; water thirty feet deep overtopped headstones, apple orchards, clotheslines, maple trees, chimneys. All the fenced and tended places wrecked.

*

A hundred years ago, many of the workers in these mills were the first in their families to leave the nearby mountains for town. Agents attracted them with rental houses owned by the factory. Simple places by today's standards, but most eventually had electricity and running water, and little yards in back where folks kept patches of corn, peas, and greens to supplement what they bought at the company store. And many of their thrifty mountain ways they kept, not from sentiment but necessity. Make no mistake: the start of this was the end of something else.

But the accounts I've read speak of a sense of shared life that marked those years. People didn't have much to spare, but none of their neighbors did either. The whistle regulated daily life, from the 8:00 a.m. start of first shift, to the 4:00 p.m. that marked the beginning of second, then third at midnight. Wednesday was prayer meeting and Sunday was preaching; the mill built the church and paid the preacher. If you had athletic talent, you played on the mill baseball or basketball teams. When people say they miss the mills, part of what they mean is they miss community. Easter-egg hunts, fishing contests, nicknames: Pokey, Mongoose, Ding Dong, Humpy. Jet Oil, Obb, Chili Bean, Gumlog. We wish we knew the stories behind the names; we want to belong to a story ourselves.

*

On *Led Zeppelin IV,* Page, Jones, Bonham, and Plant share Levee's songwriting credit with Memphis Minnie. And Jimmy Page produced it in 1971, but for all the special effects in the song—playing the harmonica echo slightly before the actual melody, slowing down the replay for a "sludgy" effect, panning the instrumentals around Plant's howl so everything swirls around him—the most powerful trick might also be the most simple. They set up Bonham's drums at the bottom of a staircase. The drums sound prehistoric but the kit was fresh from the factory. It's not just the heads (plastic) and the sticks (hickory) you hear, it's the building, the tall, narrow space that you could, by some lights, think of as a tower.

The microphone is your ear, listening from high above to the roar and pound from below. Of "Levee," Jimmy Page said, "It suck[s] you into the source." Said John Bonham, "I yell out when I'm playing. I yell like a bear to give it a boost." In the pauses between notes, the beat presses itself against your body like water. You can't touch bottom but you know if you could, deadfall branches would snag your ankles. Said Bonham, "I like it to be like a thunderstorm."

*

That rainy summer turned into a glorious fall, and because this is a small town, I discovered that the current mill owners—whose property I had, yes, trespassed upon—were good friends with my supervisor at work. Unaware of my sin, they invited me to tour the mill, which they planned to turn into apartments and had gotten listed on the National Register of Historic Places.

The mill owner took a key from its hiding place and

unlocked the front door. When we stepped over the threshold, the temperature dropped and we blinked in the sudden darkness; the windows were bricked up, the doors
covered with plywood. The looms had been auctioned
off long before, but when I played my flashlight across the
floor I saw the square bolt heads that had anchored them.
The boards underneath were lighter than the aisles, which
had been darkened by the tread of countless feet. As the
owner explained how the apartments would be arranged,
I thought instead of how crowded it must have been, girls
pushing carts down the narrow alleys and replacing full
bobbins with empties, the machines' thunder and clack.
High above us were the pipes that had sprayed mist to
keep the cotton mellow, and dead lightbulbs draped with
old lint.

In the office, a giveaway calendar clung to the wall: a
full year with no pages torn out, January 1990. I had almost
expected to find that—but not the skein of plastic garland
from the last Christmas party, nor the memo on the lunchroom floor detailing the exit-interview procedure: FOR
THOSE EMPLOYEES WHOSE JOBS WILL END TODAY.

The newel post on the staircase was raised in the middle like a blister, its paint polished away by thousands of
palms. We headed upstairs, where a training room held an
old Draper loom. I shone my flashlight over it; the beam lit
up a circle of threads, both filling and warp. It had been
someone's job to wind the thread in taut parallel lines
around the teeth of the beam. "I loved drawing-in," one
skilled patternmaker said in an interview I read. "I enjoyed
it more than anything I've done . . . honest to goodness, I'd
rather draw in than eat when I was hungry," she said. "The
only thing I ever done in my life that I really loved."

I'd seen an old photograph of a loom fixer seated in

front of a frame like this. In his right hand he held a crescent wrench, and his left hand bore no wedding band, maybe because of the tight spaces in which he had to work. A ring could get caught in the machinery and then he'd lose the finger. She must have known he didn't love her the less.

I imagine the lights flickering and the workers diving under the machines; when the power surges, the looms get out of whack, and the arm throws the heavy shuttle hard across the weave room. I see the man fix the loom and the weavers get back to work, cotton sheeting with a figured pattern of striped blue and red around the edge. The shuttles fly back and forth and the cloth grows and grows and when the roll is full the doffer razors it free, runs it downstairs to ship.

And the sheets stretch tight over beds sick or marital or childbirth. Cut in pieces they shroud okra and tomatoes from the garden and catch the pump water where the housewife shakes the vegetables dry; stitched in a line they make curtains and bloomers and pillowcases; quilted in layers they diaper infants; torn in strips they bandage the hurting. The banner on the truck that rolled down Main Street in the 1919 Armistice Parade read, WE MADE BANDAGE CLOTH FOR THE BOYS WHO BROKE THE HINDENBURG LINE. Rafters and floors of yellow pine, red brick walls, iron machines enameled green. Shuttles dark and quills pale poplar. Cotton so white after bleaching, and fat coils of roving going narrow as they seine through the needle's eye. One worker said of the old days, "You sucked the thread into the eye of the shuttle with your mouth." Workaday kiss.

We walked the floor together, moving slowly through the darkness like people floating in deep water. My flashlight picked up dim forms and shapes—broken pallets, a barrel of bobbins. Like the divers at the bottom of nearby Lake Jocassee who swim past the porch of the old summer lodge, two hundred feet down, or the cemetery, its gravestones pale teeth looming in the murk. When we turned to leave, we passed an open door scrawled with spray paint. TURN BACK, it said. YOU'RE NEXT.

*

The trouble with creating a song that depends so heavily on production is that it's almost impossible to recreate live. After a few attempts in early tours, Zeppelin abandoned the effort. So the version of "Levee" I listen to must always be a relic, seven minutes and eight seconds snatched from the past.

*

I had a hard time getting a big picture of what the mills had been like. I scoured archives, read oral histories, left messages for folks who didn't call back. It seemed like people wanted to forget what had been.

But one day I met a woman who'd worked in the mills her whole life—started out sweeping floors, moved up to the opening room, and had made it all the way to weaving instructor by the time the mill shut down. Third shift. Getting ready for her workday, she told me, she'd drape her tie threads around her neck like a scarf, for easy access when fixing broken warp. "You got your scissors," she said. "All my blue jeans had a little hole where the scissors cut. Reed hook in your back pocket, rubber bands. No belt buckle, nothing to get hung up in the threads. . . . Masking-tape strips on your pant leg, to hold the thread until you tie it." If you cut your fingertips, paint them with clear nail polish, lest the threads slice them clean open.

She'd spent her childhood on the mill hill in a haze of need, moving with her mother and siblings again and again just ahead of rent day. No tidy garden in the back— no time to tend it. One afternoon when she was four years old a man holding a badge promised her all the dimes she could imagine if she would just follow him a piece down the railroad tracks. Even that young she knew enough to run like hell, and got away.

We talked about what years of mill work would do to a body. Her back still troubled her, and her shoulders were out of joint from wrangling machinery. Growing up, she'd known healers, and it would be a help to find some now. "God gave people the gift," she said. "Guess what? To take care of the people on the mill hill. But you had to believe or it wouldn't work. They'd ask, do you believe?" Once, when she was burned, someone talked the fire out of her.

It's been ten years since her mill closed. Of the noise and the pace, she said, "All I could ever do was dream of getting out. That to me was hell. And when you get home— you can't go to sleep, you're too exhausted." But then again, she said, "I think it made people better. Respect, honesty. It bought the clothes. It built the houses."

Before I left, she showed me a picture of herself with the rest of her crew. She'd posed with her coworkers on the mill's front steps, as generations of workers had done before. Her group would be the last. She pointed out each person by name, punctuating the list with "you understand"— a habit of her speech. When I asked if she was sorry the mills closed, what she said surprised me. "Yes," she said. "I wouldn't hurt like I do now if I hadn't stopped."

✳

Say the names.

Platt Saco Lowell made textile machinery and replacement parts. In 1979, it employed 1,527 workers; it was razed three years ago to make way for a new Wal-Mart Supercenter. American Spinning made synthetic fabrics. In 1979, it employed 479 workers; today it's used for storage, a Tweaker Extreme Energy bottle flattened on the cracked parking lot. Poe Mill burned to the ground, and now skateboarders slide and jump off the wrecked foundations. Union Bleachery dyed cotton and synthetics. It employed 487 workers; it burned in 2003 and is listed as a Superfund site because of chromium contamination. Woodside Mill, once the largest textile mill under one roof in the world, made polyester/rayon and polyester/cotton fabrics and employed 1,150 workers. Today it's abandoned, its bricked-up windows covered with vinyl to make it look like they still have glass. Fooled me. "Hey," yelled the kids getting off the school bus as I stood there on the curb, staring at the quiet building. "Hey."

*

Builders used to site mills along riverbanks to harness the waterpower. That was in the early days; capital follows cheap labor. The mills here replaced the ones in New England, so it's only logical that a century later these mills were supplanted in their turn by those in Mexico and Central America. Same song, different verse.

In 1903, when the nearby Pacolet River flooded, six mill buildings were heavily damaged or swept away. Collapsed timbers and empty space where the spinning rooms had been. Tongues of muddy water and slick boil over stone. The waters rose so fast that a shopkeeper who slept in the raw had just enough time to escape from his bed above the store and clamber naked onto the roof; a neighbor lady gave him her apron to "restore his dignity."

One man ferried people to safety on a raft made of cotton bales, one soul at a time; he saved ninety-nine, but when he went back to make it a hundred, the current pulled him under. Whole families drowned. When the Pacolet subsided, one body was given away by an errant knee protruding from the clay, others by streams of flies. Many were never found.

Memphis Minnie would have grieved, would have understood. Her given name was Lizzie Douglas, but her family called her Kid. After Langston Hughes heard her play a show one New Year's Eve, he compared the sound of her electric guitar to "a musical version of electric welders plus a rolling mill." After she died, her grave went unmarked for better than twenty years until Bonnie Raitt bought a stone.

When my friend from the weave room was a girl, she'd spend her bottle-deposit nickels on banana Popsicles and jukebox songs. "Wooly Bully" was her grandma's favorite, "Mustang Sally" her mama's. Even had that last one played at her funeral. Preacher didn't understand, but it wasn't for him to say. Ain't it a comfort to hear a familiar song again? Somehow it helps to sing along.

And I think now that the genius of "When the Levee Breaks"—no matter who's singing it—is how it retells an old story. Not just this flood, but the Flood, whose waters swell to envelop everything: tents and robes or trucks and kitchen towels, sheep, parents, haircombs, dipper gourds, billfolds, panicked children; the daily routine you once kept to, dreamlike now in retrospect. Ink, rain, leaves. Even drought, the dry bone hid at the bottom of things. Memphis Minnie escaped somehow, in a boat I believe she built herself and daubed with pitch. Floated to safe harbor and knew that it could have been, could always be, worse.

✳

When I left home I didn't want to go, but told myself if I came back it would be because I chose to, not because I had to. In every other town I've lived I've reckoned distance by how many miles' drive it was back to here.

I see a boy weep as he wraps his dead dog in a terry-cloth towel. I see a daughter fold a washcloth with ice and apply it to her mother's forehead to break a fever. I see a woman unroll a stocking over one foot, then the other, and secure them at the top with stays. I see knitted socks balled on the floor beside a bed. I see a woman pull a day dress over her head, clip on her earrings, and set about her marketing. I see a woman fill a pillowcase with cotton batting and stitch shut the end. At the hospital a man lays his head down and will not raise it again in this life, but has this comfort at the end.

I see a man doff the last bolt and box it for shipping. After his shift is over he comes back and strips the remnant to take to his wife. The concrete holding the fence posts cures in a few days, longer if it rains. I see the maintenance crew staple the chain link into place, stretch barbed wire over the top. I see the man take the slack out of the chain, tuck in the ends, and snap on a lock.

Icy Norman spent her whole life working at a Southern textile mill. I read her story in an oral history. After she retired, she said, "When I come out of that mill, I know that I done the very best I could. Somewhere along the way I felt a peaceable mind."

✳

When the mills closed, one owner had the machines cut into pieces so that nobody could steal his technology from the scrapyard. Workers had to take photographs of the torches cutting the frames apart. Another owner sold the machines to salvage dealers who picked them clean for parts.

I like thinking about the salvage warehouses, dim hangars lined with shelves and bins full of cotter pins and drivetrains, motors and rotors and spinners and travelers, little staples you clip onto bobbins of ring-spun cotton. Smell of old grease and electricity and tang of rust. Hard lumps of steel waiting their turn.

I know the dyes colored the river blue on Tuesdays and red on Wednesdays. That the waterfall downtown sudsed and bubbled; that the riverbed silt is still poisoned. That as a monograph published in 1933 put it, "There has never, in the history of the industry, been a protracted period when workers could not be replaced fairly readily with people anxious to get jobs." That the mill hired young—and plenty of kids, even kids I knew, quit school for that reason. But I also know it was about more than the cloth. Yes, it could kill you. Fires, accidents—I read about women scalped by speeder frames, a man caught in a belt that bashed his brains out on the ceiling. Lint filled lungs, clatter dulled ears; hands splayed, backs broke. Work takes your life, one shift at a time, and what choice do we have? Honest wages for honest labor, but you might as well acknowledge the cost. Restore its dignity.

A former supervisor at Riverdale Mill in Spartanburg described the day he had to tell his workers that the mill was going to close. "I started calling their names," he said, "saying you been here this many years, you been here this many years, and you know we did a good job. 'You've done

it. You have bought us this much more time we would not
have had. You've got sixty days, and we're gonna do this
sixty days just like we've done it for the last hundred years.
We're not gonna do it one bit different, and when we go out
of here we're going to hold our heads high.'"

I see you, man who painted the sign that reads NO
ADMITTANCE. Brushstrokes still clear after all this time,
laid on steel you'd coated with primer to stay the rust.
Nailed to bricks made of clay that some other man had
poured into forms, sent through a kiln, and let cure in the
sun. Sun that even now licks the rainwater off the gleaming
weeds. You could make something here, a life that would
last.

No wonder I felt a shiver, standing in the stack, inside
a thing that telescopes from past into future. You could
stand on the top rung both in the clouds and hemmed in
by red clay. This could be the seat of life, or a hold gaping open to an underground cave. A man who watched
Union Bleachery burn told me the dyes painted the smoke
clouds brilliant blue, green, pink. Dark rainbow, sign that
appeared only to him, and just that once.

✳

Afterward, I felt sorry about trespassing. It wasn't the current mill owners I hoped to sneak past, but the doffers,
canteen mistresses, cleanup woman sweeping with two
brooms. Crawling inside the stack had been like entering a
mausoleum, a narrow room with an oculus cut in the ceiling. Proof positive of how dead the mill is; were the boiler
lit, you'd never dare.

I think the workers would forgive me. They locked the
gates against themselves, too, knowing they'd become out-
siders in what used to be their place. If nobody sings a

song for long enough it dies. We throw it away like a faded blouse.

The flood of 1927 was the worst river flood in the history of the United States, and we remember it now primarily because Memphis Minnie wrote her song. This is the verse given to us to sing. TURN BACK, said the graffiti on the door. YOU'RE NEXT. So I'm taking this story and saying it's mine, ours. I'm clinging to the wreckage with Shem, Ham, and Noah's wife—her name lost to time, but if you claim the story, she's mother to us all.

✳

You could say the song retells an even older story, of moving away from a loved place to seek bread by the sweat of one's brow. (I didn't think I'd ever come back; there weren't jobs.) Zeppelin's drumbeat sounds like hitching footsteps, the trudging tread of those turned out of a first home.

I followed work all over the country and what is my aim now but to try and make sense of things and to help others in their attempts. Here with the fallen world's cadged gleams of beauty: dark reef of cloud behind Echols Oil, mimosa trees blooming in sprays of floozy pink, hawk beating hard in a rising wind. Overhearing a man say, *I feel so good, I'd give twenty dollars for a headache.*

You understand, my friend from the weave room kept saying. *You understand.* She keeps a big garden now—watermelon hills in old tractor tires, tomatoes in cages, staked beans, roses. She said she'd give me a seedling, but when I tried to thank her, she stopped me short. "Don't thank someone for plants! They won't grow!" she said. "Now cut flowers, sure. You can thank someone for those because they're already dead."

*

Years later, Jimmy Page stood in the staircase at Headley Grange and rested his hand on the newel post. "I was quite overwhelmed when I went in," he admitted in an interview. Of course Headley Grange had been, at one time, both an orphanage and a workhouse. Think of the scores of others who went forth from there to their jobs, sliding their palms down the polished rail as they left. Something of that smooth surface comes through in the recording of the song, in the drumbeat's massive echo. All those workers shaping the space that in turn shaped them. *Come along then*, they murmur, *next shift's starting*, not that you can hear them over the rising pound of the flood.

And when Robert Plant sings the song's last lines, they sound like the cry of a drowning man. "Going, I'm going to Chicago," he wails, the distortion making his words slip and snag. Even though I know it's an effect Page engineered, listening makes me uneasy. "Going to Chicago," Plant sings. "Sorry but I can't take you. Going down, going down now." The guitar and drums wheel around his voice, the center of a whirlpool, a gyre, an overwhelmed sluice. That voice is all there is to hold onto—*Going down, going down now*—but by the song's end, the undertow pulls the singer down into muddy, opaque silence.

*

Rust can bind wounds, Pliny wrote, and maybe he was right. Rusty nail heads stain the mill floor; rusty paper clips hold forgotten bills of lading, formulas for dye lots. Mix a draught of well water and bitter powder; drink it down and feel it anchor you here. To these bricks in a heap, bricks in a pile. *You have to believe or it won't work,* said my friend from the weave room. Bricks without holes and chalky to the touch. Bricks edgeworn from weather. Bricks burnt orange but for the side that had faced the weave room: pale green. Stacks of bricks in the busted parking lot, forgotten so long that little weeds rooted in them. Clay shearing off in red leaves.

Consider the brick's beginnings. Clay dug from a flat place and poured into forms, slid into an oven and burned hard, a decade of summers in a single slow trip through the fire. Cool them slow lest they split: channel bricks, air bricks, plinth and coping. Squints, jambs, bullnoses; rough stocks, grizzles, and my favorites, shuffs and shakes. Bricks are dirt, our dirt, turned to stone strong enough to withstand any weather. "A thoroughly good brick," I read in the excellent *Modern Brickmaking* (1911), "should give out a clear ringing sound when struck either with a stone, another brick, or a piece of metal." Yet for all their strength bricks are friendly; we're clay too, and I feel the kinship when I run my fingers across a brick's face.

The empty lots and burned foundations, the cars streaming past, the sparrows flying through the super-store's Home and Garden Center carry no memory of the factories that used to stand here. But if you pay attention, you'll be reminded by the brick smokestacks, built a century ago by steeplejacks who were themselves far from home, floating high above the ground as they worked.

It grieved me to learn that for so long, Memphis Minnie's grave had no stone. But every time I sing her lyrics, I call her back, and every time I see the stacks I remember. Not Memphis Minnie alone, but Si Kahn, who wrote "Aragon Mill" about a mill in Georgia: "There's no smoke at all coming out of the stack," the song goes.

For the mill has shut down and it ain't coming back
There's no children at all in the narrow empty streets
Now the looms have all gone, it's so quiet I can't sleep.

I think of the old photographs: the loom fixer, the boys on the baseball team, the tired children (boys in caps and suspenders, girls with thin, clasped hands) of the Spinning Department, 1901, who leaned against the same brick wall that I would, more than a century later. I think of the laughing women standing under the mill's oak tree in 1931, and what it might have been like for the sole black man in that group of two dozen.

Like a grave marker, the smokestack is a monument. When you drive past one, you have a choice. You can overlook it, as I used to, or you can think about the masons who built it. About the families who lived in the long shadow it cast. About the suffocating feeling of standing inside it, or about the fact that an escape ladder was always right there in front of you.

✳

Before the final levee breaks, the speaker leaves. But it was given me to go back after the waters receded and walk the ruins. I knew what it meant to miss home but it was a new thing to return to a changed place and be pulled under by memories, not bad ones: watching a boy in a white-and-green uniform play shortstop on the mill field; hunting treasure at the junkyard with my father; a slow hike up Georges Creek on a hot afternoon, orange silt blooming in the water around my feet. When the train barreled over the trestle, the creosote-soaked girders shook.

✳

Somehow, even when I stand alone, mill stairwells always feel crowded to me. These were the channels that bore the heaviest traffic, men and women hurrying, always, from the raw cotton of the basement opening room to the first floor's carding and spinning, weave rooms on the second and third, Quality Control on the top. People called these "vertical mills" and it was literally true; what started as fiber on the ground floor turned into finished cloth by the rafters.

And even in the mills that have had all the spirit dry-walled out of them in the renovation process, the stairwells still hold a charge with their smooth banisters and waffle-tread steps. If developers want to keep a building on the National Register of Historic Places, they must leave the stairwells intact. Here you sense the rush and hustle; wherever you're headed, you're not yet there. The stairs at Headley Grange worked so well for Zeppelin's purposes because they were "dead space." But I wouldn't call them that myself. This feels like the most alive space in the whole building, electric with bodies. Here you can run up to the sky or descend into the mud. This is the ladder in the smokestack made public, accessible to scores instead of just the lone boy shinnying up the bars. This is the stand of poplars, peeled and painted, that bears the mill's weight. This is the tent camp set up in view of the levee, populated with people wearing the only clothes they managed to save, people throwing dice to pass the time, people—one woman in particular—taking notes with a pencil.

✳

You don't realize how many bricks it takes to build a textile mill until they're heaped in windrows stretching two city blocks. Brad called last week to say they were tearing down Alice Manufacturing. (Product: synthetic print cloth, employees: 354.) He'd heard the walls fall, weird thunder on a bluebird day. By the time we got there, a rubble field of tar paper, cast-iron pipes, tatters of fiberglass, and splintered lumber spread from the sidewalk to the railroad siding. Teenagers sat on a front porch watching us, and every few minutes a man eased past in a shiny black pickup. We figured he was a supervisor. NO TRESPASSING, said a sign. THIS BUILDING CONTAINS LEAD. The smell of dug dirt hung around the neatly stacked bricks, shrink-wrapped and ready to be sold as reclaimed.

A man in a Bobcat bashed beams against the ground, breaking off old cement. Down the way, someone running a giant clawed machine dropped tangles of rebar into an open railcar. There were tongue-and-groove boards four inches thick in careful piles—the subfloor, heart pine, good for three millings for fancy lake houses. And the scrap metal was bound across the ocean to the smelters in China.

Where had the smokestack stood? We couldn't say, nor find any sense of scale. The only everyday things I could latch onto were a busted office chair and a plastic Gatorade bottle. "I wish we could have found something like a bobbin," Brad said, "or a cotton-bale tag, something textile-related." But we were too late—all of that would have been buried by the wrecking ball.

I found a handle from a coffee cup and dropped it in my pocket. Pigeons wheeled around the north wall. Behind us, the kids muttered on the front porch. Rusty nails stuck up from popped-out planks, and bricks from the inside walls, painted Sanitary Green long ago, glowed in the mellow light. What would become of the huge poplar beams that had borne the weight of everything? It was past five on a Friday, and the man in the Bobcat took a last turn around the lot. I turned to David and Brad and said, "Does this not feel like the end times to you?" A train slid by, headed into downtown and going slow. "The end of something."

Brad said, "It's always the end of something."

Call me Fence-Jumper, Sneaky Snake, Dr. Scrutiny. David is Cake. Brad is The Instigator. Afterward we sat at a table in a Chinese restaurant and I took notes on the back of a paper place mat printed with the zodiac, clothes from three different countries covering my body. The place mat said I'm Dragon but I know from other investigations that I'm Wood Rabbit: ambitious, a collector, lover of peace. These mills—built from our clay, trussed and floored with our trees, still shedding our rain—spun our cotton bolls into cloth that would wrap you in life and shroud you in death. That's done now. All I have left is a coffee-cup handle still seamed from the glass factory's mold and a story about the time we stood inside the smokestack, just after picking enough wild blackberries for a cobbler. Blackberries thrive along roadsides and waste places. This time of year, if you know where to look, you'll find them everywhere.

It is written, *The Lord can raise up these stones to give praise.* So these tree boles, too, clay poured into forms; iron cut into nails, now rusted? In my mind's eye I see the mills packed with all the people who worked there over the decades. Windows open wide and yellow Carolina morning sun pouring in. A boy walks down the aisle with the dope cart, its can of iced tea so big that when he stirs in the sugar, he has to use a boat oar. When the whistle blows and his workday ends, he's free.

Brain Sweat and Blueprints

Before you drop that quarter . . .
Play a song for me.
—Alan Jackson, "Don't Rock the Jukebox," 1991

When I fell for jukeboxes, they were already sliding toward oblivion. At an icehouse in Houston, someone played an old Marty Robbins song, "El Paso," but what I remember is a guy in tight Levi's teaching women, other women, to two-step. I took a shot or two at the pool table and pretended I hadn't had to scrounge to buy my single Shiner. Set it down too hard and the foam burbles out the neck— so embarrassing, but nobody notices, nor pays any mind when you get up to leave.

Like calling a radio station to dedicate a song—an act that feels very old-fashioned now—choosing a number on a jukebox gives you a brief share in the tune's ownership. You didn't write the music or record the words, but you selected it over the others, changing the evening from what it would have been into what it became by giving it a sound track. Exercising your authority over song and community takes only a quarter.

But the Plexiglas-and-pot-metal consoles I knew were just pale descendants of machines that had been, once, both beautiful pieces of furniture and marvels of engineering. In the 1950s, Wurlitzer was a leading manufacturer of jukeboxes, and a factory film from the era—*A Visit to Wurlitzer*—shows what the process was like. An unseen narrator intones, "A quality product, did you say? Well, you can say that again—and still again! For that's the way Wurlitzer builds them," as the camera hovers outside the factory, lingering on beds of vegetables and zinnias, a holdover from the Victory Gardens of the then-recent past. "Pretty hard to imagine anything *but* a quality product coming out of a plant like this," the narrator says, and after a stop at Research and Development—"brain sweat and blueprints"—it's on to the woodworking department, annual consumer of 10 million feet of veneers and hardwoods. Even in black and white, the shapely cabinets gleam with wax. A slow pan shows the vast hangar of the work floor, man after man paired with his juke and rubbing hard with white flannel, putting his back into it, slow-stepping in a tight circle.

In the decades that followed, jukebox sales declined, squeezed out by television and other distractions; I was late to the party by about fifty years. During the long solo road trips I used to make, I remember diners snug as ships afloat, their windows streaked with rain. Inside the diners looked warm and dry, people bent over cups of coffee appearing happier than they ever actually were. Walk inside and shake the rain from your jacket, glasses steaming up from the griddle's heat; the waitress greets you without looking up, and you take a seat at the counter. RESERVE BOOTHS FOR TWO OR MORE, reads the sign. Once I eavesdropped on two men talking about work; the clean-shaven one was the local undertaker, and young for it, I thought. *Just not for me*, he said, eyes fixed on some point on the floor. The skinny cook dipped raw egg onto the griddle and dealt out slices of sausage that spat when they hit the heat.

Try and stick it out awhile longer, his friend said, *later you can take stock.* The cook grabbed weights and pressed them onto the sausage to keep down the fat. Someone had picked the bouncy "Mambo No. 5" on the jukebox, its brassy riffs and catalog of conquest pouring out of tinny speakers. *You can't run, you can't hide.* Outside, cold rain poured down, and the sound of a big rig's Jake Brakes came squealing up from the off-ramp. *You and me gonna touch the sky.*

That night it was Georgia, but I remember scenes just like it from Jacksonville to Tucson, tired faces and sighs, the awkward combination of babies and cigarette smoke. And the jukebox against the wall had a presence like a sleeping animal, promising to help the night along if only you'd let it, pressing those satisfying square buttons, the albums in their sleeves slapping against each other as you flip from beginning to end, telling these strangers and yourself *Here's who I am.* The night outside so dark, but you go back into it, filling up with gas at the station next door and pushing on toward the next big town. A stretch of interstate in southern Mississippi so empty I had the high beams on for miles, asphalt stretching away into shadowy stands of pines. Part of I-10 just outside Pensacola, where the road dove down under the bay and the tunnel's cold lights made the roof tiles gleam. Somewhere outside Nacogdoches, where I was so tired I thought I saw a faded barn uproot itself and slide across the road in front of me. Now there are times I crave those drives like some women crave earth, with a dark and secret want. Of all the faces I saw there were none I wanted to know. But for his, existing for me then only as a dim hope. I miss not solitude but this: I had been a good girl and am now a safe woman but there was a time between when no one knew my name. Cutting it close with not a dime to spare. Looking back

I claim every mile I drove alone, keeping afloat with the frail stays of ignition spark, old song lyrics, reflections in finger-marked chrome. Gritted my teeth and accelerated onto the freeway.

Time passes, and we select the selves we become. Now I go with him to the diner down the road; it's rainy and cold, but we don't have far to drive. Six plays for a dollar, and lots of Johnny Cash to choose from: "Were You There (When They Crucified My Lord)," June Carter singing the eerie counterpoint; "Folsom Prison Blues," live, inmates cheering when Johnny sings the line about shooting a man in Reno. Shared things, communal as a train whistle. A woman at the booth behind us closes her eyes and sings along. Drunk? We can't tell. Then a kid with choppy hair slumps over and picks Stevie Ray Vaughan. We nod. Good choice, respectable choice.

What now of the Wurlitzer plant? The men worked there for years, and always together, tending machines in the metal shop, poring over plans that unspooled for miles. Complicated pin mechanisms, coin drops, selectors. Five years after the war ended, and what had they seen before? Better not to say; better to punch in, take your smoke break, lunch outside with your pals when the weather's fine. Spend your day assembling parts that mate exactly with their partners, or clamping layers of veneer and pushing them through the quick-baking kiln. As somewhere in the Adirondacks an oak grows a little taller, and someone hones a blade. "Wurlitzer knows its woodworking all the way from the forest primeval to the finished phonograph," says the narrator. The North Tonawanda plant stopped making jukeboxes in 1974. Gone the arguments of nickel versus dime play, gone the bill proposing Congress split the difference by minting seven-and-a-half-cent coins. One of the most popular selections was the blank record, a long-lasting 45; your coin bought you three minutes of quiet. But not silence. That hiss so like the sound of tires on a road, a pop as you drift over into the rumble strip, muted but not empty, full of what could be, precious and fading. Over before you know it, without you even listening.

Coathook in an Empty Schoolhouse

We stepped across the railroad tracks, over two long-dead deer lying on the gravel, their ribcages bleached white. Behind us, men fussed over big machines, shiny yellow Cats unspecked by bird or mud. They must have seen us walking toward the old town, but they paid us no heed; they had work to do.

I'd come to North Dakota with my friends to look for abandoned towns, but the line between living and ghost wasn't always obvious. One town categorized as a Class D—semi-ghost town with small population and many empty buildings—still had the doing-a-good-business Rusty's Bar, and in another place, tidy prefabs sat chockablock with collapsing houses, busted windows, lilacs crowding the porches.

And all day long I felt watched, unable to hide on the wide prairie. White pillows of stone in pastureland. On the roadside, a crumpled pair of jeans, raveled skeins of hay. A billboard picturing an empty highway between cornfields read NORTH DAKOTA RUSH-HOUR COMMUTE. Rifle shot dimpled the road markers. BUY A PRINTER, GET A FREE WATERMELON, said a sign in Mandan. Sunflowers and yellow clover, emerald fields, glittering cottonwoods along streamlines. It started to rain. We ate peanut butter and jelly sandwiches in the middle of a dirt road in Lark. Someone long ago had planted that poplar at the bend in the road.

We drove on, stopping in front of a green-shingled

schoolhouse on a hill. Through the storm door, you could see the cellar flooded with dark water. Desks were heaped in the classroom, and a slate chalkboard lay in pieces by the front door. The beadboard walls looked to be oil-rubbed walnut; the foundation was fieldstone chinked with mud and cement. A desk outside had a circular depression for an inkpot, and black-seed rodent droppings where children had once kept their books.

In another town, beside the railroad siding with the deer bones, we stepped over a wire fence, through tall grass, and under the low-branched Russian olive to the schoolhouse. Up the warped steps and into the cloakroom, where hooks waited on the walls. Most of the windows were gone, their fragments crunching under our feet. I stepped carefully. Part of the ceiling had fallen down, and the hole in the plaster revealed ship-lathe and a dark attic. A new aluminum ladder stood in a corner. The desktops were gone but their wrought-iron frames remained, curlicues of black metal stamped with MPLS. On the floor, a piece of swallow's nest, mud and straw. The blackboard still had multiplication problems on it.

Like a good student I daydreamed, standing there on the threshold. School would have started in another month. New coat of plaster on the ceiling, pale-green paint on the walls. The jackets just light ones or sweaters, hanging easily on the hooks. The barn coats of November far off as a dream of snow.

The barrel stove was a neat cylinder covered in basketwork. White flames would have been visible in the seam where the door fit, streams of heat pouring out through the gap. Did everyone feel the urge to touch that bright line, or to slip in a scrap of paper? Pencil lead softening in the heat, blistering yellow paint.

The press had stamped out one desk leg at a time, baroque curl of iron, the metal gleaming orange, darker around the edges. He was the artist, he who carved the mold out of plaster, his the well into which wax and then hot metal would be poured time and again, the seam a little lip where the halves of the mold had fitted together. And in the schoolroom a boy thought of that, maybe, tracing the iron with his finger and feeling the little pits in the metal, listening to the wind push the alfalfa outside the window and jumping when the teacher said, *Ray, give the correct sum.*

And what of the teacher? What furnished her workdays? Smell of rain on the field grass. Chalk dust, smoke from the stove, hot metal. As even now the wind shakes the wheat and lightning arcs in the gray sky, south of here. And after she'd set the students moving along their paths, stoked the stove, marked the spelling tests and poetry themes, what did she think of then, in the early-falling December darkness, while in the woodbox an earwig crawled in the splinters and dust, woken by the heat, a shiny soldier left from summertime and doomed to burn? Before she left, she'd pulled the shades to hold the heat, the canvas unrolling with a shriek. The thermometer at the door registered sixty below.

School seems as though it will go on forever, some afternoons in particular. And then one day it ends, and what do we leave behind? To visit an abandoned school is to visit the past, to know that someone hauled beams from the railroad to the cleared place, that someone made a foundation from stones the earth gave forth in rounded biscuits and loaves, mortared between with clay and broad thumb. Someone folded the glowing wire back on itself and nailed it to the wall. They're all gone now, but this place remains, saying, *We worked here together.*

*

We spent the night in Bowman, a county seat in the state's southwestern corner. SMALL TOWN HOSPITALITY WITH BIG-TIME STYLE, its billboard said. We ate in a supper club and emerged after good bison burgers to a bright afternoon and the feeling we had slept through the night—or twenty years—and walked out into the past. A loudspeaker relayed the day's stock report to the empty streets. Rubbery red worms curled on the sidewalk. Kids brought books back to the library in grocery bags from a store whose name I didn't recognize. Sometimes you find yourself in a place that is not your home, try to imagine living there, and can't do it. OUR CHOCOLATE DIED AND WENT TO HEAVEN, said a note taped to the window of the ice-cream shop. COME BACK NEXT YEAR.

The no vacancy sign at our motel was SORRY spelled out in neon. Good thing we'd called ahead. "I got a crew," the manager said; they worked in the hydrofracturing fields two hours north of town. In the Gideon Bible in our room, someone had dog-eared the page with Luke 15, the parable of the prodigal son. What it really means is *My child, come home to me; I miss you.* The students these schoolhouses wait for will never show. By the time we woke next morning, the workers' mud-streaked trucks were long since gone.

The Scissorman

He comes around like the change of season, once every three months. It's May now, rainy and cool, and this morning he's working his way through Greer, South Carolina, a foothills town known once for its peach orchards and now for a car factory. At the day's first stop, a beauty shop wedged between a grocery store and a Chinese place, there's just one stylist working, finishing a man's cut while the man talks about baseball. Empty chairs, neat rows of bottles, a meager pile of gray hair on the floor. The Scissorman takes the stylist's scissors and tests them, leaning down and pinching a twist of fallen hair between the blades. "You're really having to work with these," he says, and she allows as they need it bad, her eyes on the reflection in the mirror, her fingers drawing the customer's locks into points. "Go ahead and take them," she says, and he walks out the door, leaving her to finish up with her spare pair.

He covers all of South Carolina, from the upstate's skinny back roads to the barbecue joints and slow rivers of the Midlands, to the cotton fields and pouchy swamps and saw grass of the Lowcountry, past junkyards and elementary schools, farm stands and warehouses. Every year, he puts twenty-five thousand miles on the white van with the SCISSORMAN tag on its bumper. He's converted the interior into a workshop. A curved plywood tabletop holds sharpening wheels and task lamps; jeweler's pliers

and screwdrivers nest in tidy racks. A ragbag swings from
a hook, and an old wet-wipes box holds spare hair for testing the blades. Everything's in place, all of it tied down
with bungee cords, a stay against sudden stops. His little
Chihuahua/Yorkie dog, Dixie, rides shotgun, listening
along to WESC, Big Country.

✳

I'm following the Scissorman today, trying to keep up with
his van in my aging Crown Victoria. The last time I got a
haircut, I asked my hairdresser who sharpened her shears.
"Call the Scissorman," she said, handing me his card,
which was a Band-Aid stamped with his phone number.
"He's a character." When I called him up, he was soft-spo-
ken and gracious, and we made a plan to meet for breakfast
at a local diner. He pulled into the parking lot right on
time, and ducked into the diner out of the rain. He wore
his hair in a long gray ponytail, neatly tied, and he was tall
and rangy, folding himself into the booth across from me.
But it was his eyes that struck me, gold and hazel and keen
enough to spot a nick and chase it clean off a blade. By
the end of breakfast, trust established, we set off down the
road, toward the morning's work.

Maybe I'm interested in his job because it feels like a
throwback. Like the journeying tinsmith or ragman, he's
someone who travels from town to town, whose arrival
bestows an almost holiday flavor to the workday. And like
those earlier travelers, he's someone who helps a community make the best use of what they have, instead of teaching them to pitch something as soon as it shows wear.
The Scissorman's van moves down the highway, defying
our built world, passing signs for Bank of America, Jiffy
Lube, and Pizza Hut.

✳

"Scissors are like men," he tells me. "The steel is hard, like our heads, but the edges are fragile, like our egos." The scissors he sees are meant solely for cutting hair; what's worse is putting them to uses they weren't meant for, like snipping a price tag. His sharp eyes find the snick. It takes 150 strokes to raise a new edge, then ten licks on the ceramic waterstone to whet the blade. He counts in his head; consistency is the key. "You can always take off more," he says, "but you can't put it back once it's gone." He takes the scissors apart and sharpens each blade, replaces the pin that holds the shears together, limns each edge with oil from a needle-pointed bottle, and tests the balance. *A sharp edge reflects no light,* I've read, and as he turns the blade in his hands, hunting the gleam, he confirms it's true.

✳

The salons have lighthearted names like A Cut Above, Hairsay, and Pat's Palace of Beauty. We're on the morning's third shop by now. As the Scissorman chats with the manager, I watch a stylist work, thinking how she can walk miles without leaving the shop, pacing circles around the chair, pumping it higher with her foot, dropping a comb into the jar of blue Barbicide, slamming drawers closed with her hip, flicking hair from neck and shoulder with a soft-bristled brush. A full-body workout.

At her workstation, a jar holds a sheaf of brushes, cans of mousse line the counter, and a daughter's school picture is taped to a mirror's edge. Her scissors are by far her biggest work investment. Three hundred dollars a pair isn't unusual. But it's not just that. Her favorites must feel like an extension of her hand. They're the claws we sometimes wish we had, sharp and efficient. They've cut her thumb clear to the bone before. Wicked. Their power is hers, and people give her a little extra for wielding it well.

*

It can't be easy to make a living like this, always hunting work. People try to stretch things as long as they can, and in this economy, you can't blame them. "Just don't try to do it yourself, I tell them," the Scissorman says. "That does more harm than good." He makes his way one job at a time, carrying the years in his hands, in their healed scars and fingerless gloves.

He comes around like the change of season. Sometimes one long summer day passes exactly like the one before, and what's to show for the time the stylist's spent? Then he shows up, and she needs him bad because of her past twelve busy weeks—sixty shifts, five hundred heads of hair. Her work seems invisible, until he measures her labor by what he takes away. "Hair's mostly carbon," the Scissorman says, "and so are shears. In the beginning, the steel wins, but it's a losing battle."

*

At the day's last stop, a converted bungalow in an older part of town, a stylist combs sections of an elderly woman's fine hair onto rollers and pins them. The client's rosy scalp shows through the neat rows of white curls, a tender place that nobody but her stylist sees. As we move through life, we're held by strangers, dependent on their skill, on what they know about nape and temple, how they dance the line between job and generosity. Across town, a midwife bathes a newborn, a nurse wraps a joint with tape, and here, now, the stylist teases out the set to hide the thinness and sprays it to hold. The woman is "put together" now, elegant and respectable, ready for church or dinner with friends. You'd never suspect how little hair she actually has. The stylist leans back against the chair as her client makes her careful way out the door, into the bright afternoon. Like the Scissorman, she'll be back.

We All Drink from that Fiery Spring
(Ode to Heavy Industry)

As the plane banks over Houston you will see the refineries of Texas City. If it is day, there will be a pillar of cloud over the smokestacks; if night, a pillar of flame. The plane's engines drown out all sound but their own, but you will know the deep thrum the flares make. A sickish tint hangs over the city, sometimes whitish, sometimes yellow or brown, but remember: the fuel the refineries decant holds the plane aloft. I see in the refineries something I recognize. Dangerous, necessary. Here's where we make things. Here's where I'm from.

Dad's factory sat between the railroad tracks and SC Highway 183. I worked there the summer before I moved to Houston, first shift, packing parts. The loading door stood open to let in the breeze. Kudzu crawled over the railroad siding. Check for chatter by running your fingertip across the barrel's lip. Keep a red rag to wipe sweet kerosene from your hands. I could finish a box in twenty minutes, arranging spark-plug shells shoulder to shoulder, spraying each layer with a silver can to keep away rust, tucking one cardboard spacer between each layer. Five layers to a box. Sponge the kraft tape wet, pull it taut over the box's seam and press it home, ink initials and date in the top right corner.

First shift started at 6:00 a.m. Barbara, my supervisor, kept a first-aid kit tucked under the counter, and a poster pinned to the wall that said, I'VE BEEN BEAT UP, KICKED, INSULTED, LIED TO, AND LAUGHED AT. THE ONLY REASON I STAY AROUND IS TO SEE WHAT HAPPENS NEXT. The secretary in the front office had air-conditioning, Gatorade, and access to the front restroom. We had to use the shop restroom; second shift smoked while they pissed and stubbed out the filters on the cinder-block walls.

I would move to Texas in August. I had never been there before, and for me—for everyone at the shop—it became a fabled land, a mirage that shimmered just out of sight in the heat waves that rose from the asphalt of the employee parking lot. One day during break, LaTrina, who ran the counterbore machine, said, "When you get out there on your own, whoo! You'll be your own lady. Ain't got no man to tell you what to do, ain't got no kids to tie you down. I'd go in a minute."

Friday was payday, and I'd deposit my check at the bank in town. Always there was someone in the teller line who'd turn around to see who smelled of old grease, sweat, hot metal. Always I'd look her in the eye and give her a tight smile. I don't owe you a nickel, lady. A thousand miles to Houston meant forty gallons of gas, and I could pay for it. We all drink from that fiery spring, hear the refinery's dull roar when the engine scrapes to life. Barbara said, "Once you get out there, you'll never come back here. You won't know us no more."

Orders fell midway through the summer, and I got laid off. Cletis, the floor manager, said he was sorry to do it. Not long after that, Dad sold the factory out to a conglomerate from Connecticut, and they moved the machines from the shop beside the railroad tracks to a new white-

painted building in town. Heavy-duty haulers moved
the big green screw machines to the new factory and the
workers bolted them to the floor. One of the machines, a
chucker, had been stored in a cave in Kansas for decades.
The federal government had had it built in 1947 to make
parts for bomb detonators, tooled up and ready to go in
case of another war. Engineers tested the machine at the
factory in Connecticut, sprayed it with Cosmoline to keep
it from rusting, wrapped it in heavy paper and burlap,
and trucked it cross-country. Hundreds of these machines
waited in the cave until 1993, when the government auctioned them off for a song. While similar machines would
retail for better than a hundred thousand dollars, these
sold for sixty-five hundred.

Strange to think of the old shop sitting empty now,
the machines gone, Barbara's first-aid kit and I'VE BEEN
BEAT UP poster gone, the thumbtacks that held it to the
wall gone. But curls of scrap must still be there, corkscrews
of brass and steel pressed into the filth of the shop floor.
And the smell of kerosene caught in the insulation. And
the workbench I leaned against as I worked.

My old boss Cletis is gone, too, gone to glory. The
last time I saw him, he was in intensive care in the hospital, recovering from a triple bypass. I would move to
Houston a few days later. "Be careful out there in Texas,"
he whispered. The tubes in his chest made it hard to talk.
"Remember, when you marry one of them rich oil barons,
I want to be the gardener in your mansion." Bougainvillea,
cycads, Chinese tallowtree. None of them plants that we
knew. But I would learn them on my own, rich air pressing
me down, the smell of roasting coffee from the Maxwell
House factory swirling over my little garage apartment,
and sometimes when the winds changed, the bitter fume

of the refineries' hot metal. I married not a rich oil baron but another writer, poor as me, and for years we have lived first carefully and now extravagantly together, today back not far from that railroad siding, where last night's hard frost killed the kudzu back until next summer. Last time we visited Houston, I noticed a label on an air conditioner that read ALPHA AND OMEGA AC REPAIR. I am the first and the last.

Yesterday I asked if the old cave machine chucker was still around. "Kind of," Dad said. "Made a new machine out of it. Took the original head out and scrapped it, put a new head in. Same frame." Still running.

Hammer Price
(Song of the Auctioneer)

The auctioneer remembers. What it cost him to learn to chant ($37.50 for a class in 1978). The year this house was built (1946; the deceased laid the bricks himself after returning from the War). What this bidder, a trim lady with carefully permed hair, will pay for a McCoy planter shaped like a bird-of-paradise ($80). "One more time, believe I would. Believe you'll get it," says the auctioneer as another man bids higher. "I was wrong," the auctioneer says. "I have ninety, who'll give a hundred, hundred, hundred? Nice piece," he says. "Don't shake your head. Don't walk away."

I like this auctioneer, and I go to all his sales. A big suntanned man with a neatly trimmed silver goatee, his chant is a pleasure to hear and easy to follow: playful, a bit of a twang, and a tobacco-auction echo in the soft-*r* way he sings "quarter." By the sale's very nature, we don't want the same things, and yet he's such a good salesman that I feel we're on the same team. We need each other.

I love auction day's carnival atmosphere. It's an efficient treasure hunt; the place is flushed empty in a day's time, and we each leave with what we wanted most. The auction saves waste by keeping goods in circulation. But for me, the best part is the chant, which rests on one note even as the auctioneer's words dance and dip. On auction day, I rest inside the chant, and feel it bear my weight.

✻

Most of these sales take place at old farmhouses along narrow roads; we park on the shoulder and unfold our chairs under shade trees planted years ago by somebody long gone. But today we're in town, the Hotel Easley, a two-story brick affair with striped awnings, halfway between the high school and the funeral parlor. Like always, the auctioneer snaps on the PA at 10:00 a.m. and starts in. First item: a six-drawer dresser with attached mirror. He tries twenty-five dollars, "twenty-five, five, five." No takers. So he drops to twenty, "twenty, twenty-dollar bid, all right, ten, am I bid ten, ten, ten. [Sigh.] Gimme five dollars, people, five dollars to start." Someone hollers, "Two-fifty!" and six hands shoot up. It's gonna be that kind of day.

When I grew up here in the 1980s, the Hotel Easley still drew textile managers visiting from out of town. But by the time I started high school, the hotel had turned into an old folks' home—I remember a woman sitting on the deep front porch in the same chaise longue that waits in the dewy grass with a number zip-tied to its frame. When I moved away for college, the hotel was a halfway house for people who'd just gotten out of jail. And for years now it's stood empty.

Its furnishings reflect that history. Dozens of dressers and nightstands, box lots of sherbet dishes, slippery old *National Geographic* magazines. But other items are harder to trace. Pillbox hats with traces of makeup staining their grosgrain insides. Pocketbooks, empty but for little mirrors in waxed-paper slipcovers that crumble under my fingertips. Slide rule, topo map, and a dissection kit nested in a case that snaps shut with a click. In a box lot, if you want one item, you have to buy the whole grab-bag bunch.

As the morning wears on and we shift to stay in the shade, I see bidders I recognize from other sales: the trio of white-haired sisters, the city dealers in the navy Jeep, that ponytailed guy whose shirt says, I COULD TRY TO CARE, BUT MY GIVE-A-DAMN BROKE. Auctions aren't anonymous; when you register, you give the clerk your name, phone number, and a copy of your driver's license. We must be a little ruthless to do this, haggling over possessions of the dead. But to buy at an auction is to start a new conversation with an old piece. I'll remember this afternoon's particulars long after I've forgotten a thousand other summer hours: the sudden downpour, pecan tree dropping pollen down my neck, boy pushing a toy bulldozer through the gravel.

*

"It's like playing a banjo," the auctioneer says, sitting across from me at a local diner where we've met to talk. "Start out, you can only play one note at a time. Then, over time, if you practice, you're playing 'Foggy Mountain Breakdown.'"

I like him as much in person as I do on the block, where he sings, sometimes, for eight hours at a stretch. His hands are workingman's hands, wedding band on one finger and a Mason's signet on another, and the rise and fall of his pitch generates the power of the chant. "People get anxious when an item they're interested in comes up," he says. "You can sense it. Whether you say 'hypnotize,' or 'get into the joy of the auction,' the tune soothes people."

At the sale last Saturday, I watched as his five-month-old grandson rode in the crook of his arm, staring at his granddaddy's face while he chanted. Auctions are family affairs: his wife clerks, his son is a ringman, a daughter and a daughter-in-law calculate totals when buyers close out. But it's more than that. "You'll see families break up over stuff," he says. Once a man had to buy back at auction a silver dollar his mother had promised him, years ago, and paid more than it was worth because his brother kept bidding against him. "When he won that thing, he held it up in front of everybody, said 'I got my dollar back.'"

I love box lots for their quality of surprise. How does the auctioneer build them? "You got to put the good, the bad, and the ugly in there," he says. "Something to catch that person's eye. Think of a husband and wife. Think of a mother and a daughter." That way, you run a better chance of getting multiple bidders involved. "All you got to do is spark a little interest. Old jacks they remember playing with, key chain with 'Chevrolet' on it. Anything to spark some memories back where it used to be."

✳

Oil lamp crammed with dead wasps, filling-station watering can, card table with two folding chairs repainted yellow. Canning jars starred with seed bubbles. Potluck casserole dish still labeled with her name. Hammer price does not include sales tax; all items sold as is, where is. Homemade toolbox, '79 Ford, nightgowns. Child's tea set, still in the box.

"Tew, tew, tew," cries the mockingbird from the upper reaches of the pecan tree. "Five, five, anywhere five—HEP", yells the ringman—"gimme ten, ten, ten." The women in the front row murmur to each other, and out on the highway, a car slows down, then speeds off. Below all this is the sound of my heart beating, the house's floorboards creaking beneath strange feet as people step into the attic and pull the chain on the bulb. Hiss of electricity, slap of the Porta-John door. The auctioneer keeps three things in mind: the have, the want, the next. The have is the current price, the want is what he's asking, the next is a click past that. His guiding star is *more*.

What must we, the gallery, look like to him? Our faces worried or wanting, bored or at peace. As my eyes shift out of focus and I tuck my card under my thigh. As the woman next to me fidgets when the lawn mower comes on the block, and bids high. As that city dealer carries off an armful of hand-stitched quilts. The auctioneer mops his brow with a handkerchief and sips lukewarm water to open his throat. When learning to chant, try filler words such as *Whatabout, bettaget, gottaget. Believe I would.* "I like to drove my family crazy," the auctioneer said of learning to chant. "On car trips, I'd sell telephone poles, cows, cars coming down the road. With repetition, you can do anything you want to do."

Even when I forget that these objects once belonged to a living person, the auctioneer remembers, moving between the quick and the dead and striving to do right by both. "I want to do the best I can by the seller," he told me, "but I want to protect the buyer too." I remember a sale at a little house by the railroad tracks. She'd kept a garden. Even the rusty tomato cages were tagged and numbered but those purple irises bloomed for nobody but her.

*

When the sale day ended at the Hotel Easley, I paid for a set of jadeite mugs, a little cross painted with GOD BLESS OUR HOME, and what I wanted most, a bundle of old keys. One for each door at the Hotel, plus a master.

How many times did someone else do as I'm doing, rolling the key slowly between thumb and forefinger? People call it a skeleton key but really it's a bit and barrel, and any lock it fits is easy to pick: bow, shank, bit. Now I can claim every room it opened. The tidy bed that waited for the widower, the pile of street clothes stiff with starch, the hook holding the bride's traveling cloak. I can step over the threshold, knowing that once I do, someone here will look after me. Mount the creaking staircase, set down my suitcase, and shut the door as the afternoon fades. Stare out the window as ripples of heat rise from the undertaker's smokestack. And when night falls on a Friday you can hear the marching band play, *Here we go, Easley, here we go*; hear the crowd yell when a call goes their way. Later, after the late train runs, you'll hear keys knock against each other as the hotelkeeper replaces one on its rightful hook.

Keys are for the living; to turn one against the outside is to stake your claim to everything within. The time will come when I will long to be unburdened, necklace to paperback, and when that day arrives I want someone orderly and calm on the block, someone honest, good-humored. Someone who earns his pay wiping my life as clean as he can so someone else can get her use of it. *Believe I would*, the auctioneer says. *Believe I would.*

Pacing the Siege Floor

Mark the smoke on the horizon and follow it down to the factory on the riverbank. May be winter outside but in here it's always summer, sweat-drenched men moving slowly around the thrumming furnace, twirling rods whose ends burn with molten glass.

Say you spend your working life making objects of someone else's choosing. You turn your attention not to the thing itself but to the process of making, losing yourself in repeated motion. By shift's end, the lehr is lined with your work, dulling as it cools, the belt ticking it slowly toward the shipping floor.

You might sign your work; some do, neat script on the bottom of the candy dish, distinctive stamp attaching handle to basket. But this is the exception, not the rule. The closest I've found is the divot dimpling the bottom of the amber drinking glass, the mark where the blower broke the hollow rod free.

Sometimes when I hold that drinking glass (swirled from foot to rim) I think on these things, how someone made it with fire and sand plus flux, once called "salt," to ease the melt. Seems like magic but really it's skill I don't have, its steps like rituals learned from an elder, and to ignore those superstitions is to lose a particular history.

"With all thine offerings thou shalt offer salt," Leviticus 2:13. So salt your newborn to keep away the devil. Boil and halve an egg, pack salt into the hollow where the yolk had been, eat it, and go to bed to dream of the man you'll marry, or the day you'll die. To protect your house from thieves, set aside a glass of water. All night it waits on the table, resting on its pontil scar.

*

In the factory on the riverbank, I stood on the siege floor and stared into the white-hot maw of the day furnace. "Like a swimming pool," the tour leader said, and nobody could look away. Cold as it was outside, I was grateful to be there, coat folded over my arm, furnace warming my cheeks, combustible air shivering with heat. Another Monday at the plant.

I'd been on this factory tour plenty of times before. On family road trips, we'd go out of our way to stop at Fenton Art Glass, and I loved it all, from the glowing furnace to the handlers to the painters in the basement. At the end of tour, Mom would let us pick out a little something from the gift shop. I still have a ruby vase on my mantel at home, and an iridescent carnival-glass clock rests on the piano.

It was good to be back, but things were different. "Tour times are subject to change during very busy days," said the *Welcome to Fenton* brochure, but it had been printed long ago. As we walked down the steps into the art department, our guide said the shop would close down for half the week because of slow demand. All but one of the painters' tables were dark. Brushes waited, bristles up, in reject vases of robin's-egg blue and white hobnail. The canisters of paint lined up beside them were screwed tight shut.

We moved along to the shop floor, where a man worked on a series of cat figurines. "He has no way to measure, just years of work and experience," the guide said as a gatherer twisted a clot of hot glass on the end of a rod and stuffed it into a mold. The cat would cool to a custard yellow edged with pink, made with depleted uranium, and it would cost less if it had a bit more pink than others, or listed a little to one side. I've always liked noting the slight differences between seconds and perfects. Humans made these.

*

Look at the old paintings and see how we furnish our paradise with glass. An apostle dips a pen into an inkwell; angels hold an hourglass, grains sluicing from one bulb into the other; an offering of first fruits rests in a translucent bowl.

But glass has links to dark magic. People said that the Venetian glassblower who first invented the famous *cristallo* had connections to alchemists. How else could he have created that clear, lustrous stuff? Black magic the only explanation, unless it was, as an old manuscript claimed, the very air of Murano, "purified and attenuated by the concurrence of so many fires," twenty furnaces at a time, burning "perpetually, for they are like the vestal fires, never going out."

Yet if glass is a thing of fire, it is also a thing of earth. Glassmaking is a trade rich with lore, practiced in more or less the same way for hundreds of years. People used to say a monster called the salamander lived in furnaces, feeding on heat, and that if you looked in the glory hole you'd never look away. Back then, when it came time to replace the village glassmaker's old furnace, men in animal-skin costumes gibbered and danced through town, making children scream. The maker formed the new pot from pieces of the old one, pounded to dust and mixed with fresh earth from particularly favored spots. He worked the clay with his bare feet and could feel in his skin when it was ready.

There's humanity in the glass begotten by the breath that passed from the blower's lungs and through the tube into the bubble of molten glass that swelled and split into a hollow column that caught the light. The blower set it on a shelf and heard it tick as it cooled. If you could test that trapped air, breathed in another time, what would it reveal? There's something in it nobody can explain. And in the old days, the makers couldn't tell anyone else their secrets, under penalty of death, until their sons apprenticed with them.

German glassmakers used to roam the forests, setting up and moving on when their fuel ran out. They called their ware *waldglas*, forest glass, and it had a greenish cast from trace elements in the sand they used. This is a thing of our place, and grows from it like a tender plant would. This accent, this turn of phrase, this flower, this dirt-smelling air. Those who know how can tell from which bight in the river the sand came.

✳

The massive pot furnace, scorched and patched, dominated the middle of the factory. Each door was labeled with the color of the glass inside; there was no way to tell the difference otherwise, since the lava all glowed the same red-white. Ever since glassmaking's beginning, the furnace has been critical. To keep the glass malleable, the furnace gorges on fuel. Today, Fenton spends one hundred thousand dollars a month on natural gas, and the furnaces run day and night, keeping the glass at a constant twenty-five hundred degrees.

In Biren Bonnerjea's *A Dictionary of Superstitions and Mythology*, I read that "Salamanders are the spirits of fires and live in them. They seek the hottest fire to breed in, but soon quench it by the extreme chill of their bodies. Should a glasshouse fire be kept up without extinction for more than seven years, there is no doubt but that a salamander will be generated in the cinders."

Cold beings live in the heart of the fire, then; are spontaneously generated by it. In the blue plasma that floats over a split of well-aged oak as it burns. In the pig iron forced into red melt. In the scrubber flames that roar atop the refinery stacks. Since Fenton has been open for better than a hundred years, that would make fourteen salamanders, give or take, created by the furnace. Quite a family by this time. And in old Constantinople, people believed that the salamander "makes cocoons like a silk-worm. These cocoons, being unwound by the ladies of the palace, are spun into dresses for the imperial women. The dresses are washed in flames, and not in water."

The one time the furnace goes dark is when you change the pot. This has always been and still is a tough job. Molten glass fuses the pot to the floor over time, forcing the men to wrench it free. Worse, changing a pot forces downtime. This is not something you want to do any more often than you must. I keep thinking about the pot-setters in their animal skins. It would have been a sight to see, wouldn't it? Ogres huffing and straining in the red firelight.

*

Finally the tour comes to my favorite part: the handlers. All of the Fenton jobs impress me, but this one seems especially challenging, because it requires several steps in quick, practiced succession.

Picture the basket body attached to a long pole, a punty, that rests on a steel-plated marver table. With a gloved hand, the handler twirls the punty, crimping the basket's edge at just the right moment. Then he attaches the floppy handle, stretching it out and up with a bar during the twenty seconds he has before the glass cools. If he needs to use a paddle for shaping, he'll choose one made of close-grained apple- or cherrywood, so it won't stain the glass at those high temperatures.

But what I like best is the stamp he uses to attach each end of the handle. It presses his particular mark into the soft glass; the basket goes into the world with his signature, legible to those who know how to read it. His stamp retires when he does.

✳

Later that day, a half-hour's drive upriver from Fenton, I walked among piles of busted glass at the marble factory and marveled. The cullet—beer bottles, reject marbles, broken art glass—was separated by color. Fox face in opaque cornflower. Puckish mouse with oversized ears. Shards signed in a flowing hand, blushing coral around the edges—the firepolisher's mark. Heavy, cold-cast starfish in orange and lemon, part of a set, the soap dish long gone. But melt this down to save, stretch a drip of honey into a feather.

Later, someone with a front-end loader would scoop up the glass and drive up the ramp into the Marble King factory, but the furnace was down for repairs the day I visited, and the broken glass waited in the rain. This was the perfect spot for a marble factory. Natural gas waited under the ground; sand collected in the river's oxbow; the river itself would carry the product to market. Better still, the scrap from Fenton would make gorgeous marbles. It is the nature of glass to break, and once it does, it can never really be made right. You can choose to deny this basic fact or you can face it head-on.

A man named Berry Pink faced the truth, and by so doing became the Marble King at a time when that still mattered. A hundred years ago, marble factories lined the Ohio River on both sides, turning out aggies and taws, clearies and mibs by the ton. Berry Pink, son of a liquor manufacturer, turned teetotaler after nearly drowning in a vat of shine as a child. ("Can't stand the smell of it," he said.) When he lost his job in the crash of '29, he continued his habit of riding into Manhattan every morning, either for appearance's sake or for his own sanity. In the city, he met a mysterious man who rented him an office, cheap, and gave him piles of used glass. Milk of magnesia bottles, smeared ink bottles, yellow patent-medicine flasks, shards of ruby dinnerware.

At this point in the story, I think of the weaver's daughter in the fairy tale who had to spin straw into gold, and couldn't do it. Rumpelstiltskin came to her aid, although like anyone, he had his price. She had a place to work, and plenty of material, but she just didn't have the right touch.

Berry Pink had no such trouble. He built a machine that could perform magic, creating toys from trash. He must have had a furnace to remelt the discarded glass, a shear to cut the molten stream into slugs, and rollers to shape those slugs into orbs. Let them cool and they're ready to sell, smooth little globes clear or opaque, dotted with bubbles of air like pips of mercury.

On the ground outside the Marble King office door, someone had spread marbles instead of gravel. People used to call marbles from around here "West Virginia trash," but that's hurtful, and wrong besides. Dozens of factories in this region made micas and melon-balls, slags and corkscrews, bricks and beach-balls and bumblebees. Today almost all of the marble factories are gone, and who remembers how to play conqueror, eggs in the bush, bounce eye, skelly, or cherry pit?

Marbles seem to be humble things, but in fact they put the world in a poke. Burned trash, junk transformed, art so cheap kids can buy it by the bagful. Marbles take no obvious signature, their skins too smooth for writing. But those who know can tell what made them: an orange starfish, fine-ground river sand, what it all comes back to. Knowledge snared in a line.

*

I can't quite figure out Berry Pink. People snickered at his name, but he said it was a combination of old family names. Quite common in the South, he said—yet he was from Passaic, New Jersey. I ponder the picture of him that ran alongside a *New York Post* profile in 1938, when he was thirty-seven years old. In the article, it says Berry Pink wouldn't take off his hat until he went to bed at night—lest his bald spot show. "The kids would know he's not one of them," the reporter wrote, "and that would spoil his fun." But of course the kids knew better, hat or no hat.

He was a self-made millionaire, even during the worst of the Depression; he was a man who played the kids for keeps, "deploring the fact that it's necessary—to make Jimmy know how Johnny feels when he loses all his reallies!" He seems like a chiseler, despite the bags of marbles he'd give away at schools to kids who got hundreds on their spelling tests the day he visited. In the photo, Berry Pink's looking straight at the camera, a little boy next to him biting his tongue and squinching his eyes shut with the effort of aiming. The look on Pink's face says *Trust me,* which of course makes me suspicious. Something about him doesn't square.

Is it that he's a hustler? Instead of conning people his own size, he cheats little kids and says he's doing them a favor by showing them how the world works. Maybe part of him didn't want to sell the million marbles his factories turned out every day. Every cloth bag handed out for an aced test cost him something. Part of him wanted to take it all back.

Walking through his world, he clicked marbles in his pocket "like other men clink dimes." Here was someone who gave himself over to one idea. He was in love with the marble itself, not the particular colors or sizes—let the kids pick the ones they like best, order a million of those, drop the ones they don't like. He made the marbles from leftovers, what other folks stumbled past.

I can picture the rented office the "kindly old man" loaned him for a pittance every month. How it filled with boxes of broken glass as he thought about what to do. He must have cut his hands time and again. His thumbnails must have been starred with white from sharp impacts, or darkened with blood. To release the pressure, heat a sewing needle in a candle flame and press the needle into the nail, clear past the quick, and blood will fountain up like oil. Were his hands scarred with stripes of pink and white? Were his knuckles wide and stony? There's something loutish about a grown man competing with children in their games. He has his own realm of play, called business; why should he need this too?

Yet: "The national prizes will include a gold-plated crown studded with marbles as jewels, and cash prizes." He paid for all of this himself, at a cost of fifty-five thousand dollars a year in 1940 money. He said the marble tournaments, which emphasized good sportsmanship and helped keep kids off the streets, were "his life's work." I have a soft spot for another photograph of Berry Pink, not the one where he stands next to Jack Dempsey holding a mesh bag of marbles, but the one with the newly crowned Marble Champion, a boy whose shirt proclaims PITTSBURGH, a boy cradling a substantial trophy topped with a figure of a marble-shooting child, a boy whose face wears an expression of shy pride. Berry Pink looks straight at the camera. His ever-present fedora is dented a little on the side, which gives him a kind of salesman's look. His jacket sleeves don't quite cover his cuffs, and his pockets are roomy enough for a spare handful of marbles. There are worse ways to spend your working life.

When Berry Pink died of a heart attack at the Bridge and Whist Club, aged sixty-two, his obituary ran in the *New York Times*. In the accompanying photo, he's not wearing his hat, and his face is neutral—gone the toothy smiles of earlier years. "He hopes to be married one day and have some [kids] of his own," the article from 1938 had said. He never did, and the tournaments faded a decade before he died. But today Marble King is one of the few marble factories still running in the United States, and the woman who runs it, although no relation, is named after Berry Pink. He had been her father's business partner and family friend. She keeps the furnace lit.

✳

The big shooter rests in your palm and is warmed by it. Little seeds of air bubbles caught inside, a creased leaf brilliant red. As a child I loved to sort marbles into groups by color and size. Dad had a big coffee can full of them from his childhood. He grew up with nothing but still he had this. Plunging my hands into their cool stony roundness felt like wealth. A little seam where a breath of air had displaced the molten glass, a swirl of black on yellow. *Hold on to these*, Dad would say. *Might be worth something someday.*

And now they are. Today people dig up their gardens in West Virginia and find old marbles put there for fill. It was cheaper to dump them than to pick them up, but now collectors fight over them. Say you bought a little white clapboard house down by the river, pulled your spade from the toolshed, and set about digging a garden. Under a few inches of dirt, the carroty roots of Queen Anne's lace, and the scrawling stitch of crabgrass, the spade turns up marbles by clutch and cluster. So smooth they shed soil, crumbs sliding off their slick sides. Ruby red, flecked with gold, blue as island water, black and yellow like an old highway, crizzled by heat. Wash them under the spigot and see how lucky you are, heir to this bounty that was once cheaper than dirt. Dumped and covered and waiting all this time for you.

Not long ago, a boutique marblemaker in West Virginia ran a special batch of marbles for serious collectors. I saw some of the results online. Beautiful swirls of salmon and gold, oxblood and amber and milk. "This one's name is Bud Platinum," the blogger noted. "They named it that because they used Bud Platinum bottles to get the blue glass. It worked well." Gorgeous, common, beer-bottle sapphire. What are we but swept-up specks of this and that? Curls of brass from the shop floor? Space dust and sand, water and a spark of flame. Destined to break but our pieces can be remade as long as the furnace lasts.

✳

Not long after I visited, Fenton shut down for good. It's the same old story, cheaper imports and customers who crave variety. Most people don't want to look at the same vase for fifty years. A few beadmakers do lampwork in the mostly empty building, the gas tongues that melt the glass threads the only ghosts of the great furnace that once blazed day and night.

I yearn to do good work that will last. I see this in other people and in these rituals. Once the workday is over, what remains?

Most people never heard of end-of-day pieces—also known as whimsies, friggers, trifles, or whigmaleeries. Made from leftovers, they're scarce by nature. At shift's end, if there's a dab of material left, you might make a little treat for yourself. A glass top hat. Balloon-ended darner. Paperweight a simple slug of jar glass.

Most whimsies are unsigned. That seems humble, but don't be fooled. It takes nerve to make these, swiping time and material for something the boss can't sell. The work you do during the rest of the shift prepares you for these few redeemed minutes. Who else can stretch glass thread-thin and twist its end into a buttonhook too fragile to use? Who else can pull a hank into a yard-long cane to brandish in the glassmakers' parade, when men carry glass crowns studded with colored jewels, or hats in whose tops spun-glass plumes nod as a glass orchestra sounds its tune? No ears now listening, I fear, have heard the glass bugle's four-note song, and all eyes have dimmed that watched the player's breath condense within the clear tubing. That watched him turn the horn carefully, counterclockwise, and pour the warm water on the ground.

Blow a witch-ball to hang by the fire and stay the devil; shape a hollow rolling pin to fill with salt and give to a bride. In the great Chicago World's Fair, in 1893, Libbey Glass Company's exhibit included a glass dress made for actress Georgia Cayvan. "The dress would have proved too uncomfortable, heavy and irritating to wear for long," reports the history book *Fire and Sand* I read, "but it shimmered with a luminescent beauty that made the lady visitors catch their breath." Not mass-produced or even useful, just a gorgeous idea made physical.

When the World's Fair came to New York City, in 1939, Berry Pink wanted to build a house of marbles there. I can't find pictures, but I like to imagine the scene. No mortar, just marbles poured into wire forms to hold them, the sun shining brightly through, and bits of color snagged inside the first cat's eye marbles manufactured in the United States. You could call Berry Pink the ultimate end-of-day maker. He fashioned himself from scraps of truth and made a new man, whole cloth.

Somehow the end of the day expands to hold what precedes it: rising from the crumpled bed, driving to the shop, your hand pulling the time card from its slot. There's your name, typed at the top. The day's first piece a little reintroduction to the work, clumsy but hopeful, dew still on the grass. By midmorning the familiar routine reasserts itself, and you're a different person than you were at the start of the shift, closer to who you were yesterday. The stack of boxes grows. There is a dread inherent in 3:00 p.m. that nobody mentions. Here's what we've contracted to do: trade our hours of luminous possibility for wages. What choice do we have?

But even though sweat darkens your shirt and oil smears your goggles, though your legs shiver from standing and your eyes burn from checking measurements, you could still have some of that morning optimism left in the tank. Could decide to use up that last little bit and finish the day off right. The coreless sulphide marble cools in its nest of sand as you carry yourself off, to the promise of shower and supper. The end-of-day piece spans the gap between work and home. Making it, you remake yourself.

And work can be a gift. I read an interview with an old-timer who called whimsies "off-hand work," and I like that. "Off-hand" speaks to the worker's casual mastery; it makes it sound easy. If you know how to make the most of what you've got, you'll always have something to spare. Give the figured spittoon bowl, glowing like amethyst, to Grandma. Give the girl the tin pendant reading TO BETTY FROM GRANDPAP in trade for the hours you spent away from her. It's not enough, but you'll make it do. With something to sell, something to swap, something to pay yourself back for being so damn good.

*

The man dressed in animal skins glowers and moans as he dances through town. There's no salamander in the fire, he knows; the men who left were stolen away by better jobs, not monsters. But if it comforts the townspeople, let them blame the creature instead of the foreman, who could well be someone they know. *What's this philosophy that takes me*, he muses, cobbles cool against his bare feet, body damp inside the suit. Children crying but that's old too, he knows. They'll relish it someday, that acquaintance with a fear that's strange to the younger ones.

And after all, idleness is the monster everyone fears, what he tries to frighten away with holler and hair shirt. Let the furnace dim for the time it takes to break the old pot free, but relight the flame quick as you can, lest necessity depart. Dead ashes, cold grate. He sacrifices to the fire with scarred hands: hours, oak, treading the siege floor.

All the vases, goblets, bowls he's made are a blur. But for that one pitcher he favored. Its thin lip where water streamed. Out in the world somewhere, resting on a table.

Half-full of water and forgotten, perhaps, yet protecting its house from burglary just by being there.

A soothsayer passed through town long ago, dancing like this and swinging lit firebrands. He'd tell your future by reading the sparks. *What would he have said of me*, divining pine knots' fatty bursts and kicks? Something of the fallen world in this trading of time for lucre, and something of the divine. To make, even of particulars not of your choosing; to start a job without knowing quite where it may finish. As even the good Lord makes score after score of people, minor changes on the great mold.

INTERMISSION

My strength was that of a giant!
I tell you ladies, you don't know how good it feels till you
begin to smash, smash, smash.

CARRIE NATION, COFOUNDER
OF THE WOMAN'S CHRISTIAN
TEMPERANCE UNION, 1900

Girl Power:
Ode to the Demolition Derby

For my mother-in-law

"I'm going for Dr. Death," the little boy next to me said. We'd gone to the fair with my in-laws specifically to watch the demolition derby—the only reason to bother. The rat-trap midway wasn't worth much; one year, my sister fell out of the Tilt-A-Whirl and had to get stitches. I could've skipped the livestock, just a couple of goats in makeshift pens, and a sad-looking elephant kids pelted with treats. Worst of all was the clown, a sleazy character working the dunk tank. Eyes ringed with dark, cigarette stub parked in the corner of his mouth, laugh ratcheting like gunfire. He had an angle, insulting women so men bought softballs to throw. Wolf whistle: "If my mommy looked like that, I'd never've left home." Hoarse undertone: "Gimme a flash-light and a bottle of whiskey. I'll do it for my country." Mocking singsong: "Mommy's little moron, mommy's lit-tle moron." The whole time I watched, nobody could dunk the clown. They were too mad to aim.

We found a spot in the stands and sat down. The man behind us said, "All day long this fair made money." In front sat a skinny kid, bald already, and a girl I sensed was preg-nant even before I saw her belly—that resigned look. The teenagers leaned close together. Part of the racetrack had been sectioned off with concrete barricades; using the whole track would let the drivers build up too much speed. A man hosed down the pit to make it slippery and to reduce the fire hazard. The announcer said, "Are you ready for some smashin', bashin', and crashin' at the Upper South Carolina State Fair, this annual upstate tradition?" We sure were.

The cars lined up, twenty or so, with names like *Kat Dog, Just a Little Crazy, Punisher,* and *Doom.* I noticed an '84 Cadillac and a Ford LTD, but the others were too beat up to identify. The drivers faced off in heats of four or five while the others waited. The last car moving won each heat and became eligible for the finals.

I learned later that most derbies have lots of rules. No windows, windshields, or headlights; no hearses, 4x4s, or filling your tires with cement. No hitting on the driver's side— first time warning, second time removal. No cars over forty-eight hundred pounds ("No pre-1973 Lincoln Continentals") and, obvious as it sounds, no cars under twenty-six hundred pounds (Gremlins, Pintos, Datsun 280Zs). Passions run high over the 1960s-era Chrysler Imperial; some drivers swear by it, but many events specifically ban the Imperial because of its subframe, which has no weak spots or "crash zones." One expert said that if an Imperial crashed into a contemporary SUV, the SUV would be inoperable while the Imperial could drive away. Not having a crash zone actually makes the car more dangerous in a collision; the driver's body bears most of the impact.

Finally, after a guy in a tiger suit led the crowd in a weak rendition of "Tiger Rag," the derby started. It looked like a free-for-all at first, and although some patterns emerged, luck mattered: ricochets, chain reactions, misfires. Sometimes two cars faced off, only to be interrupted by a third, joining forces with one to batter the other. It was either complex or chaotic; I couldn't tell which. All I knew was that there was something very satisfying about seeing one of the cars get a running start and ram into another. Like pitching a soft-ball and connecting with the clown's bull's-eye. My mother-in-law and I clutched each other's knees and squealed; the woman beside us gave us a mean look and put her fingers in her ears. A female driver from North Carolina, the first woman to compete, won her heat (fifty dollars and a trophy) landing blows that crumpled fenders and crashed trunks. A good strategy, I read, is to back up into your opponent and smash his hood with your rear. She was expert at that, but during the finals, two other cars sandwiched her big gold Caddy—*Girl Power*—until she couldn't move. Teamwork is against the rules but impossible to enforce. When *Girl Power* had to forfeit, we were disappointed, but cheered for the driver when the announcer called her name. Then it was all over and everybody scrammed. Tow trucks lined up on the field to load the wrecks.

I've never gone looking for a crash, but as I watched the woman in the gold Cadillac I wanted to be her, driving hard with nothing to lose, rich as a dozen junkyards. What if you coasted down the mountain into a foothills town? Shift past the others and hit your enemy hard, dodge and veer as hot wind roars past your helmet. A scrim of other bust-ups as from the corner of your eye you see him barreling toward you. He hits and the impact shears your tire, rim skidding out showers of sparks. Burned rubber and blue exhaust, humid air, and afterward everyone walks to the parking lot, saying words they can't hear, deafened by ruck, raw-throated. Here's the secret: to crash in a derby is to gull the bloodthirsty road gods. It's a bluff, a gin, an empty sacri-fice, a tinsel death. So bust what's careful in yourself and see what comes. See if there's any play left in the wheel.

ACT THREE

If we had a keen vision and feeling of all ordinary human life, it would be like hearing the grass grow and the squirrel's heart beat, and we should die of that roar which lies on the other side of silence.

GEORGE ELIOT,

MIDDLEMARCH

What the Body Knows

I will say to the north, Give them up, and to the south,
Do not withhold; bring my sons from far away and
my daughters from the end of the earth.
—Isaiah 43:6

In the beginning, waiting outside the Fairbanks train station, I had the feeling the whole thing could fall through.
When our guide Carl showed up, we shook hands, slung
our gear into his van, and headed up the Haul Road before
anyone could stop us. We were bush-leaguers, my husband
David and I, lugging grocery bags full of canned stew,
Chef Boyardee, boil-in-bag rice. All night Carl drove as the
sun shone through burned-over black spruce, the Alaska
sky glowing an apocalyptic red behind charcoal trees. A
blur of jolt and jounce, the silver pipeline always leaning
over my shoulder, big rigs barreling toward us, skidding
on gravel. Midnight, and after midnight. Could he stay
awake? Past 4:00 a.m. by the time he pulled into Coldfoot
and killed the engine. We made camp beside the skinny
airstrip and crashed into sleep.

I had tried to prepare—trained, researched gear, plotted distances—but, as the little plane surfed and dropped
in the thermals, I saw that it wasn't enough. "What made
you want to visit the Refuge?" the pilot asked, and my
throat closed. Cliffy mountains on either side, and below.

Snow caught in their creases, and marks where hooves had struck stone. "Got a bee in my bonnet," I said, and as soon as I heard the words I wanted to take them back. Why did I want to go? I wasn't sure. More than just curiosity, although I wanted to see what all the fuss was about. Wanted to see a place with a bounty on its head, a place outside my ken, a place with no trees or roads or (now, midsummer) darkness. In the cockpit, a locket swung from a knob, and a picture of the pilot's kids covered a dial. He belonged here, not me. But the truth was, I had to see the Arctic National Wildlife Refuge for myself; if we waited, I somehow knew that it would be too late.

The plane touched down on a flat place littered with bones, and after we unloaded our equipment, the pilot slammed the door and took off, making for a cleft between mountains.

✳

Time to inflate the raft, rope down the gear, and go. If you fall in, point your feet downstream, and protect your head from the boulders with your arms. Let the current carry you into a side channel where it will be shallow enough to stand. Six inches or more and you'll be swept off your feet. Carl tells us this as we're separating our stuff into drybags with HULA HULA and GOLDEN EAGLE and KONGAKUT inked on the sides. I'm trying to hide how nervous I am— I'm a decent swimmer, but white water scares me—and after all, this is what I've signed up for, scrounged and plotted and saved for; we're 140 miles south of Bird Camp, and there's only one way to get there. No road but the river, and two weeks to reach the edge of the world.

Perched on the raft's edge, one leg wedged beneath the taut rubber roll and the other splayed for balance, I clench the paddle in my hands and shove into glacial water opaque with rock flour, so cold I can feel my bones inside the dead meat of my hands and legs. I squint in the bright sun on the water, looking straight ahead as David and Carl banter in the back of the raft, their words blurry in the steady stream of wind and water.

At night—I need no flashlight—I write in a notebook with a waterproof pen, a frail stay against the onslaught of detail that threatens to swamp me. Can you draw up Leviathan with a fishhook? Not here, in this place out of time, where the sun never sets and our passing leaves no mark. Everything tends north: following the river, we paddle from the mountains, where the current is swift and deep; to the plateau, where the Upper Marsh Fork and the Canning River join to make a wide trunk; to the coastal plain, where the water spreads out thin and silted, draining into the ice-clogged ocean. Along the way, we spot shorebirds and raptors, caribou and earwigs; see the riverbank strewn with the tracks of many beasts. Moose scat like marbles. Cast antlers beneath low, stiff bushes. We spend hours on the river, soaked and shivering, and one night when we haul out, I ask David, "Have you ever been so cold you think you're going to puke?"

"Here," he says, "have some tea."

✳

A friend who'd visited the Refuge years before spoke of the place reverently, but with few specifics. "The landscape there is . . .deceptive," he said, and as we paddled the river, I saw that he had spoken well. I'd sweep my eyes across the rolling tundra and would have sworn the place was deserted, until caribou or musk oxen emerged from a line of bright green willows. Things were sewn up in seams there, and while sometimes we saw the animal itself, more often we saw its mark, which we read as best we could. On our day hikes, I'd consult my field guides, noting what I'd seen and when, but soon realized that science was not enough for me to make sense of the place. I needed something more, something like magic.

✳

The river shapes us and our days. We sleep on its banks, drink it in chalky quarts, dip our cook pot into it to boil our noodles, soak our feet in the raft's self-bailing bottom. We bear right when we can and read the water ahead, trying to dodge the shallow places that send us swinging, or shelves where water pours strong over submerged benches and snagging there means getting dumped. Water slides quick against ice banks sharp enough to slice your hand. Pay attention! The mountains don't move and neither do you, paddling hard for hours in an unwieldy current, and when finally you stop, you can't tell how far you've come. Sun high in the sky but it's nigh on midnight. Time to make camp; time to eat, macaroni and cheese mixed with canned chicken, a chewy, salty feast. Open a can of spinach and cram it down, dark juice and all.

✳

The doctrine of signatures, which once dominated medical thought, holds that a plant's appearance reveals its use. Nettle has milky sap, so it's good for lactating women. Pine needles resemble front teeth, so a tea made from them promotes healthy gums. This is the same idea behind what anthropologist Sir James George Frazer calls "sympathetic magic" in *The Golden Bough,* his landmark study of belief and ritual. The key tenet of sympathetic magic, he says, "is that like produces like . . . an effect resembles its cause."

So if shape indicates purpose, what to make of the Alaska cotton blooming outside the tent? I roll it between my fingers; downy and insulating, it could be a buffer against cold, or with its white hair, a bulwark against early death. That's not far off, my field guide reveals. Nursing caribou rely upon it for protein, their milk-warmed colts staving off weakness and wolves, at least for a little while.

Like produces like, and certain images repeat themselves. The vole track pressed into the gray riverbank sand is shaped like the grizzly's, but smaller. A willow twig swaying in the wind leaves a jagged scribble, and the gull above us teases the jaeger by flying up and down, up and back. The fine mat of grass roots is lank and brown as musk-ox hair; clouds over the Brooks Range pile themselves into a second set of mountains in the sky. And as I stand there on the bank, the river leaps along, slicing a new channel for itself, carrying ancient meltwater and grit, catkins and leaves, swelling after rain, tugging the valley this way and that. I cup my hand and drink, wipe grime from my face. *Make me different* is the thought I can't put into words. I don't want to be the same after this trip. Bolder, maybe, less concerned with things I can't control. I turn a blue cobble over in my hands; it's honeycombed with chalky white, fossil coral. Individuals do best in community, it says. I tie it to a line and guy out the tent, in case of rain.

*

We're rocketing down the river, balanced on the edge of the raft. Dig deep and pull, front to back, torquing with the belly and not the arms, making for deeper water on the right, the banks blurring past, mountains above them unmoving, and then we're caught on a boulder the size of a recliner, solid in the current. The river pushes the back of the raft; we're perpendicular to the bank now, and the water's lifting my side of the raft higher. If it flips, we're all going in, and the current is strong enough to sweep us all downriver. I'm riding high, trying to press myself and my side of the raft down, wrestling water as Carl works the paddle, trying to dislodge us. The riverbed is too deep to touch, but he searches the side of the boulder we're stuck on and leans against the paddle with all his weight, and then the blade slips against slick stone, the raft moves a tick, he keeps pushing until the aluminum paddle bends double and breaks, and then we're over the hump, sliding down the other side.

Soon after, it's time to make camp. We unroll the tent and spread it flat, thread the poles through their sleeves, and pop the ends into the grommets. Home appears, a bright orange dome tucked into a stand of willows. We've done this so many times that we don't need to speak; one step follows the next. It feels good, knowing exactly what to do, unzipping the door and laying out the sleeping pads, bags, the books we're reading. The sun warms the nylon wall where we tuck the bear spray. Everything we need and nothing we don't, wallets forgotten in a dry bag with LYNX on the side.

I crawl out of the tent to fill my water bottle, stepping over the mountain avens growing just outside. A small plant with a white, daisy-like flower, the aven means good camping, and legend calls it "the blessed herb, which stops the devil from entering." Here's home, for a while, a dry place on the tundra. We share it with wolves, one of whom surprises me as I crouch by the river. He locks eyes with me, evaluates, decides to move on, and lopes easily along the gravel bar, glancing back now and again. In the pause after he's gone, I hear the hum of billions of mosquitoes. One clings to the tent screen, clapping her front legs.

Brooding over these things, eyes scanning the tundra, I sense something strange taking root deep within myself, an insistent wriggle of thought I dare not speak aloud.

*

This is midsummer, a powerful, auspicious time. The line between waking and sleeping is porous now, dreams more real than waking, hours of paddling front to back, front to back, staring at layers of cobble-striped light, sun vinegary on thin water. The clearest sign is the absence of a sign.

Clouds race across the sky, and a rain smear hovers over the mountains, but we hear no thunder. You see her too, don't you? The lone caribou staring at us from the gravel bar. Then the hawk floating overhead. Look at these piles of yellow hay drying in the sun, left either by arctic voles or ground-dwelling birds, and it seems vitally important I find out which. Sometimes I'm breathless with the sense of time tumbling past, but when paddling we're caught in a moment that never ends. The shallow current tugs us north, the wind off the Arctic Ocean presses us south, and we're caught, vertical needles pointing straight up at the coppery sky.

Old accounts, written by sober men employed by the US Navy to map the coastal plain we're traveling, tell of mirages so sharp that the men saw their distant camps hovering above the horizon. The angle of the light and the curve of the Earth made their far-off colleagues seem to walk upside down, heads to the tundra and feet treading thin air. The accounts speak of driftwood polished and old, and survey markers that turn temporary, tundra working the concrete loose by freeze and thaw, heaving the heavy plugs free. One afternoon I could swear we're alone when a herd of thousands of caribou appears, crosses the river in front of us, and vanishes. They leave hoofprints in the dark sand, snatches of hollow hair, and a scent like beef jerky in the air. I'm the only one who can smell it.

Months later, we'll watch her pale bones appear on a dark screen: skull, vertebrae, and sacrum, what lasts longest of any of us. I'll realize then that what I sought in the Refuge is as close and unknowable as my own belly. Images taken during the earliest days of gestation show a shape that resembles a tongue. Nubbled, bumpy, a crease where the spine will be. While I craved spinach and liver, her brain knitted together. While I paddled and paddled against the wind, shouting with rage and strain, her body was rocketing through a whole host of changes, and I hardly knew.

Praised and cursed be the thread-legged horde, singers of the monotonous whine, filchers of blood, for keeping us always in the moment. They hatch before the snow melts, rise in clouds from the tundra, drive caribou onto snowfields, and are ever with us, their hum as constant as the wind on the river. We wear head nets while eating, snaking spoonfuls of grub under the mesh as fast as we can and extricating our hands, bitter with DEET and pimpled with bites. They bite through our pants, our shoes, our neoprene socks; they bite through our head nets where the fabric brushes our temples. At night, we unzip the tent and roll in quick, then set about killing the dozens that have swarmed inside. Yet without the mosquito, the jaegers and longspurs and buntings would starve, and the wolf and the bear. They're the wide base of the food pyramid here, billions of pounds of protein on the wing.

We paddle past midnight and sleep until noon, and one bright morning brings me my grandmother, gone and buried under Ohio turf these many years and yet now, somehow, seated across from me at a table covered with a white cloth. We're at a banquet, and the air between us hums with the low talk of other guests; later there will be a keynote speaker, but right now I'm telling her about some apartment my sister wants to rent. An ordinary conversation. *I am so happy we can sit here and talk like this,* I tell her, and she smiles. We hug each other and I wake shaken; I could swear she's visited me.

The light and water and cold shake loose everything I carried here with me—the cities of my adulthood, then the small town of my girlhood, and now the farm country of my childhood, vast ripples of green and gold, and stubble after plowing. Dark earth. My grandmother lived all her life in that place. She worked hard, borrowed trouble, made the best of what little she had. And foresaw things, both bad and good, before they could rightly be known. Her husband's sudden death, yes, but also children, and other things I can never now ask her.

Later, after watching a herd of musk oxen vanish into a stand of willows, I find a twist of soft underwool, *qiviut,* snagged on a bush and tuck it into my field guide to save. It would have been better, maybe, if I had left something in its place—not to pay for what I took, but to acknowledge a certain reciprocity. The Dena'ina, a Native tribe who live in central Alaska, teach that "when a person harvests a medicinal plant in the mountains, besides speaking correctly to it, he should also leave a small gift, such as a thread or match or bit of tobacco, in place of the plant." What should I have given? A bone; a hank of my own hair? A pinch of loam from a fallow field; a thing that might,

over time, become part of here? We pass clumps of dwarf
fireweed, also called river beauty, whose purple florets are
just starting to open. When the last blooms fade, people
say, you've got four weeks until first snow.

✳

By this point in the trip, we are keeping it very real. We've
been on the river ten days without showering, and the
coastal plain is so flat, there's not even a hillock for privacy.
Between these physical demands and the conversations we
have, we've become a band of three with our own lingo
of inside jokes and games. We roll down the river singing songs from our youth, like "Eye of the Tiger," "Purple
Rain," and our anthem, "Beat It."

Michael Jackson goes to *work* in that solo. He sings it
all—lead, backup, and the offbeat *hee-hee*s. But Eddie Van
Halen plays the guitar solo, thirty seconds so indelible I
bet you could lay it down right now. We did, barreling
downriver, Carl howling the guitar line, David singing the
rhythm, me whapping the side of the raft. The solo starts
guttural and ends in a keening scream, and by now, a gen-
eration after its creation, it's spread across the world, gone
circumpolar, like some lichen species. Four verses and a
chorus: some fights you win outright, others by avoidance.
And then the knock on the door. They've come for you.

It's not the song so much as the contrast it provides,
the gap between Michael Jackson and this wild place. It's
a way to be silly, a relief from the cold and exhaustion,
and a distraction from the fear we seldom speak aloud.
We're paddling the Canning, the boundary between the
protected-for-now Refuge and the disputed "1002 area";
we make camp on the Refuge side, and gaze across the
river. It's quiet now, except for the current and the gulls,

but what's next? What can we do about it? Right now, here's what we can do: bear right, dig hard to slide past that gravel bar, and suck down enough air to sing the next word.

We sing other songs too, but keep coming back to this one, and as we repeat its lines they turn almost tangible, calling up a feeling of warmth on my shoulders, hills sliding past, spray on my arms. I am not going to drown while singing "Beat It." Here's how the body calms the mind: perform a repetitive task, repeat a familiar litany. In the old days, people built bonfires on Midsummer Night and danced around them until dawn. The only fire we have is the hissing Jetboil, but after we scarf the day's last meal, we jig around the raft to get our blood moving and howl till we're hoarse at the floating sun.

✳

Without trees, the mountains seem disproportionately high, and when we go hiking, land that looks smooth and unbroken from the river turns out to be boggy, tooled with gullies and seeps. So I find myself looking down, at things small enough to focus on, and discover lichen in amazing profusion. While David and Carl read, I go a-hunting for powdered sunshine, rippled rockfrog, and fairy puke. Here's elegant orange lichen splattered across a stone, but no frog pelt or rock tripe, nor pixie cups, a club lichen that looks like minute goblets. Their species name, *pyxidata*, comes from "the Latin *pyxis*, 'a box,' perhaps because the tiny cups looked like miniature containers," muse the writers of the wonderful *Plants of the Western Boreal Forest and Aspen Parkland*. "A pyx is a box in a government mint in which sample coins are kept to be tested for purity or weight. Are the tiny scales in the cups of this lichen fairy coins?" I recognize rim lichen from back home in South Carolina. Flat and bluish-white, it's called "manna" by some. According to my book, "Local people believed that it fell from heaven, and in times of famine they followed the example of their livestock and used it as food."

Lichen gnaws stone, making earth from raw quartz and flint. It grows slowly, sometimes as little as 0.02 millimeters per year—a hand-sized patch can be a thousand years old—and scientists studying lichenometry can uncover details about glaciation and what the planet's climate used to be like. Lichen reveals the air of the past, too, taking heavy metals into itself and giving knowledge to those who know how to ask. Fabulous secrets, kept since the world was young, and I step over them, leaving them behind as I bounce across the tussocked plain, eating of bitter dock and looking for ragged paperdoll and granulated shadow.

Something here sings to the body's stony bones and wrinkled veins, pulls at the blood's piling tide. The iron-rich stones wipe clean the details of the life I somehow used to know, with its rooms and its lightbulbs. Why had I stayed indoors so much? Why had I believed that it mattered what people thought of me? Taste how sweet is this chalky water straight from the river. Feel how good is this sleep in the blessed bag. Do you see it too, the plateau sliced into red books of shale, tangled branches of a rough-legged hawk's nest, fox tracks? Sometimes my own name sounds strange to me. How could I need it here?

＊

Eventually, we'll register for gear at the baby superstore, staring gobsmacked at the wall of wipes and rubber nipples and nail clippers kitted out with tiny flashlights. If only we were outfitting a trip to the Arctic, I'll think. At least then we'd know what to pack.

Memories of the truck stop at Coldfoot will come flooding back to me. A framed collage of disaster snapshots hung on the wall next to the pay phone. Big rigs jackknifed in a ditch; tow trucks loading a mangled SUV. Someone had pasted dialogue bubbles to the glass. Beside a crumpled Tahoe: "Will my insurance cover this?" A man chaining a big rig's undercarriage for a tow: "Relax, I'm a doctor." Gallows humor, exactly what you need when you're halfway to Deadhorse. In for a penny, in for a pound; if the inclines don't get you, the frost heaves will. But what can you do? You can't stay here.

✳

Our last day. From afar they look like animals, but up close I see they're oil barrels, dozens of them, black and rusty, left from exploratory drilling twenty years ago. It's jarring; for two weeks, the only human-made things we've seen have been what we carry with us. Across the plain, in the distance, beads of light burn above Prudhoe Bay. Too easy to imagine drilling platforms here, gashes ripped by wide tires, a rime of frozen smog. I turn away from that and out to sea, the yellow grassland running up to the water's edge and falling away.

Piles of dry wood mark the tide line in silvery drifts. Here, where land begins, bear tracks mark the soft beach, and I step aside with an unconscious deference. These are barren-ground grizzlies, Carl tells us, smaller and less numerous than their Kodiak cousins, but hungrier. There are no streams jumping with salmon here, and they have to make do as best they can. The beach is littered with skull-pans and vertebrae of long-dead caribou, stained dark by the sand. The Arctic Ocean, what we've been making for all along.

As for that deep-seated fear of being swept downstream: Cast it off, along with your grimy clothes, and run naked into water so cold it shorts out thought. Ha! Dog-paddle out to the nearest chunk of ice. Slap it, bob in the water, and swim back to shore, sand giving underfoot. Stagger out onto dry land and rub down with a little towel; stand bare-skinned on the damp sand, baying with joy. "What a rush!" I holler, heart booming in my chest. "What a rush!" Warm rays of sun on your back. An arctic fox's bushy white tail. Telemetry station, steel pipe listing to one side; under-feathers from a snowy owl. And atop the rise, a graveyard with markers cut from gray wood. It had been edged with a low fence once, but now the palings lie on the ground, worked loose by animals or frost heaves. But the wooden markers are dry and sound, and the characters carved on them read plainly:

NASON

DIED

FEB. 10 1933

ANGOPKANNA

DIED

MARCH 23 1936

JIM O'CAROOK

BORN

MAY 19 1933

DIED

SEPT. 4 1934

An old whaling camp, Carl says, and I try to think what it might have been like for the people who lived here, keeping snug in sod-built homes, eating strips of blubber from bowheads they'd caught, bearing babies and trying to raise them right. We stand in the wind, looking out over the ocean stretching north clear to the Pole.

Maybe the closer you get to the top of the world, the greater your risk of madness. Move beyond the life you once knew and into a new place that breaks with the past. Into this new body, arms lean and trembling, palms black from the paddle shaft, feet fluent in the safe path hid between stone and current. Into this place where the very stones grow bread, speak of ancient warm seas, crack open where yarrow sprouts. Cups smaller than a baby's nail hold precious samples waiting to be tried; I assay the value of a thing by bathing it again and again in glacial melt, exposing it to sunlight for weeks at a stretch.

And in the pink sky at 3:00 a.m., the sun floats, a pale bubble. We lie on the grass at Bird Camp; we'll leave in the morning. Early July, and spring is just beginning to green the grass stems, though the wooly lousewort's already blooming. All of it passing away—rivers carrying mountains out to sea, lichen eating stone, the spinning earth hauling the long darkness closer, one minute at a time.

✳

Morning. Coastal fog could have given us another day, but the air was clear, and the pilot skidded to a landing right on time. We loaded our gear and climbed inside, and the Beaver lifted, banking over the shallow lagoons lousy with loons, rising over gleaming braids of the Canning delta, the double lines that meant caribou trails, grizzlies' brown humps. I grieved to go, and all that afternoon's long drive back to Fairbanks I felt sensitive as a peeled egg as we skidded past hillsides of purple fireweed, gorged on gigantic Boo Boo Burgers dripping with teriyaki sauce, drove through rooster tails of road dust. On the radio, Bob Marley sang "Redemption Song," and I worked hard not to cry. *Won't you help to sing.* Our last hours together, our band of merry singers about to split. *All I ever had.* And somewhere along that busted road another heart started beating beneath my own ribs.

The fluorescent lights in the all-night grocery store hurt my eyes as I hunted a pregnancy test to confirm what I already knew. We said goodbye to Carl and watched his van disappear into traffic. Something had ended.

And something had begun. Back in South Carolina, her heartbeat pounded like wave after wave of skirling wind. Like that Arctic wind, coming from a far distance and hauling with it the chill of great change.

I believed that landscape to be far behind us, but during those lengthening nights I dreamed it close, seeing again the hills and divots I'd quietly named First Raft Put-in, Prince's Purple Meadow, Hypothermia Beach, Mew Gull Bombing Range, Sunny Draw Piled with Hay. Campsite Where I Told David My Suspicions. Last Place, Which I Mourned to Leave. The Gwich'in call that coastal plateau Sacred Place Where Life Begins.

✳

Those musk oxen we watched in the bright midnight must now, early February, stand in clusters in the howling dark, as wind scours the snow from low places on the tundra and they feed on the grasses exposed there. Soft underwool streaming in the gale. So are you, my child, eyes opening and closing in the black. A glow now and then toward which you turn your face. I do not know when to look for you but what I imagine is a time belonging to no hour.

In *The Golden Bough*, Frazer tells of people from Bombay to Transylvania who believed that unlocking doors and opening windows would help a woman in labor. Back then, men would unbraid their hair, uncork bottles, unlid pots. David and I prepare as best we can. If it would help to unsnarl the extension cords, straighten the garden hose, unclasp necklaces and lay them flat, we would do it. We crave something useful to do, a song whose every word we know by heart.

✳

It will begin after midnight, the old stories say. As the time draws near, I dread nightfall, and every sleep is surrender. I long for the constant sunlight we had in the Refuge, but it's winter now, and darkness falls early. Here in our bed, David sleeps beside me. He will do what he can, I know, but mostly I'm in this alone.

Or so I think. When the pain begins, I know what to do: set it aside to get more sleep, rest I will need to do the work this day will require. At the time appointed it shakes me awake and wracks me with cold, and I say, *There you are, my enemy, my fear. Let me wrestle you as with a lover.* One at a time. This I can do. As the wrenching starts, low in the belly. As it catches and strengthens and pulls me into itself, tight. More, more. As I climb the steep side of the wave, and higher. Breathing through my throat, ah. Pain a burning cold that builds on itself and burns out from the marrow. Caught upon the tines of it. Whirled into a dense core. No words for this, but a moan and huff. A gleaming, blinding center, glaring as sun on ice. And from the peak of it, to slide down the far side. It wanes and I wax, aware of myself again, laughing at how it took me. And here comes another, crawling up my belly to my heart.

They come, they come, a few breaths apart, then two, then one. My body wringing like a twist of cloth. We gather our gear—towels, Vaseline, *The Joshua Tree,* a snapshot of a two-lane highway—and go. David drives the car down the road. It was not this tidy, but to leave it unwritten is worse. It diffuses into the air, leaving flashes of images behind: squinting in the sun. A harsh birdcall. Swirl of rock flour in the cook pot. In the moments between I become aware of the seat belt snug under my belly, fluorescent lights in empty offices, bare sidewalk. 5:00 a.m. on a Monday. And then: yellow grass. A mosquito cloud rising from the tundra to find a haunch and settle. I have done this, have fattened with life and split, my labor inseparable from the place where I first divined its coming. This is the difference between spirit and flesh, the idea of a place and its reality. Beyond the mind lies the visceral: what the body knows. I have taken pleasure in the steaming mug of tea, sun on my back, springy earth pressing my feet. Look: a miniature forest of tiny golf clubs, short as a knuckle. And this: a gnawed antler, half-buried, tooth marks like little ditches in the bone. This lasts a long time, until the others take what they need, and this calcium turns into a vole nestling, from that into an owl's eggshell, and from that into a thieving fox's belly, where kits overwinter in the stretching dark.

Slow. I walk down a hall. I lie down and relax a muscle at a time, neck to shoulders to back to belly, and the pain comes in wave after wave that I slip up and onto and over and down, up and onto and over and down, and when I glance over to gauge my progress, I see the same bedside, the same cutbank as before.

When the final press comes I'm ready. "What we come

twenty thousand miles to get is worth saving," Starbuck says to Ahab, the chase hard upon them. Starbuck, always too careful. Doesn't he know? When the time comes, you have to give it all; hold nothing back. Ahab knows this, and so do I. Breathless with the relief of finding, at last, the long-sought one, and after all the rolling of line and sharpening of points, anticipation and dream, nausea and swelling, ready now to stare and throw. I strive with my work as with an opponent outside my body, and wrestle myself to the mat. Can't sit without help but I'm strong, feral, working through a body that doesn't feel like mine, a curl of muscle and sinew, cut loose from a narrating mind. I lose speech during this repeated action; spells fill the space. What a strange glow marks this seam between life and death; one hand takes the other and grips.

Pray for those who labor, the old ritual says, for danger holds them, and they must give themselves up to it, moving outside of thought into a place that splits them clean open. I drag myself forward a stroke at a time, by turns crabbed and lean with the strain, making for a place meant not to dwell but to witness things beyond time's usual span. Eyes squeezed shut, I reach out and slap the slick of a broken berg, bobbing in an icy humor that blanks out thought and burns all over. With numb toes, I push off the bottom and make for land, blind-stumbling and staggering, choking with cold, gasping up and out and onto the beach, falling onto something that knocks the wind out of me, a solid thing that is not an idea but a fact on its way to arriving, a fact that sings *I BE* in a rising stream of notes that is a cry.

And then I laugh and laugh, David will tell me later, but I have forgotten that. I remember only her here, warm and slick, holy dirt smearing her crown, clinging to a scalp that pulses with life.

There is a logic that the body knows. The head gets in the way, most of the time. But not the red night we danced at Bird Camp, and not now. Soon, the midwife will wash and wrap her, but for now we hold tight to each other, curded with the river I drank to swell our first shared blood. She was with me all along. Child from far away, my daughter from the end of the earth.

The World Is On Fire:
Cave of the Apocalypse

Patmos, Greece

1.

Women keep their own secrets. These four sit together in a dim room, polishing silver, door open to let out the kerosene fumes. Laughter and talk, none of which I can understand. Three of them polish with rags but one uses her bare hands, the pads of her thumbs flat and blacked with soot. Rubs her finger in the cranny to catch the stain.

They see me standing in the courtyard, holding my little daughter in my arms. Because of her they call out to me in love and friendship. *We do this every three weeks*, they say when I ask. Wicker baskets piled with finished lamps rest on the cement step. French curves and cutouts through which the candle flame will shine. Metal blinding in the sun.

2.

John had climbed this very hill, hands bound, tunic dark with sweat. When he tripped and bloodied his toe against a stone, he managed somehow to keep silent. Guards surrounded him, men with short tempers. He had once been like them, not that they would dream of such a thing. Son of thunder. But that was long before, these boys not yet born when he had begun his discipleship on the banks of a faraway sea. He had woken that distant morning thinking only of the catch. Twist rope, mend net.

The sun here was strong, the air dry and sweet. The guards turned off the main path and led him through a stand of junipers, resinous and perfumed, up to a dark hole that opened in the slope. Their captain gave him to understand that this would be his place until such time as the emperor extended mercy to him—a day unlikely to come. John stepped inside. The cave was small, its walls gray stone shouldering out here and there into knobs. He thanked the guards for his rations and sat down on the cool floor to eat, blessing God before breaking his fast.

When the vision came to him, was he awake or asleep? A line of light, brighter than the sun's keen edge. Thunder, perhaps, and a gust of wind that blew into the cave and scoured the room, making bits of refuse fly.

Or maybe none of that, but a change he sensed in himself. The skin on the back of his hand went porous and he saw there scenes from his past. Fine wrinkles on his wrist like the net of braided rope rising from the skin of the lake, heavy with fish. Fig tree in leaf but not in fruit, for the time of figs had not yet come. Aaron's breastplate set with precious stones. Sense impressions but no words; those would come later. All he could do now was open his eyes to see the thing as best he could.

3.

Three men, half-tight but still in step, stride down the old road in front of our little patio. *Kalispera,* good evening, they say as they pass, *'spera, 'spera. 'Spera*, we reply. A fat red moon, missing a rind, rises slowly over the monastery and floats like a bubble in syrup. Sure, it all feels like an omen if you try, but then what to make of the motorbikes speeding loud around the switchbacks, or the FUCK POLICE graffiti by the public basketball court, or the SMOKE CANNABIS? *The moon became as blood, and the sun black as sackcloth of hair.* I stand on the patio and watch as the red fades.

We're on the latest stop of a long journey. The Corn Palace in Mitchell South Dakota, the Black Hills during the big Harley rally at Sturgis, the fallout shelter beneath the Greenbrier resort in West Virginia, my grandparents' graves in rural Ohio, the Spanish Steps in Rome, a Capuchin crypt walled with bones, Florence. All very earthbound, and I don't know why I think this will be any different. You can find Patmos on a ferry schedule and buy a ticket. You can step off the boat at midnight and catch a cab up the hill to a rented room. What do I think I'll find here, on this little speck of an island in the middle of the Mediterranean?

I've come to Patmos, along with my husband and our eighteen-month-old daughter, for the same reason most people do: to visit the Cave of the Apocalypse, where John the Beloved Disciple, also known as John the Apostle or John the Evangelist, is said to have written Revelation around 90 A.D. I had been a bookish kid, raised in the South during the late Cold War, in a church that preached a fair number of sermons about the end times. These factors had combined to make Revelation a book with which I had a strange relationship. I'd avoided it as an adult but read it as a child, believing it was a foregone conclusion that the world would end soon. Fireballs, nuclear winter, cancer, starvation. We'd make it through the initial blast, I sensed, but would live only to suffer and scrounge for years.

None of this would seem to make for a carefree Mediterranean vacation. But since becoming a parent, I've realized I need to come to terms with this book somehow. Is the age of miracles past? Traveling here, could I make a vision of my own?

4.

To get to the Cave of the Apocalypse, take the stony old road up the hill, follow the left fork through the woods, and pass the trash heap by the abandoned house. We trudge along, sweaty and dusty, and pass a group of matrons heading down the road to the harbor town. Something makes me look back, and I see one of them squatting on the side of the path, relieving herself. Then she pulls up her drawers and runs to catch up with her friends.

The Cave is smaller than I'd expected, like a living room dug out of the mountainside. We step inside and sit down to catch our breath on a narrow bench, unsure of what to do next. I'd been so focused on getting here that now I'm kind of lost. A small window looks out over the dry hillside, down to the sapphire water. Right in front of us there's an icon, Jesus with a potbelly. To our right there's the hollow where John would lay his head, the corner set off now by a brass fence. You can see the cleft where he'd put his hand and help himself up. The headrest and the handhold are haloed with hammered silver. And straight ahead, the stone ceiling dips lower, and I see the break through which the awful visions entered. When the baby gets squirmy, David carries her outside, cradling her head so she won't bump it on the low hip of the three-part crack.

5.

I eavesdrop. The tour guide says that here is where John began to write, pointing to the white napkin spread like a tablecloth over a rock. Then she opens a leatherette-covered binder with L'APOCALYPSE printed on it in curving letters. "Apocalypse" is a Greek word meaning "unveiling."

Theologians note the spiraling pattern of the narrative in Revelation. The stars fall from the heavens and you think it can't get any worse, but instead of the story ending, it starts again with fresh modes of destruction. The narrator returns again and again to this story he can't escape.

Revelation is a book in three parts. While exiled to Patmos, the narrator has a vision of Christ, who tells him about the end of the world. He charges the narrator with telling what has been, is, and will be—past, present, and future—and although the narrator's first audience is the seven churches of nearby Asia Minor, in a larger sense, his audience is everyone who will ever read his book. Three times, Christ or an angel orders the narrator to write: "Write the things which thou hast seen" (1:19); "And he saith unto me, Write"(19:9); "And he said unto me, Write" (21:5).

"What has been" is the vision he's just had. "What is" are the shortcomings of the seven churches. "What will be" takes up the majority of the book, and it details the end times, with seals being ripped off of scrolls, rivers and oceans turning to blood, and terrible suffering coming to anyone unfortunate enough to be alive.

"What will be" is what makes Revelation a scary book to read. It purports to be not history, but prophecy, and unlike the prophecies in the Old Testament, this one hadn't come to fruition. We were waiting to see what would hap-

pen. Waiting for the moment when the story and our reality matched. The match might be coded; we had to watch
closely or we might miss it. If we read it right, we could
be on our guard, and as prepared as anyone could be.
But reading the story implicated us, too, made us responsible. *You know what to do. Live perfectly.* Even as kid, I knew
I couldn't manage that. So maybe I'm here for a clue, a
closer reading that might let me off the hook.

6.

John doesn't make much use of Patmos except to name it at
the beginning as the place of his exile. *I, John, was in the isle
called Patmos; and I was in the Spirit on the Lord's day.* For me, this
passage neatly lays out the book's central duality. He's in
Patmos, but he's also in the spirit; linear narration doesn't
apply.

So I circle back again and again, returning to the Cave
over the course of the week we spend in Patmos, not knowing what I hope to find. Whatever it is, it's tied up with
what I think is the most chilling verse of the whole book,
Rev. 10:6: "that there should be time no longer." The words
call up a primal dread from my childhood, a fear that used
to hit me at a particular time of day: summer evenings at
eight o'clock.

In South Carolina, in July, that's when the sun starts to
set. That's when I knew, even then, that the brief time allot-
ted to me was slipping away, and I had nothing to show
for it. It wasn't solely a fear of the world ending that scared
me—my parents wisely forbade me from watching *The Day
After* and movies like it, but even from the ads I knew that it
showed entire city populations being vaporized by atomic
weapons. No, mine was more of an inward fear of not hav-

ing real faith, of trying to make myself believe something absolutely. Sometimes I couldn't do it.

If the Rapture came at one of my moments of doubt, I would be left completely alone for measureless time. I knew that was coming, had felt it even during children's choir practice on Wednesday evenings. Yellow light poured in through the west windows of the choir room, and the director sat splaylegged on a stool. His khaki slacks were tight in the crotch—you couldn't help but notice—but I was ashamed of myself for noticing, and knew that I was lost.

Looking back on it now, I have some questions. Did he really have to sit like that, feet propped on the rungs of the stool, spreading his legs like a lazy dog airing out his merchandise? I couldn't have been the only one who noticed. We were in elementary school and knew little or nothing about sex—even listening to Joan Jett at the roller rink was suspect; I still remember someone's mother leaning in and telling us, *That is a bad, bad song,* when "I Love Rock 'n' Roll" came on the speakers. It wasn't attraction I felt, looking at him, but fascination and embarrassment. Here was difference made unforgettably visible, a weird combination of pride and vulnerability.

He was trying to teach us a song about the new heaven and the new earth: "For the first heaven and the first earth were passed away," Rev. 21:1. The song was supposed to comfort us, but it chilled me. This first earth seemed pretty great. We used to drive down to the creek and wade in the cold water along the slick stones. We used to drive to the dump and heave our bags from the trunk into the pit, and once I found a book of poems there, and once a little table with a drawer set into the side. I painted the table pink and covered the worn spots on its top with picture postcards of places I had never been. In the backyard, puffballs squirted brown smoke out of their tops when you pressed them, and pill bugs motored along under the holly bushes. Could all this cease to be?

Yes. The children are grown, the house sold, the creek diverted to feed a water-treatment plant. Was the awful dread I used to feel just an intimation of the brevity of life? Possibly, but I think the unease was something more. A realization that even the most dreadful story could come true. That an even worse story—one you hadn't read yet— could likewise become reality. The world of Revelation is still peopled and vivid, filled with action and therefore the potential for change. Worse yet was the threat of a wordless existence. The idea that a time could come when there was not even a terrible story to hold on to. My gut went hollow when I thought of that on those hot summer evenings. It was hard to explain to my parents, impossible to share with friends. This secret I had to bear alone. Its face was a blank sheet, bleached-out in the light.

7.

Is that monk Windexing the Bible? No—just the plastic sheet that covers it. There is much to do to prepare for tonight's services. He tucks a loaf of bread into a napkin-lined basket, plucks spent tapers from the tray of sand and dumps them in a box, which goes outside to wait for trash day. Someone's spread the rugs on the big rock outside for an airing. I watch the monk and he ignores me; I am just another visitor, sitting on the Cave's bench. Nothing for me to do but pray or write, which is praying with your hands. You have to believe that someone's listening.

The view would have been the same. This dry air, this steep hill, terraced now with olive trees. Lichen splashed across lumps of limestone. Junipers, eucalyptus, and thorns, surely, dry like these and begging to burn. *The whirlwind is in the thorn trees.* Simple food he depended on someone to bring him. It's a dry place and never bore much. Probably he ate fish, clams, now and then a bit of bread.

Strange that his year of privation would lead, later, to the island's becoming one of the richest in the Mediterranean. The monks of Patmos were wealthy for centuries, thanks to a chrysobull decree granted in 1088 by Emperor Alexius I Comnenus of Constantinople that exempted them from taxation and gave them the right to own ships that plied the waters and gained treasure. It's a desert island and would seem to be naturally poor, devoted to an ascetic way of life, but an important story started here that's attracted pilgrims and tribute for centuries, and you can see the wealth in the monastery at the top of the hill with its richly worked silver and gold icons, the treasures in its museum, its tapestries, the costly lamps I watched the women polish. The Cave itself can feel like an afterthought.

But the only treasure John carried out was the one wrung from his own mind. The words unspooled and he followed the trail they made.

Here God spoke. In a gray room that looks like a highway underpass. If here, why not anywhere? Walls of stone pliant as dough under your hands. Hollow out a place for your head to rest, and a grip to help your hand as you rise. What we take to be solid can turn soft and you sink, the earth's skin breaking under your weight.

As many times as I visit, I never sit alone.

8.

The group filing in must be Russian Orthodox. The men gather in a circle and start singing an ancient-sounding song, led by a baby-faced priest with frizzy red hair. The women wear their hair wrapped in scarves of many patterned colors—print, paisley, white, turquoise. Nuns file in, wimples framing their faces and covering their chins. Now they're all singing, men and women both, *Kyrie eleison*. The women kneel and then put a hand on the bench as they rise.

It occurs to me that this shiny, wobbly bench is holy too, and ought to be edged with silver. That the bottle of Windex is as transformational as holy oil, and more subtle. Kisses wear a smooth place into the bottom of Jesus's robe, and shuffling feet press a trail into the floor. I breathe in and the tour group's collective stale breath gusts into my lungs. *So teach us to number our days, that we may apply our hearts unto wisdom.* On an old cane-seat chair behind me, the monk murmurs to himself in Greek, going over accounts.

The three-part seam says that the Word is powerful, fearsome. Be wary; inspiration can strike anywhere. It's dangerous that way, destroying what you had believed, demanding a new place for itself. Inspiration carving itself onto the warm clay of hand and brain. Inspiration strong enough to split stone. Who hasn't prayed for that? For a word that, even if inscrutable, is loud enough to transcribe?

Watching the pilgrims, I see what I'm supposed to do. Cross yourself; buy a candle; kiss the icons; drop a coin in the alms box. It makes no sound when it falls, muffled as it is by other gifts. All of us are searching for a way to express something—reverence, delight at having arrived here safely, gratitude to God for the inspiration to do work, awe at the beauty of the dry hills and the dark sapphire sea. We share, I think, a desire to show respect to the monk, whose job it is to take care of the place, who domesticates its wildness by living here. I can barely greet him in his native language, and am abashed when I try. I envy the silver-polishers; they have a job that needs doing. The Russian women unwind their scarves and touch them to the crack. I want to participate, too, but what do I have to sanctify? I look down and see my hat and my notebook, and stand up to take my turn.

The Cave could provide an example of the compromises of a good life. Yes, the terrors of world's end—which you can decide not to believe. It's too awful; make it untrue. Distance the Beast to the historical past, Nero, ancient Rome. Yet there's part of you that knows the Beast can change himself into the thing you fear most. Think what that is; don't speak it. To say it could bring him to life. The fear of Revelation is the fear of death. You know the end is real, much as it torments you. Once you find out, the trick is trying to forget about it. At best it becomes like my memory of the choir director in the khaki slacks—always present, often underground.

But this is the other half of the compromise: going over accounts so you can use the coins left in the box to buy candles for tomorrow's prayers. Carpets freshly beaten. *Whang, whang*, the sexton bangs the brass candelabrum to make the taper fit. Wraps the base with a paper towel and tests it. Secure.

9.

During our days in Patmos, we eat our faces off. Octopus, prawns in melted garlic butter, green beans. Slab of feta and a spoonful of yellow oil. Glass tumbler of ouzo, steel cup of salted potato chips. *A measure of wheat for a penny, and three measures of barley for a penny, and see thou hurt not the oil and the wine.*

One evening in town, I see the Russian Orthodox priest

with the red beard, his face open and frankly relieved that
his work is over for the moment. Enjoy yourself in the tourist shops, young priest. Buy an olivewood spoon, bricks
of soap, a child's dress edged with white lace. Buy a cardboard box of incense the same size as a pack of cigarettes.
Buy a gold-smeared icon of potbelly Jesus, a plastic mag-
net picturing the Cave, a postcard of a naked satyr dancing
joyfully with his enormous erection.

We visit the grocery store, where we learn that the Greek
word for diapers is *pampers*. Toot Toot is a popular brand of
sandwich bread. Along the road, I steal seeds from blooming four-o'clocks and stash them in my pocket. When evening falls, the air fills with the sweet smell of juniper and
eucalyptus, hay and warm stone. This is my favorite time
of day here; though it used to bring me dread as a child, in
Patmos, somehow it doesn't. The buildings the faintest of
pink in the fading sunlight; the grumpy sexton driving up
the hill in his little car. No portents of destruction, only the
world we would grieve to leave.

I conflated my old fear of apocalypse with the place
its story began—a natural mistake for a Cold War kid, for
whom place names have the power to convey a physical
chill. Alamogordo, Frenchman Flat, Jornada del Muerto.
The Cave of the Apocalypse is a popular site for a particular kind of tourist, but what kind? One whose mind is on
the things of heaven and not of earth? Who venerates the
site of a story's beginning? Or who is confused by something in herself and believes that taking notes and pinching sand into a plastic bag will let her in on some secret?
She strains her ears to hear that secret over the whining
mopeds, the generator that rattles one hill over, and the
reruns of *The Nanny,* dubbed in Greek. The clock on the
wall reads, permanently, 10:01.

10.

I thought everything written was true. *Give me the little book. Sweet as honey in my mouth but as soon as I had eaten it my belly was bitter.* I was always looking for a sign, asking myself what it could mean. Trying to interpret things I found in my daily life, which can get you into trouble. What does it mean to let a story scare you? I went to Patmos because I had read about it. I knew the story, and believed that gave me an insight into the place. At its root, this impulse wasn't so different from the desire I'd had to visit Nantucket Harbor, or New Bedford, Massachusetts: "How cheerily, how hilariously, O my Captain, would we bowl on our way to see old Nantucket again!" But there's a difference if you believe the story might be prophetic.

Look at these fragments. Shards of ironware. Green thumbnails of sand-scoured glass from Kampos Beach. After five on Sundays, the buses don't run, and you have to borrow the cell phone the tavern owner gives you to call Patmos Taxi. An old story says that John gathered sticks and pebbles from the seashore and transformed them into gold and pearls and rubies, to teach his followers about the folly of trading eternal grace for the transient riches of earth. After a month of penance, his disciples turned the gems back into common stones and left them on there on the beach, where we found them.

Remember this: the child asleep in the cleft between beds, pushed close together. This: how the rat running under the tables in the *plaka* makes us all scream and drop our potato chips. This: a German tour guide stops me in the courtyard to read my child's face and palms. "She is destined for a great work," she says, "but she must be surrounded by people who support her."

As she walks away, she turns back and calls out, *"Agapemo,"* my love. "She will have a large dream-world," she says.

Potted plants grow in the courtyard beside the steps leading down to the Cave. Tea roses, jade plants. Shaded by the whitewashed wall, sheltered from the sea wind. The saucers beneath the plants hold water; it must be some- one's job to refill them. Who knows how long we have? In the meantime, tend the flowers till they bloom, and pinch them when they're blown.

11.

A year or so after his arrival, John left Patmos, his book finished, the emperor who exiled him dead. He would have walked down the steep hillside path he'd climbed before, heading for the harbor. A little boat would have taken him to Ephesus, where according to tradition, he died of natu- ral causes at a good old age, the only one of the disciples to avoid death by crucifixion or torture. In the last letters he's believed to have written, John says again and again, *Little children, love one another.*

We walk through town on our last night there. A sign in the goldsmith's window reads: JEWELRY COLLECTION INSPIRED BY APOCALYPSE. Strings of pearls, coral figu- rines, lapis lazuli pendants, beads of onyx and tigereye. John spends much more time describing gems than he does on his one bare mention of Patmos. Jasper, sapphire, topaz, amethyst. I buy a silver ring inscribed with rubbed- black characters in ancient Greek. *He shall wipe away all tears from their eyes.* Not exactly the inscription I wanted but it's the one that fits my finger. If I could pick any verse it would be: *What thou seest, write in a book.*

Tradition says that John performed many miracles after he left Patmos. In one of them, a man shattered priceless gems into shards to prove that he did not care for riches. But John said that this was pointless, because it did not help anyone. He put the fragments back together again, and his followers sold the gems, giving the proceeds to the poor.

Diamonds can be set afire. Diamonds can shatter if struck a certain blow. Rough diamonds are greasy, gray, onion-skinned. Little pebbles you'll throw out with the mudwater if you don't take care. Rub them between your fingers to know them.

Pearls demand special care, and love to lie against the skin. True amber smells of resin. Zeolites, known as "boiling stones," bubble when heated. Emeralds are cool against the finger; reject warm stones as false. Emeralds are also known for their flaws. Were John's shattered gems emeralds? Did they keep their seams after their miraculous repair, like the crack in the roof of the Cave? John had a fondness for that kind of thing, could have decided purposely to leave one, to tell the tale of the break to those who knew how to read it.

12.

Those four-o'clock seeds I pocketed have taken root in the clay here at home. My flowers of the apocalypse, blooming in late afternoon on heart-shaped leaves. *Mama, the pink flowers have started*, the child said to me yesterday as we weeded.

And I believe the act of having a child flies in the face of actual belief in apocalypse. If you really think that extended suffering and an awful end must be our portion, you don't want to bring a child into that and sentence her to such pain. If you have a kid, you're betting that it's at least unlikely. And that maybe it won't happen at all.

The people who live in the shadow of the Cave of the Apocalypse aren't more aware of the brevity of life than people anywhere else. They don't possess some rare secret that walking the streets of their towns might let you in on. It wasn't religious reasons that pulled me to Patmos, exactly. More like a funeral for my childhood dread so that I wouldn't pass it along. If I could go back to the child I used to be, that serious girl even then keeping track of everything, trying to do right, I would take the Bible out of her hands and close it on the desk. I would tell her that eternal things matter, but God loves you, and so do I. Nothing you do can separate you from that truth.

I was onto something when I went outside and hunted the ground for treasure as a child. I didn't know it then, but seeing the beauty in a chip of colored stone and knowing that stone's name is a gift. I was able to see the love of God paving the world around me but I distrusted this knowledge because it was concrete. I believed in bodiless dread, but not in the physical reality that I could see and touch. At the end of Revelation John writes about the stones that furnish paradise. He must have known his readers would need the relief of the physical after all he had put them through, and he might have needed the relief himself. There is something more than what we see and know in this mortal life. And our days are precious; I knew it even then, reading the line "when time should be no more."

If there should be time no more, let it end here, paused in this moment. Our last afternoon in Patmos. The child eating green beans and tomatoes from a thick ironware plate until she's full and sleepy, then tipping over in her high chair to fall dazed into the yellow sand. Sleeping in her father's arms under the ailanthus tree as the afternoon wanes. Then we peel off our clothes and swim in the warm bay until the man with the boat calls out to us that it's time to go.

Touch the Bones

Come and see.
—Revelation 6:1

Walk with me down a narrow hall.

There are worse things on display at the Mütter Museum of medical curiosities, in Philadelphia, but start here, with the glass cases of Things Swallowed. Jade bead, enameled Greek cross, lozenge of lapis lazuli. The cross would catch in your throat, but the lapis would slip down easy and root in your gut, a blue seed. Note the pair of toy opera glasses, a charm shaped like a football, a wee ship. A safety pin.

And if you walk from room to room down a narrow hall, you can double back on your tracks and see if you missed something.

GRAZIE HO FAME
—Sign held by a beggar, Florence

The La Specola museum, in Italy, is known for its collection of anatomical models. Made of wax in the late eighteenth century, the models are detailed to a fanatical degree, and many of them were cast from molds made from cadavers. The unsettling quality about them, though, is that they don't look dead. Not even the ones without skin, or the

218

ones with muscles pared away from the face. It's partly because the artists were so meticulous—in the poses they chose, in the shaping of each lacy vessel and nerve and bony landmark, in the staple of the model's muscle fibers. And it's partly because of the wax the artists used. Even after all these years, the figures seem almost to sweat.

Something about the place makes me queasy. It could be the smell of dead birds, on display elsewhere in the museum, or the warm day; we walked across Florence and crossed the shimmering Arno to get here. But it's more than that. You can't help seeing yourself in these figures. In the gesture of the hand of the standing man. In each carefully placed hair, rooted in its socket on his brow. In the half-closed eyes of the woman they call Venus, lying naked on a silk sheet in the Pregnancy Room.

Here's a case filled with pigments and tools that the artists used. A glass decanter holds a measure of blue-black ink for painting veins. Pink powder, meant to impart the blush of life to skin, fills another bottle. Here's a jar of black liquid, labeled with letters too faded to read—turpentine. Open dishes hold stubs of wax, translucent as honey or opaque as jasper.

Liquid wax would have flowed through the spout of this copper pot. The wood-handled scrapers and spatulas lying nearby could have come from a present-day studio, but others are strange to me: a handled iron spoon; a thin bar knobbed at one end; a ring-handled syringe, meant for applying wax onto small areas. Like the ropy veins that twist all over the swollen surface of *uterus gravidus,* "uterus of a pregnant woman."

Some of these are hard to take. "Fetus with thoracic and abdominal cavities laid open" looks like a sweet little sleeping baby, lying there on its silk cloth, eyes closed, arms at its sides. But from chin to thighs it's disemboweled, the liver turned up so you can see the stomach and intestines. Under the museum lights, the surfaces of the lungs and heart shine.

> Seal up those things which the seven thunders uttered, and write them not.
> —Revelation 10:4

You wouldn't know it to look at her; it's too early. Observe Venus's face, her head tilted. Dark hair falls halfway down her back. She wears a pearl necklace to help hide the seam where her body can be taken apart.

Remove her skin by taking hold of these white satin tabs. And see her veins, swollen with blood, and the mammary glands preparing for the work they soon must do. "Apocalypse" means "unveiling." Her right breast detaches by means of another satin tab, this one red.

Remove her lungs by grasping another set of red satin tabs. Remove the greater omentum, to see her intestines, by the same method. Remove the various parts of her heart. All she can do is lie there on the silken sheet, face turned away. Remove the small intestine. Remove the top of the uterine wall and see the little one curled into a ball, head covered by tiny feet crossed at the ankles.

> A dissection was regarded and experienced as a special public occasion which one not only attended but paid to attend.
> —Monika von Düring, "The Anatomy of the Human Body: A Unique Collection of the Late Eighteenth Century"

Theologians note that one feature of apocalyptic writing is its tendency to write about past events in future tense, as if prophesying.

And so you will walk from room to room, barefoot. Wake in the night to find yourself standing at the front door, checking the dead bolt.

The first two weeks are free—you haven't conceived yet!—but they still count. The initial cell division happens during week three; in week four, if you're paying attention, you find out; in week five, the two-part split between skin and inner organs takes place; by week seven, nostrils form. And as for you, you will long to lick salt in glittering mounds. The very idea of kale, crumpled and dark, will turn your stomach.

And you will wake in the night to see a dark figure standing beside your bed. Wake and see and gasp aloud. Watch the figure dissipate as you stare.

Right now nobody will know it to look at you, although you feel dead in the marrow, sleep overtaking you at unguarded moments, like chloroform in an old movie. Things are happening inside your body that you can sense only through signs.

And you will wake in the night to see the dark figure once more. Standing next to your bed, a glowing lamp in one hand.

Remember things you had forgotten. Like standing in the Pregnancy Room in La Specola, looking at the woman they call Venus and thinking of yourself as you carried your daughter, a toddler now. You want to hurry up and get to the end of this new pregnancy, when you will be dramatically large and the baby ready to live on its own.

But there are many weeks to make it through first. And the depictions of the early embryo and fetus are one of the few things the Italian artists got wrong. They made homunculi that look like plastic babies for a king cake. The earlier in the term, the smaller these models are. A baby the size of your fingernail, fixed by slender wires to a square of polished wood.

And you will wake in the night to see your pillow alive with roaches; another night rats; another night a pair of keen scissors gleaming in the streetlight.

You are at seven weeks, nine, eleven. Twelve. The wax model claims the young one looks like this, but you know from your reading that it looks like that. You think you know, but you are wrong.

And you will wake in the night and see nothing, but hear a dark conversation. The bodiless figures talking to each other in the hallway, plotting hurt to your child. Get up to drive them out of your house and come back to yourself walking down the hallway, naked, on the way to check the front-door dead bolt. Trying to secure the house.

> I was in the Spirit on the Lord's day.
> —Revelation 1:10

I was not in the Spirit. I was in the body.

Tradition holds John the Beloved Disciple to have been a virgin. So this story is not for him. Even though *The Golden Legend,* a medieval collection of the lives of the saints, tells us that the name John means "one to whom a gift is given, and in John's case this gift was the revelation of secrets. For to him it was given to know many profound secrets." This particular mystery he never knew.

This story is for you, woman. Will we know each other at a glance, see in each other something we recognize? Some invisible mark on our foreheads? Maybe you, too, woke in the night and saw a dark figure standing in the hallway. Staring at you as you slept. Gesturing with one hand for you to come along. *Come and see.*

No, you tried to say, but silence clotted your mouth. *I will not come with you.*

For the time is at hand.
—Revelation 1:3

As in a dream, as in Revelation, just when you think things can't get worse, the torments begin afresh.

And perhaps the perspective can shift.

Wake early on a Monday in April and find a drop of blood. Over the phone, the midwife will ask, *Dime-sized or quarter-sized? Quarter,* you will say, taking down the address for the ultrasound office, deciding to believe nothing is wrong.

Lie on the paper sheet and turn your head to one side. Acoustic ceiling tiles above measure a foot square; this room is twelve by twelve. *I just want to know if the baby is alive,* you will say. The technician snaps the video screen to black and mutes the sound. *That's all I want to know,* you say from your place on the table. The technician's mouth is a firm line. She keeps her eyes on the screen, says, *I can't tell you anything.*

This is the only time they'll behave for you, jokes the man at the reception desk. Close-up photographs of angelic infants cover the waiting-room walls. *They stop listening soon as they're born.*

And you will go to sleep that night still believing there can be some other explanation. But when morning comes and you wake tasting blood, warm river smell rising from your skin, you will know. Why go to work? Because you crave routine; because you are a woman of habit. Because you do not know how bad this will get. During your first class, the contractions start, sharp pains forcing you to pause as you instruct your students. They're sweet girls, and they work hard all hour, pausing to whisper intent suggestions to each other about thesis statements and transitions.

Things deteriorate quickly. Walk down the hallway, where your colleague insists on driving you home—a good thing, because you nearly black out in the car.

Okay, you're not yourself. Lying in the bathtub, currents of blood beating out, room spinning as you try to sit up, head between your knees. Something not recognizable as a baby, but something you instinctively know was once alive and now is not, caught halfway outside your body. Oh nobody speaks of this, do they? Grieved by it and somehow shamed, but this is labor's dark double, like what you went through to bear your living daughter, yet worse: the pain, nausea, and weakness, yet no joy at its finish. No finish. Lying on the floor, the afternoon wind singing through the half-opened window, and sunlight that pains your eyes gleaming on the skin of your hand. Observe the fine mesh of lines and creases there; you are porous, the image comes unbidden of grasses shivering in the pink light past 3:00 a.m. Three in the morning is the hour of the wolf but three in the afternoon is the hour of the curtain rending in twain, top to bottom. The body wrings itself dry with pain and nobody knows but you.

Walk down a narrow hall again and into the room labeled OSTETRICA, where the woman they call Venus lies on a silk sheet edged in silver embroidery tape. This silk, torn from age and dry rot, says nothing lasts forever; it once was dyed a brilliant green but now has bleached to white. Wax purling down the cold candle in sooty drops. The silent wick. Her teeth are less convincing than her lips, which gleam with varnish that looks like saliva. She lies naked on the table, waiting these past two hundred years to bear her child. The child that will never grow larger than this, whose lungs will never swell with breath and whose voice will never rise in a cry.

Woman, will you go through this alone, or will someone you love stay in the room with you? Will he cover you when you shake, read you psalms when you ask? Will he carry you to the car and drive you to the hospital? The bliss of lying in the backseat, rocking back and forth as the big car slows for stoplights, letting go. Nothing more you can do. There is a crease for grief in any day but usually we turn from it. It is a narrow room into which your body will just fit.

You can take Venus apart, lift her belly out by the satin tabs, but don't do it. I want to cover her; she can't do this for herself. At the hospital your teeth will shake, your knees will shiver, the patella looks like this when replicated in wax, you will retch, here are the trachea and the root of the tongue. Tears will edge from your eyes. You will call down blessings on the orderly, a saint performing daily kindness, who unrolls the warm blanket over you, starting from your toes, up your legs and your belly and your heart and under your chin.

What do we say?—if we say anything at all. *How far along were you?* Seven weeks, twelve, twenty. We say, *Sometimes bad things happen.* We say, *It's a bullshit thing.* We spare each other the details but we know them by heart. I go over them again and again.

The ultrasound, which the technician had muted, reveals the baby had been dead for a month by the time the miscarriage began.

I thought you were with me but I was alone.

I can't tell you anything, the technician had said. And for a long time I couldn't say anything either.

Seal up those things which the seven thunders uttered. In those days my living daughter would pull away and I believed it was because she could sense death on me.

And he saith unto me, Write. Write the thing which thou hast seen.
—Revelation 1:19-20

Take a step back.

Another April, many years ago. Middle school. We sat cross-legged on the gymnasium floor. Blond hardwood laid down in narrow strips, thick with lacquer and dotted with tiny frozen bubbles. A red mark on my ankle when I shifted. The speaker had come to talk to us about staying in school, maybe, or staying off of drugs, something so obvious as to not need repeating. But here's what I remember:

He had worked in a slaughterhouse. Every day he waded across a factory floor flooded ankle-deep with chicken blood. The blood was a by-product, used to produce makeup. The floor was slick from the rendering operation, and when clumps of fat stopped the floor drains, the speaker unclogged them. There's blood in in everything, he told us, urine too, disguised under clinical-sounding names. Like in shampoo it's "urea." Read the side of the bottle when you go home. We sat and listened, totally silent. Outside, the pear trees' new leaves shivered in the bright spring morning. The fire door stood wide to let in the breeze.

Sometimes, walking with the rest of my class to the lunchroom at our appointed time, we'd see a line of eighth-grade girls waiting outside the locker room. I held my breath as I passed. These girls knew something I didn't. They knew about blood, as I myself would soon, drops of it falling in the bowl and spreading into overlapping rings, skeins of it purling from their bodies and slipping heavily into the drain.

Women knew these things. They knew how to put on their faces, dabbing foundation on their cheeks with fingertips or triangular sponges, the foam oozing oily drops. Women slicked their lips with lead and copper. Women darkened their lids with ashes ground fine and stretched their lashes long with tar. Blood was at the root of it all. Blood with the red drained out so you could forget what it really was.

The man walked out of the slaughterhouse each night and left dark boot prints on the asphalt of the parking lot. Working there was the worst thing that ever happened to him, and he used the story of it to try and scare us straight. What must our teachers, women young and old, have thought as they listened to this man who was paid special to come share? They didn't say, not to me and maybe not to each other.

Take another step back.

One afternoon in Rome we stopped at the Capuchin monastery to see the crypt covered with bones. The walls were stacked with femurs like cordwood. Finger bones, nailed to the plaster, decorated the ceiling with kaleidoscopic patterns. The lamps dangling overhead were lightbulbs caged in bones and wire. A sign on the lintel of the door read:

IT IS STRICTLY FORBIDDEN:
TO SMOKE
TO TAKE PHOTOGRAPHS
TO WRITE ON THE WALLS
TO TOUCH THE BONES

As we walked slowly past each alcove, it got quiet. The last room had a small skeleton on the wall, a child, holding a scythe in its bony fingers. LA MORTE NON È LA FINE MA L'ALBA DELLA VITA, the sign says. Death is not the end, but the dawn of life.

Years ago, I used to dream of a baby who shrank tiny and vanished. Would wake myself searching the bed-clothes for the lost one.

Now I know who it was. It was you, slip of a child. All I have of you is the tale of your dying. Death at the dawn of life.

Make me not explode.
—Prayer written on a scrap of paper,
Chiesa di Santa Maria de'Ricci, Florence

There was no way to preserve the bodies as the artists worked. They needed up to two hundred corpses to make a single model. So the individual woman they call Venus must stand for many more.

To tint her skin, melt grains of pigment and thin beeswax with turpentine. Paint her thigh with a series of brushes that go from stiff to soft, ox to marten to badger. Beeswax they imported from China; think how it traveled over mountains and down rivers to reach them here in the sunny rooms where they worked beside the riverbank. Traces in the wax of flowers from plants now long gone.

The bees made that. In the skin of her thigh, you can imagine the sun shining through the bees' glassine wings.

I would lift that afternoon from her shoulders if I could. Silk faded from green to white. *You didn't do anything wrong,* the doctor said, but I didn't believe her. My anger was slippery; it threw out sharp hooks but could find no purchase, not on the doctors nor on the technician nor on the grinning man at the desk who said, *They stop listening soon as they're born.* Not on God nor on those who refused to grieve with me nor on the roundly pregnant walking joyfully (as I had) down the cracked sidewalk. The maple tree whispered lushly as spring turned to summer. I knew the statistics: one out of three pregnancies ends in miscarriage. I knew the facts: many miscarriages are biology's way of weeding out genetic problems. I knew these things and they mattered not. I had failed to protect you even from my own body. Well-meaning people said, *Relax;* said, *Try not to worry about it too much*; and I knew that swimming beneath those words was the belief that my very thoughts had strangled you.

I see her lying on the table. I lie down beside her and whisper in her ear:

I'm sorry. Something choked and went cold but you couldn't feel it. Your own breathing so loud, and the blood pounding in your ears saying regret, regret *or* God, God, God. No answer came that I could hear.

A measure of wheat for a penny, and see thou hurt not
the oil and the wine.
—Revelation 6:6

Yet it is worse than that.

The wax woman they call Venus looks alive. All of these figures do.

But at the Mütter Museum, the cases are stocked like a warehouse with parts that are very dead. Heart, lung, penis, ear bones of mouse and vole. A thumb, "amputated for caries," suspended like a pendant, wrinkled and bloated white. I gasp when I see it. Venereal warts strung on floss like beads on a necklace. "The body is nature's book," says a sign.

I walk those dark-paneled halls and observe many displays. Tidy hair balls of man and beast stored in tall glass jars. Dissection kits, a collection of skulls, a daily book bound in the skin of "Mary L., Irish widow, died 28 years." Pancreas in a glass container, sealed shut with tape. In order to see the deep jar holding the conjoined livers of Chang and Eng, you must kneel. One room is filled with fetal children, some in alcohol, some splayed on wires, I turn away. The doctor checked a box on my chart. He tried to be quick but I caught him; the box said "habitual aborter."

I stop in front of a glass casket. People call her the Soap Lady; farmers discovered her in 1875. Back then people called her the Petrified Lady because it was believed she had turned to stone. She is an example of a rare phenomenon in which a dead body succumbs to adipocere formation, aka saponification, aka grave wax. As the years went by, she turned to wax. Her toothless mouth is opened wide; her nose is short and piglike; her jaw is broken on both sides, as though she died screaming. If an embryo develops in your abdomen instead of your womb, your body might fill it with calcium and turn it into a lithopedion, a stone baby. Sometimes even after the lithopedion is discovered, if there are no symptoms the patient will choose not to have it removed. Not long ago, a woman in Colombia discovered she had been carrying a stone baby in her belly for forty years.

Tidy charnel house, filled with bones neatly labeled. A

heart of granite would crack for this. I have been a sepulchre carrying quiet death within me.

And I know what I am missing. Those first mornings when our living daughter was newborn and pollen sifted in through the window screens and joy clung to every surface. Paul Simon sang, *These are the days of miracle and wonder, and don't cry baby don't cry.* And camellias exploded in bloom, and forsythia, and the weeping cherry tree released clots of pink lace that floated in the warm air. People brought us food and I tried to thank them enough and could not remember how, being confused by happiness, and people laughed because they understood.

Instead of that there is this. These are the nights of walking down the hall in a dark house.

When you crave black nights of no moon.

When you become the husk the plant casts off even as the plant itself withers.

When even the gray sun of an overcast day pains your eyes.

Beware the impulse to seek a vision and a sign.

You might find one. And then how to tell it. I smelled blood like wet dirt on me.

Come and see. And I saw. Haven't I seen what I didn't know to beg heaven against?

Thus, each of the good friars, in his turn, enjoys the luxury of a consecrated bed, attended with the slight drawback of being forced to get up long before daybreak, as it were, and make room for another lodger.
—Nathaniel Hawthorne, *The Marble Faun*

I dream my throat is stitched shut with porcupine quills. I must reach back over my tongue, carefully, and unhook them one at a time from my tonsils. I lay them flat on my palm and when I wake my throat is raw and dug.

There was nothing much to bury but we cut the clay with a spade. If I could sing I would sing Psalm 51, *The sacrifice of God is a troubled spirit*. ("Miserere," by Gregorio Allegri.) I was your only home and then I was your grave. Cerements a rich red, scalloped at the edge. Sleek stitch purling in the bowl.

The descant floats above the melody in a wail. On this night someone must clear the flowers, the candles, the scriptures from the altar, yes, and the prayers left there too; sweep aside the loose pile of scrap papers, some folded, some lying open with just a word or two written there, *Make me not explode*, or, *That I can heal my heart and feel happy again*; clear it all away and leave the flat slab, burn the prayers to ash and as the poor flame rises one should sing that song, *Cast me not away from Thy presence; O give me the comfort of Thy help again*.

What does it mean to make a habit of something? Provide examples. I read my Bible every night before bed and have done so ever since I was six. I have read on airplanes, during overnight flights, in hotel bathrooms when others were sleeping, in tents, cars, bunks. Habit. The Capuchins in Rome wear habits of brown. Later I read that the bone crypts began because of an absence of space. When a monk died, he was buried in the graveyard behind the monastery, which was filled with earth brought back from Jerusalem many years before. But Rome is and was a busy city, with space at a premium, so each monk could only rest in the ground for twenty years or so before they had to dig him up to make room for the newest body. Hence the bones lining the wall. Hence the numbers inked on joint and shank.

There was nothing much to bury but we cut the clay with a spade. Yet this belief in holy ground is a tale for the living, not the dead. How could it mean anything to you, who never breathed air nor touched ground, never felt any kiss? You had no time to find a favorite color, no time for any memory, no time to build any habit. If I find this red clay sweet, and I do, it is for me now, to think on when my turn comes.

> Is not my word like a fire, and a hammer breaking
> rock in pieces?
> —Jeremiah 23:29

Listen. I had feared childbirth for as long as I had known what it meant to be female. Yet the day I bore my living daughter I saw I need not fear labor nor even death—not my own. Only hers. There could be no pain like that.

And now I ask. Haven't I paid out the measure of sorrow for the joy I have had? For all the light and shuddering transcendence of her birth, haven't I drunk deep of this bitter draught? By day and by night haven't I prayed to heaven for mercy, the end of longing, to stop the loss that blooms from me time and again?

Haven't I listened with all my strength and heard no answering word?

Haven't I prayed for a vision so that seeing, I might understand?

What means the beast with seven heads? What means the flying thing with a tail like a scorpion, with which he does hurt? What means this, the clear shape cut from water? A tiny heart ticked and went still. A closed mouth. Make sense of this. Fit this to your story. Tell me what comes next, how I'll get what's coming to me. Waters turned to blood and a third of the creatures living there do die. My marriage bed spread with sackcloth of hair. And time shall be no more.

Or match this to your shining vision. To crystal sea and gates of pearl, add pain bereft of use or profit. What good comes of it? What lesson ought I learn, being taught it again and again, habitual? That my dear hope means nothing? Pearl of great price buried in a field. You sell all you have to buy that ground. But when you uncover your treasure to rejoice in it, you find it gone to dust. It craved the touch of your skin for life and now it is gone, vanished, and your grief, too, must be silent. What can you say? *Don't bother*, even the well-meaning advise. So you stop your own mouth.

But there is another way.

The coal touched to your lips. If no angel comes to you in the night with such a brand, you may kindle a fire and pluck from there a searing word for yourself.

ANGER IS A GIFT.
—Graffiti, Ketchikan, Alaska

We take black to be the color of mourning. I wore it every day and said not why, and nobody asked. The Victorians knew how to dress for grief, their women draping strands of onyx around their necks, or jet, hard coal that takes a high polish and can be cut to catch the light. Or gutta-percha, rubber molded into elaborate black curls and lace and very lightweight; you can wear chandelier earrings made of gutta-percha and they will not pain your lobes; the gutta-percha pendant will warm from the skin covering your breastbone but leave no mark.

But before that the grieving had worn white. White linen, white silk, a string of pearls like those worn by the wax woman they call Venus. At the pearl's core lies a swaddled pip, sometimes the oyster's own egg. It lodged in the smooth-walled room. Opalescent water bathed it again and again until it smothered round and dry.

Time passes. You find yourself aware of the date, a hot landmark in the year, grim birthday. Observe from the corner of your eye how this date (unremarked by others, unknown and unspoken) appears, recedes, then approaches again. A red coal tucked between other days, radiating.

Walk out the door of the Mütter Museum and see the sign that reads:

HARRY'S SPIRITUAL SUPPLIES
SINCE 1918
OUR AIM IS TO HELP LIGHT A TORCH FOR THE GOOD
CROSS SWORDS AGAINST EVIL

Walk out the door of the charnel house in Rome and see the woman holding an alms cup, hear sycamore leaves clattering along the sidewalk in a gust of hot wind breathed out by the city bus.

Walk out the door. Of the room in La Specola that smells of old birds and iron nails, holding the hand of the woman they call Venus. Steady her as she rises from the table, leaving the puddle of silk behind; help her as she makes her slow way down a dark street to the riverbank. Sometimes swallowed needles will pass through the gut and work their way out of the body on their own, silver quills rising from calf and throat. When this happens, pluck them free and wipe clean the beads of blood, and if you unhook a safety pin from the back of your throat, use it to hold yourself together. If you find a pair of toy opera glasses, peer through them and see a wee ship, tied with silk thread to the far bank. Press a drop of oil to my forehead and I will do the same for you, will hold your hand while you pass your hour with death.

Walk out the door of the house and hear the mocking-bird in the maple tree calling, "ten-year T-note, ten-year T-note." The mourning jewelry I choose is obsidian, black and shining and keen-edged. Lava when it cracks to cool in seawater, or lightning when it blasts the sidewalk into spatters of glass. Of course the Victorians' favorite mourning jewelry was made of hair, preferably from a deceased loved one. You worked over your grief by twisting the locks with a hooked needle and pinning the loops tidy under glass. I have seen hair woven into cuff-link covers, hair knitted into chains for eyeglasses, rosettes of gray hair in clavicle pendants. Something about this feels morbid to us today, part of the larger taboo we hold against the deceased. What does it mean that for four weeks I could sense no difference between living and dead?

Not love that fooled me, but my own desire.

And there was something in the mortal body's kinship with death that tricked me. Something about the still form that my quick body recognized.

Tonight there is only one heartbeat pounding inside me and nobody shares my blood.

Listen. Listen hard.

Why do I strain my ears for something more? Fancying a beat of that *tumtumtumtum* will make itself known. *They stop listening soon as they're born.* Stop listening. Stop.

But there beside the bed the dark figure stands.

I rise from bed and step into her. Shadow self, familiar shape of my own dying body.

We are bound, soul to clay, myself to my lost child to the one my mother lost, to her mother, to hers, hanks of light and dark, a braid reaching back. And forward.

So I rise from bed and walk alone down the hallway, securing the house in the dark hour.

> Remember I care about you.
> —Folded note found in a secondhand copy of
> Thomas Wolfe's *You Can't Go Home Again*

Let's say "him," though I can't know for sure. He had been the same age as mine. The midwife had him in a glass jar in the refrigerator, waiting to take him away and bury him, I think, though I didn't ask. Pray over him, maybe, speak his name if he had one. Eyespot cold and dim. Shape of head and wee club of arm. Now when I think of mine I think of hers, lost child of a woman I've never met. I can give her the mercy I denied myself.

Listen.

You held him close and never left him alone. With him night and day.

And even though you didn't know it, your steps as you walked rocked him gentle across the river.

He must have loved you. Love yourself back.

Somebody to Love

> If something is worth doing, it's worth overdoing.
> —Freddie Mercury

He sings the first note like a prayer. The actual word, "can," hardly matters. He sings it past language, sings it like want.

The sound swells in his mouth, a globe, compressed yet large enough to grow a world of need. Nobody invites you inside. I woke one day and found myself there.

✳

The MRI machine is bolted to the floor of a windowless room. Take a cotton blouse from the nurse and fit yourself to the narrow board; she locks you down, wrist and ankle. You must not move. *Maybe a bump on your brain*, the reproductive endocrinologist had said, *microadenoma, nothing to worry about per se, but it might be causing your infertility*. As a mask of clear Plexiglas shields your face, the machine swallows you tight, then bangs and whoops. You can't get out. Try to breathe. If your throat closes, if panic presses hard on your chest, if you can't say how much time has passed, if you flinch—you must begin again.

✳

Begin again. Freddie sings the first note alone. Then the chorus comes in, rich and harmonized, and the piano starts up with a sound like a church basement. Dust in the carpet, faded pictures on the walls.

✳

The first time I read Lorrie Moore's "People Like That Are the Only People Here," I was glad not to be in on the joke, to be excluded from close personal knowledge of that period of elevators and waiting rooms. At one point, the narrator calls her friend from the children's hospital, who says, "You've got to have a second child. . . . That's what we did. We had another child to ensure we wouldn't off ourselves if we lost our first. For a while, until our second came along, I had it all planned."

"R-O-P-E," the friend says.

Once our daughter was born, I got the joke.

You can say I'm greedy, and I won't argue with that. I loved carrying her, wanted again that knot and swim, kicks like happy nerves, myself growing large and fecund and elemental.

And the force of our attention on her. Think: tractor beam. Think: unblinking Eye of Sauron. Love her so that it seems too much for one small body to bear. We wanted to give her a brother or sister, and thought that agreeing to the idea would be enough to bring it into being.

✳

Factories produce glass vials with cunning rubber stoppers designed to be pierced with a syringe. Two needles per shot, one to mix and one to inject. In the how-to class, we sit around a conference table with other sad-faced people and learn how to mix effectively, leaving neither clump nor air bubble. Don't shake. Roll between your hands. David's ring clicks against the glass as he rolls the powder and purified water into a solution. If you hit a vein, do not panic. Pull the needle back and try again in a different location. If you see blood, do not panic. This is what the gauze pads are for. We practice injecting a cube-shaped sponge with water.

"Like stabbing?" the man next to us asks.

"Yes," the nurse says, "like stabbing. Don't worry if I go over medications you don't have this cycle. Maybe you'll never have to learn how to use them, but we'll be here if you do."

✳

About this time, I start listening to a fair amount of Queen, especially "Somebody to Love." At first, I can't say exactly why it pulls me. It's an old story, the speaker searching for love and questioning a seemingly absent God, but Freddie's vamping and begging turns it into something more.

I read that Freddie meant for the song to sound like gospel music, that he admired Aretha Franklin so much he wanted to emulate her. Just the same I see something in Freddie I'd steal if I could. I love the way he pushes the limit. It's almost a joke, the way he stretches into that upper register, and you think he can't mean it—until you hear his voice catch. That sincerity moves the song beyond camp into a kind of secular hymn. It raises the hairs on my arms as I listen.

Queen goes gospel—who would have expected it? But this is rock-and-roll gospel, amp and sweat. Grappling with God seems always to have this flavor of the flesh. Remember Jacob wrestling all night with the angel. Who touched Jacob on the hip socket with enough force to put it out of joint, and still would not reveal his name.

✳

If you vomit (blood) or (a substance that resembles coffee grounds), seek immediate medical attention. If you notice (vision changes that turn out to be permanent). If you fall asleep without warning (perhaps while driving). If you are exposed to cold, this medication increases the chance of frostbite. This medication is a clever mimic, it throws its voice into cadences remembered from early pregnancy (nausea, exhaustion, tender breasts.) May cause a (false) positive pregnancy test. May cause mood swings, hot flashes, slurred speech.

May cause bruising at site of injection. Pinch skin between fingers for subcutaneous, stretch skin taut for intramuscular. Beware interactions with other ergot alkaloid medications (LSD the best-known ergot alkaloid). May cause hallucinations. May cause believing in things that are not true.

All of these things are true: This medication is made from the urine of pregnant women. This medication is made from the cells of Chinese hamster ovaries. This is a powerful medication; do not take more than the dose your physician recommends.

FLIP OFF says the vial lid, a gray plastic coin that snaps in place. The hypodermic's lancet point, a triple-beveled alloy recommended for use where beauty is preferred, arrives in an efficient hard-shell case covered with tamper-proof, color-coded red. Neat hash marks stripe the barrel, and a drop of purified water clings to the tube's inside. Code marks the ergot-alkaloid pill, sans-serif characters graven on bitter chalk.

I research the Belgian pharmaceutical factory. Somehow it helps to think of someone taking the train to work, walking inside the windowless building, going through the "air bath" that is the first line of defense against outside contaminants, zipping herself into the first white suit and then the second, pulling the hood over her head. The white covers on her shoes whisper as she treads the enameled factory floor.

*

Note that "Somebody to Love" is far more complex than most rock songs. It contains more chords, and arranges them in surprising progressions. The song knows your desire and manages it, setting you up to long for a particular note from the key signature, the bedrock the song is built upon until the climactic "to," a high E-flat Freddie hits right before the final coda. The song's key signature is four flats: one for Freddie, one for Brian May, one for Roger Taylor, one for John Deacon.

One reason the song works so well is because it follows a pattern, though not too strictly, of making you want something—a chord progression, say—and then fulfilling that want. But if the system worked the same way every time, you'd tire of it. So the occasional 6/8 bars Freddie tucked here and there, usually before a repeat of the chorus, serve not so much as a stutter-step but as extra room, just enough for a flourish, a more expansive turn around the stage. Those bars keep you off balance.

The song works with traditional characteristics of gospel music: call and response, handclaps, even the pleading nature of the speaker's need. But there is something more. Every time Freddie sings the word "Lord," he pairs it with the highest note in the phrase, ramping up to it. "I've spent all my years in believing you / But I just can't get no relief, Lord"—that "Lord" is an upward look written into the music. No answer comes. The next note drops down, back into the mortal realm:

Somebody (somebody)
Somebody (somebody)
Can anybody find me.

If "Lord" looks up, "Somebody" looks squarely around at the other bodily, flawed, present humans, the ones crowded around the piano in the studio version, or dispersed across the stage—and in the stands—when Freddie performs it live.

He built the song's strangest section, the bridge, on a different framework from the first half of the song. These chords are a circle-of-fifths progression, and they move steadily down the register, underscoring the feeling of struggling in deep water expressed by the lyrics in this passage.

I try and I try and I try
But everybody wants to put me down
They say I'm going crazy
Say I've got a lot of water in my brain.

The rhythm of the words, the way Freddie sings them, also feels off-kilter here. He's deploying this struggle for effect, yet singing it with such absolute commitment that it's easy to forget that this is a revised reenactment of pain. It just feels like frustration, albeit with a pleasing shape and a thundering drum line and a host of other voices singing along.

And something surprising happens during the song's final build. At first, the instruments cut out, leaving nothing behind but a chanting unison of voices. *Find-me-somebody to love, Find-me-somebody to love.* From that chant, Freddie folds in new textures one at a time to create a river of sound: first a new vocal harmony, then handclaps, then drums, then bass guitar, all the different runnels and flows braiding together to make one cresting, flooding, smashing thing. Something big's coming, and even if you know the song very well, you can't help but tense up during this section.

✳

A shiny tangle of needles crams the sharps box. I lie on the acupuncturist's table, a string of cloth birds dangling from the ceiling over my heart. The acupuncturist is a stylish, sandalwood-smelling person with long dark hair tied in a knot. I credit her with special powers, and I want her to like me. She slips needles under the skin of my wrists, shins, feet, belly, scalp, and forehead, and trains heat lamps on me that glow redly in the gloom. Later, when she takes the needles out, quick quick quick quick, I ask, *How many? Twenty-two this time*, she says, and after she leaves I peek into the sharps box and stare at the bristling nest inside.

✳

Summer comes and I am on the road, teaching extra classes to help pay for all of this—it's like carrying a second mortgage—and must make alternative arrangements for delivery. Someone must be available to sign for and refrigerate the meds. Someone must provide a valid credit card number, security code, expiration date.

Standing, lost, beside a gravel road in Iowa. There's a duffel bag of meds in the trunk, clean syringes, K-Pack needles, swabs. Outside an abandoned schoolhouse sheltering an old upright piano, I meet a woman I'd say is in her seventies. "I'm infertile," she tells me, holding an orange sheet of paper in her hand. What? *What?* "I'm in Fertile," she repeats. RESIDENTS OF FERTILE is printed on the sheet of paper. So, okay, she lives in a town—a real town—named Fertile.

I have to laugh at that and it lets the air in, heat and gravel and great rafts of cow-manure smell. I take photographs of the Fertile Post Office, the Fertile Hardware Store, and the defunct Fertile diner. I take photographs of the abandoned school and the old piano. I stand underneath the town water tower, whose huge white belly is in the process of being repainted. Faint sweet smell of paint. High-pressure hoses lying flat on the ground. The belt of words around the tower's wide middle reads FERTILE. I pick up a little rock, chalky as an old tooth, and slip it in my pocket, then run away like I've stolen something.

✳

Lunaception is when you synch your ovulation with the full moon by sleeping with the blinds open. Strawberry Moon, Wild Ricing Moon, Falling Leaves Moon, I am synched, I am ready. An Ojibwe healer advises red jasper against my skin and a tea made from raspberry leaves. Friends pick leaves from their berry canes and put them in a paper bag with holes razored out so the leaves will dry properly. Chinese herbs, bitter and brown. Straw-colored vitamins. When I find a knob of jasper on the beach at Lake Superior, I hide it under my tongue.

When before none of this had been needful. Just the two of us. "Very strange," says the endocrinologist, but offers nothing more.

✳

I love the call and response between Freddie and the chorus, which is to say, between Freddie and his bandmates, and to some extent himself. Three singers, overdubbed to sound like hundreds.

The song's obsessive rerecording, repeating a chorus

like a mantra, is part of what I respond to. It echoes the circling of my thoughts, the phases of the moon, the daily charting and noting and swallowing. Hermetic, breathless.

I sing along as I drive down the road. If Freddie were still alive he would have turned sixty-eight this year. I sing along and at some point it occurs to me that I am tuning my voice against a ghost's. *Where will you be in twenty years?* an interviewer asked him in the early '80s. Freddie replied, *I'll be dead, darling!* The *darling* a tic of his speech. You hear him say it again and again.

✳

Please help me, I start asking, but in different words. I write, *That we could have a happy baby,* on a piece of paper and fold it and put it unsigned in the wooden box for prayer requests at church. I light a candle. My friend knits me a model uterus and tucks a wee plastic doll inside; the last woman she did this for bore a healthy daughter.

One hot summer night we walk downtown. People will try to witness to you there. *We already have a church home,* I say when they hand me a tract. I am used to this, I know what to do. But then there are two sweet-faced college boys standing in front of the newspaper building, holding handwritten signs that say FREE HUGS. I walk over and we embrace.

And when the boy on the right says, *Is there anything you would like us to pray for?* it catches me off guard. I know exactly what I want but am ashamed somehow to say it out loud to these two strangers. We stare at each other for a second and then I step up close to the one on the right (blond hair, Abercrombie T-shirt) and whisper in his ear, *I want a baby.*

I have always been fascinated by kinds of wind that

make you insane. The Santa Ana, mistral, foehn, khamsin, sirocco. But there is another kind of weather, internal. Unpredictable and strong. The rawness of my need embarrasses me but I can find nothing to blunt it. On Sundays after communion I try to put words together but all I can arrow toward heaven is *Help, help, help.* God seems to be on vacation, or napping, or perhaps he is in the bathroom and cannot be disturbed.

Okay, says the boy in the Abercrombie shirt. *We'll pray for that.*

*

The meds arrive in a silver bag the same bright Mylar of a space blanket, and I remember a night from long ago, on the first road trip David and I ever took together. Houston to Seattle, and this was the last leg; we drove through California all night, reading Walt Whitman aloud and listening to a call-in radio show about aliens. The Star People were the friendly ones. I suppose it was about two in the morning. Somewhere north of Eureka we rounded a curve and braked hard; traffic was at a dead stop. ROCK BLASTING ZONE, said the sign. PREPARE TO WAIT. Workers dressed in Mylar suits walked down the road under blaring klieg lights. Emergency flares burned on the tarmac. A masked man holding an acetylene torch turned to face us, and I looked over at David. Was this really happening? He was the only thing keeping it from being some weird dream.

On that trip we fell in love—with each other, and with the last stanza of Whitman's "Song of the Open Road":

Camerado, I give you my hand!
I give you my love more precious than money,
I give you myself before preaching or law;

Will you give me yourself? will you come travel with me?
Shall we stick by each other as long as we live?

And so it began.

I'm sorry, I say in the doctor's office, thinking back to those first delirious nights. *You didn't sign up for this.*

Yes I did, he says. *I signed up for everything. I signed up for it all.*

✳

Back then, we used to drive down to the refineries that lined the Houston Ship Channel and watch the scrubbers and flares burn at midnight. Black tar bubbled at the joints, and the air carried a sugary, chemical smell. Tunnel and maze, safety bulbs burning behind metal cages. I see it now in blown-out light, orange and gray, tank farms behind chain link, white globes with narrow staircases curving up their sides. Crude oil must be heated to specific temperatures to draw off naphtha, solvents, kerosene, jet fuel, sulfur, tar. If you could look inside the tanks as the crude boils, what would you see? Viscous pool shimmering with heat, intoxicating burn, tank walls sweating with beaded honey.

Now come nights of complicated dreams in which I crawl through passageways no wider than my shoulders, dim rooms of shadowy treasure, reached by a narrow cave mouth dug in a sandy bank. I'm drawn back to the cave time and again but it could collapse at any moment, filling my lungs with dirt, and nobody knows I'm here or will know where to look once they realize I've gone.

Other nights I dream a warren of windowless second-hand rooms, tables laid with dusty bric-a-brac, our daughter unwatched elsewhere. I run to where she ought to be and find her chair empty, door standing open to a crowded square and busy honking traffic; I scream her name again and again, running as fast as I can, lost. I wake choking, the air in my throat gone to sludge.

*

"People tell me, 'I don't know how you can work where you do,'" the nurse says, drawing my blood, sitting so close to me our knees touch. "They say, 'It's like you're playing God.' I say, you don't see the women that I see, the joy on their faces when I get to tell them they're pregnant.

"This one woman, I went in with another nurse to tell her, she thought it was bad news because there were two of us. 'Congratulations,' I told her, 'you're pregnant,' and she started to cry, said how her husband had prayed over her every night, laid his hands on her belly and prayed she could have a baby."

Honestly, if I could play God, I would do some things differently. Like the couple who asked if giving the shots was like stabbing. If I could play God, they'd have their baby, a few months old by now and sitting on her own, a girl with curious eyes and a shock of black hair. And the woman who sat alone across the conference table. Twins she'd name Jonah and Josh. I bless the name of Tabitha, who answers the clinic phone with a sweet-voiced "just a moment" when I call every four weeks to leave the message that it didn't work again this time. I bless the kind nurse who takes my temperature and says, *I hope we get good news soon.* I would change the news if I could. If I could play God.

*

In spite of all the interviews and discographies, the appreciations and photographs and comic books and fan-club

pins and Christmas cards and tour passes and ephem-
era, in spite of all the Queen research—which, let me tell
you, is extensive—we still don't know what it looked like
when Freddie wrote this song, the one everyone says was
his favorite out of the hundreds that he wrote. (Whitman,
another prolific poet: "I have heard what the talkers were
talking, the talk of the beginning and the end / But I do
not talk of the beginning or the end.") (Lorrie Moore: "A
beginning, an end: there seems to be neither.") Maybe it
happened this way:

A man with a felt-tip pen and a notebook. Face flat, not
arranged for anyone's view. Looking down at the sheet of
paper, glancing from time to time out the darkened window.
Safe bet that he's smoking a cigarette—he goes through forty
a day. Tries out a riff on the piano, shifts on the bench.

That's it. That's the start, the spark that would grow
large over the course of the band's careful recording and
rerecording in the studio, work by which Freddie would
transform three voices into a gospel choir of 160. Of
"Bohemian Rhapsody," made using the same method,
Brian May said, "The tape went through so many times
it wore out. We got in a panic once because we held the
tape up to the light, and we could see straight through it.
The music had practically gone." Still they saved enough
to share.

*

The "Pain Intensity Scale" taped to the examining-room
wall is a list of numbers alongside cartoon faces. Zero, no
pain, correlates to a smiley face. Three to four means mild
pain (slight frown), seven to eight is severe (big frown), ten is
very severe/worst pain (tears streaming from the dot eyes).
Check yes or no: "Are you currently experiencing pain?" If

yes, clinician should note location and numerical value of pain. A list of adjectives describes Pain Quality: Burning, Throbbing, Stabbing, Constant. Tingling, Radiating, Dull, Cramping. Check as many boxes as apply.

When the endocrinologist says, prior to a particularly excruciating test, "Pregnancy rates go up to 20 percent during the cycle of procedure," but shortly thereafter drop off to 2 to 4 percent, the average rate of pregnancy among infertile women.

When the child says, most every day, *I am the big sister. You have a baby, and I am the big sister.*

When I keep doing the math; if it works this time, we could have a May baby, a September, a Christmas. When _____ asks, "Have you thought about adoption?" When the endocrinologist hands me a brochure that says this costs $22,500, plus $10,000 for meds, but if you don't take home a live baby ("'live baby' defined as a child born who lives more than seventy-two hours post-delivery"), you get some of your money back. When I realize that I am just past the age cutoff for this special offer. The brochure has a picture of a happy infant sitting like a smiling, damp boulder in a crib.

✳

Recently, a team of archaeologists discovered the gates to hell in southwestern Turkey, at the site of an ancient temple to Pluto. Poisonous gases stream out from clefts in a steep hillside. If you were a pilgrim in ancient days, the archaeologists say, you bought a pair of birds from a seller near the temple, and released them near the gaps in the rock, and when the birds flew into the fumes, they dropped dead.

This is the kind of place I normally would dream of visiting, the good smell of hot dust, sweat, desert rocks with unfamiliar creatures hiding in their shadows. But as the months click past, I stop caring. Stromboli is a volcanic islet north of Sicily where you can bathe in radioactive mud sulfuric enough to eat through your bathing suit. Lake Natron is a soda lake in the Tanzanian desert so saturated with bacteria that its waters are red as blood. When birds fly into it, confused because of the lake's strange reflective qualities, the calcium in the water turns the birds to stone. I stare at the photographs: CALCIFIED FISH HAWK, CALCIFIED SWALLOW, CALCIFIED HERON.

Sometimes a dark thing grabs me by the foot and pulls. Do an inventory: "How many times in the past seven days have you: felt lonely, felt sad, had trouble sleeping, experienced spells of crying, been very distracted?" "According to the answers you provided in this quiz, you fall into the category of 'severely depressed.'"

Maybe it would be better if I died, I say to David. *There would be the life insurance money.* Knife, cement truck, R-O-P-E. *You could have children with another woman*, I say. *Someone younger.*

"Try a pole-dancing class," counsels the website.

Don't say that, he says. *You can't say that.*

✳

From the corner of my eye I see movement (rat? beetle?) but when I turn my head there's nothing. I watch as the wood grain in the hallway ripples and flows. I wake to see a column of light hovering beside the bed. Strange juices bathe my vitals, strange water (slipped under my skin with a hollow needle) pulses through my veins. If I slipped inside a dry hellmouth (in a windowless hospital room). Or (in a desert, cheek by jowl with other tourists). Doves piled in soft heaps on the ground. If I rowed a boat across a lake (of blood). If I crawled through a gap in the fence surrounding (any one of a number of abandoned pleasure grounds). Grinning cat's mouth opening onto a tunnel in Spreepark Berlin. Jellied green water stagnant in the log flume. Bumper cars upended at Pripyat, three kilometers from Chernobyl. Every time a length of chain and a padlock tightens around a gate it is given me to feel it. Smell of piss and ozone, glint of needle, gauze pad the junkie rips free, ancient sugar in rusted candy-floss machine, weed tree splitting asphalt beside the fotomat (fixer's sweetish chemical smell). Earwigs jostling inside the padded swing (cracked vinyl weeping phthalates), screak of dry chains, rust etching metal in powdery bloom. Waste can lidded with a clown's gaping maw (FLIP OFF): sour water, drowned sparrows. Glaze of tea-colored ice. Plastic jewel dulled from cold. I see it all, I brush my open palm over the seized turnstile. I am the snake that races into the chickweed, the brown bat nesting inside the Tunnel of Love. Spirit myself up into a bulbous dangling car, or lean against a life-sized cement Christ at the eighteenth hole of Golgotha Fun Park. I wait (like a roe deer) unseen in the tall grass at Pripyat.

Proverbs 30, verses 15 and 16: *The horseleach hath two daughters, crying Give, give. There are three things that are never satisfied, yea, four things say not, It is enough: The grave; and the barren womb; the earth that is not filled with water; and the fire that saith not, It is enough.* I crouch, silent, against the tunnel wall, waiting invisibly in the black. Flick your head to the side to see the movement you sense in your peripheral vision. Try to be quick but you won't catch me. I want, want, want. You can see straight through me, and I'm closer now than you think. I'll twist your mouth to fit the words I say.

✳

Our daughter. Squealing, happy, hair flying in the wind as her father carries her on his shoulders. Her face lit by a campfire as she devours a marshmallow I have roasted for her. Who wants more of this? I do, I do. More time, more love. Love is greed; *three things are never satisfied.* You can't get enough of the beloved. You want more to a degree that embarrasses you, the smell of her neck, her fine downy hair. There is only this, only now. Sharp little fingernails and the way she tells me she wants to be a flamingo, because "they can stand on one foot better than persons can."

She likes to help me wash dishes. And sometimes "Somebody to Love" makes us want to dance, and we spin together on the scarred old heart-pine floor as the sun sets behind the back porch. Domesticity, I don't know that Freddie ever wanted that. All I know is that lately this song is my life raft. Freddie and I might not want the same things, but we both want them bad.

✳

Because Brian May didn't have the money to buy a factory-made guitar, he built the Red Special by hand with his father. They used a knitting needle, a knife, pearl buttons, a section of cast off mahogany mantelpiece. Memory of smoke from old fires, caught in the tight grain and coloring the notes, along with the sixpence he used for a pick. They shaped it together, chisel and file.

Pearl buttons, repurposed, remade. From the (mother's?) blouse they had held closed or let fall open. And earlier, the oyster shell they had been, calcium, flat leaves of bitter chalk. Earlier still, a float of life borne on the tide. He pressed his fingertips to their round faces, warming them.

In the early days, Freddie and Roger Taylor kept a stall

in Kensington Market, selling secondhand clothes. Years later, Brian May remembered "velvet jackets, filigree waist-coats from the 1920s . . . and some incredible tat. Freddie would pull a strip of cloth out of a huge bag and say, 'Look at this beautiful garment, this is going to fetch a fortune.' I'd say, 'Fred, that's a piece of rag.' But he could sell it." Even then Freddie could remake old scraps, recast them in his story. His mother used to put together baskets of food and send them to the boys' flat once a week. She didn't want her son to go hungry.

✳

Measures like rooms, empty until Freddie fills them. Some are spare but most are crowded; that's how he likes it.

Think how many rooms must wait now—empty, we say, if no people are in them. Not void, though. Chairs tucked under kitchen tables as the clock on the stove clicks past another number: TIME OF DAY. Chairs pushed beneath school desks, or balanced atop them at week's end, for the janitor to vacuum underneath before punching out.

Chairs in darkened waiting rooms. Chairs beside examination tables. Paper sheets spread across Naugahyde bumpers. Sign advertising stuffed animals for purchase, onto which you can record your unborn baby's heartbeat. Lamb, bear cub, ducky.

Rooms in Freddie's old house, crammed with things he'd chosen. Persian rugs, Hepplewhite furniture, Dresden china. That Bavarian outfit he wears in the picture of him I like best. On anyone else it'd be absurd—is a little silly even on him, honestly—but then again, why not? For a man from Zanzibar, or India, or West London. A man who named himself, shifting as the occasion called.

Empty rooms shiver with *I was here.* Empty dressing

rooms after the show, empty hotels. Warehouses in which stacks of lumber cure, waiting to be soaked and clamped and bent into piano frames. Thrift store full of other people's clothes, releasing the smells of dry-cleaning fluid and haylike sweat. You glance over your shoulder, expecting someone to return.

And in the suburbs, in the dark, a woman rises from bed, drinks a cup of coffee in the shadowed kitchen (TIME OF DAY, clicks the clock), and takes the local train to the pharmaceutical factory, where her feet will whisper across the gray-painted floor.

✳

One night I dream I'm free diving, deep, with no need for oxygen. Way down on the stony ocean floor I find an infant, his eyes open wide, watching me. He's tucked into a hollow in a coral reef and I gather him in my arms, hold him to my chest, and kick hard until together we break the surface of the water.

We have to find out who his parents are, David says. The process of decompression has not hurt the child; he is perfect, and his eyes are blue as all newborns' eyes are blue.

We have to find out who his parents are, David says again, and I will not let the child go.

He's ours, I say, *as long as I hold on.*

✳

When we sign the consent forms before another procedure, we learn that some of the carrier fluid is sourced from donated blood. Carefully screened, etc. Extremely low risk. But still. A whisper of another stranger, hidden now in the center of me. More and more my body is haunted. I carry with me traces of all the pregnant women and postmenopausal Italian nuns who helped supply the drugs I've taken, the children I have lost and who never were and the many selves they will never become. When I crack it open the fortune cookie says, *You can have anything you want if you want it desperately enough.*

So lay out the hoard, the sacrifice this demands. Cold lab rats in tidy ranks. Vials of violet dye, of saline, Betadine, photostatic water; vials of my blood, stoppered with rubber. Vials that click, gleam, rattle. Hanks of flexible plastic tubing. Rolls of stretchy orange tape, tin-lidded canisters of cotton swabs. DublSoft tissue boxes. A well-washed blouse printed with filigrees. Its tented form recalls the shape of a ritual garment, something to be draped over the celebrant's shoulders. A cape.

Take needle and thread. Stitch one at a time each metallic sharp to the cotton blouse. Acupuncture needles thin as hairs, knobbed on the shank. Heavy-gauge needles for mixing. Hollow triple-beveled needles for injection. Secure each with a tight overhand stitch. Cover the shoulders with glinting ridges blunt on one end, sharp on the other. Double row of needles, triple row. Bristling shoulders corduroyed with silver. See how they shine under the infrared lamp, feel how the heat warms them. Remove the round tops from the vials containing photostatic water and hand stitch them in a whorl, tin coins with blue centers. Sequin, sickbed, tinfoil flash. Heavy as you take it from the form. Lift it carefully onto your shoulders and shake its folds true.

Weighty and gorgeous, wicked blister. You bear it all in your body. If you can't keep your feet under you (medication may cause dizziness), well, don't let that stop you from dancing to your favorite tune. Step into the light and see the needles glow, everybody watching as the fringe throws off sparks of frantic gold.

✳

Disrobe quickly; the nurse is waiting. The clinic isn't the red-light district—far from it, dear!—but the fluorescent-light district. Hang your clothes inside the locker stamped DRESSING NOOK. You need a song to help you through. A mantra to help you remember who you are, mojo to remind you why you care, an antidote to the grimness. A sense of humor, for God's sake! You need *Queen Rock Montreal*.

Freddie loved fabulous costumes—kingly robes in ermine-trimmed velvet, studded leather biker gear, that famous white satin bodysuit (holding, as critic Jonh Ingham wrote, "a bulge not unlike the *Sunday Telegraph*"; or, better, a "rope in repose, barely leashed tumescence, the Queen's sceptre"; for "never has a man's weaponry been so flagrantly showcased," leading Ingham to sigh, "Oh to be that hot costume, writhing across the mighty Fred!").

But tonight his clothes are simple. White Levi's, tight but not, you know, Robert Plant-tight; red sweatband on his wrist; white tank with Superman logo—that'll come off by the second half, tucked into his belt like a painter's rag.

On the piano top, go-cups and bottles of Heineken, lemon-honey tea, a scrawled set list.

Can . . . Freddie sings. *Can . . . anybody find me.* He's glazed with sweat, riffing on the piano, giving himself a breather. You could almost believe he's making it up as he goes along. The crowd's in shadow; he's all you see. At one point he glances up, looks the camera straight in the eye. Looks at me.

Whitman: "I am a man who, sauntering along without fully stopping, turns a casual look upon you and then averts his face." *Somebody. Mmmm, somebody.* Piano filigree. "Leaving it to you to prove and define it, / Expecting the main things from you." *Somebody to love.*

Okay, he says, *let's do it*. When he plays the song's opening riff, the crowd recognizes it and cries for joy.

I envy them. They don't know, Freddie doesn't know, what I do. (Says the doctor to me: "I don't want to run out the clock.") Exactly ten years from tonight, Freddie Mercury will die in a curtained room at his home in Kensington.

Before the end, his friends—the men onstage with him now, playing their hearts out on his song—will lie to the reporters ("vultures") to protect him, closing ranks to shelter what privacy he has left. "Without them," Freddie had said, much earlier in his life, "I would be nothing." During his memorial service, at his request, they will play a recording of Aretha Franklin. Grains of her voice shading their grief.

✳

Freddie takes on the sorrow that all the audience members know and sings about it with everything he's got, even if that vulnerability makes him look foolish. So what? You could have, say, prominent teeth and a background nobody understands, kids could tease you in middle school, and you could still grow up and write terrific songs (in the bathtub!) with indelible lyrics and melodies, thereby becoming a huge rock star and an international sex symbol with a ton of disposable cash to spend on fabulous old antiques at bazaars and flea markets all over the world. We're all damaged. We all need love. So say what you want; say it again. The 12/8 comes to feel like your heartbeat, in rhythm with thousands of others. Accept your flaws, own them. This brokenness, this too-short life.

Because Freddie knows: you don't always get the happy ending. Doesn't he know that better than anyone? Sometimes your body lets you down. But he also knows:

you want what you want. So give me Freddie, full of yearning he can tell chapter and verse. Give me power and sex
and energy and going too far, camp and joking and blood
pounding through the veins on his temples. Closes his eyes
like he's fighting back tears.

If I could play God, I'd make it so he never had to
endure the awful pain at the end; I'd give him peace,
strength, a hundred happy years. I'd make it so his mother
(holding him as an infant in another photograph, her eyes
warm with joy) never had to mourn him.

*

Start with the chant of need. By this late date it could be plea
or demand. This want undertows my days and my night hours
shudder and keen, yet this is not all there is. As I reread *Leaves
of Grass*, I'm struck by the way Whitman directly addresses the
reader: "When you read these I that was visible am become
invisible." I can't quite believe Whitman's gone; a whisper of
his voice whistles between my teeth even now.

> Now it is you, compact, visible, reading my poems,
>   seeking me,
> Fancying how happy you were if I could
> be with you and become your comrade;
> Be it as if I were with you.
> (Be not too certain but I am now with you.)

That's why the moment when Freddie looks directly into
the camera—into the future—jolts me. *Listen*, his look says.
Don't miss anything. Remember this. Remember me.

Remember, too, that where the capacity for sorrow is
large, so is the capacity for joy. Blush to read Whitman
singing the body electric, of "love-flesh swelling and deli-

ciously aching, / Limitless limpid jets of love, white-blow
and delirious juice," of the "well-made man," whose vitality
shows "in his walk, the carriage of his neck, the flex of his
waist and knees, dress does not hide him"—*Sunday Telegraph*
and the white satin leotard?—

> The strong sweet quality he has strikes through the
>   cotton and the broadcloth,
> To see him pass conveys as much as the best poem,
>   perhaps more,
> You linger to see his back, and the back of his neck
>   and shoulder-side.

I linger to watch David walk past in Levi's, tight but
not, you know, Robert Plant-tight. I linger to watch him
hoist our daughter onto his shoulders for a walk to the
garden. I linger to watch (again) the footage from *Queen
Rock Montreal*, marveling at how the song builds toward its
big finish. *I write disposable pop songs, darling*, Freddie used to
say, but don't believe it. What lasts? This wanting (beyond
language!) (more than language can tell!) (a heartbeat!)
outlasts the singer, outlasts us all.

You could find yourself in a desert, swooned in a poison cave. Could be consumed by the brimstone you drove
yourself to find. Could be delirious enough to fly down
instead of up, purblind in the glare, and drown in blood
before turning to stone.

Or you could write yourself a mantra, a password, a
way out. You could put your hand in your pocket and draw
out the key to an abandoned hotel. All its ghosts belong to
you now. Fit your key (bit, shank, barrel) to the lock and
hear the tumblers click.

Now I think Freddie summoned the crowd into being

by writing their part. *Find* (clap clap) *me* (clap clap) *somebody to love, find* (clap clap) *me* (clap clap) *somebody to love.* ("I sing to the realists," Aretha said. "People who accept it like it is.") Handclaps like a steady pulse. You feel it, don't you? Even just reading the words?

So sing it with me, with all the invisibly present people in the arena that night, as Freddie leaps up from the piano and strides out into the middle of the stage, the mike in his hand sending off little screams of feedback. Let yourself go, repeating the words again and again until they turn hypnotic, like the sound of quick breathing or pleasure or sobs, as sweat streams down his neck, as the klieg lights shine, as Roger slams along on the drums, as the crowd pounds its feet—

I want it all. Paper cup of lukewarm tea, crowd chanting in a sweaty muddle. Pearl buttons and knitting needle transformed into music, into glory. There is only this, only now, *keep it going,* Freddie stretching out the vamp, little horse-gallop across the stage, a breath of wind passes over your face, almost more than you can take, *Can anybody find me—*

And he slides onto the piano bench, hands the mike stand to a roadie, takes a swig from the cup—

*Somebody to—*the note vaults way up to the ceiling, above the piano and the band and the crowd, all of us holding our breath, savoring this moment we've waited so long for—

All of us on borrowed time, all of us needing someone. Child, I searched for you everywhere, I haunted the caves, my hand pushed the empty swing and set it crying. I thought I spoke to God but now I know I was praying to you to show yourself. *(Be it as if I were with you.)* Would that I could hold you, could touch for the first time your wrinkled, glowing face—

Love.

Don't feel you have to make conversation, Freddie said to his friends at the end. *It's enough just to have you here.*

When it's too much to take, dare to pray for this: the chance to speak your grief so plain that anyone listening can sing along. You're not alone.

I can do this, I can make this work, part of me dancing unseen in the shadows in my flashing silver cape; I can drop it here onstage, with the love letters and cigarettes and phone numbers and knickers, appointment-reminder cards and temp charts, perfume of sandalwood and rubbing alcohol, empty prescription bottles tinted stage-light amber. Earthy offerings, and dear, darling. No need to carry them any further.

FINALE

The wonder of the world, the beauty and the power,
The shapes of things, their colours, lights and shades—
These I saw.
Look ye also while life lasts.

MOTTO OF MARGARET AND OLAUS MURIE, BIOLOGISTS
AND CONSERVATIONISTS WHOSE MIGHTY EFFORTS HELPED
ESTABLISH THE ARCTIC NATIONAL WILDLIFE REFUGE

Some Memory of Daylight

1. HAIRY JOHN AND THE PUMPKIN FARMER

Little Greenbrier Cove, Tennessee

We forget the sons, even though there had been four of them. We forget the mother, who appears in none of the photographs; maybe she thought such things were foolish. We remember the seven sisters—especially Margaret Jane—and their father, known locally as "Hairy" John Walker for the impressive beard he wore.

He must have been grateful to live to grow that white beard. In the War Between the States, he fought on the Union side—as many mountain people did—and was captured after a month of service and sent to Andersonville as a prisoner of war, where he nearly starved. One night a Southern farmer threw pumpkins over the fence, and he ate them and was saved.

I wonder about this story. If the pumpkins were ripe, it must have been late fall, likely nighttime, because what the farmer was doing went against local practice. It gets chilly during those damp nights in early November, and the farmer's old horse would have steamed from nose and flanks, standing beside the fence palings, waiting. The farmer must have been old himself, or he would have been pressed into service. Was he halt, maimed? Soft in the head? For some reason, he took pity on these men, even though he and his family, if he had one, must have been hungry, too.

Surely some of the pumpkins split from the fall, but John ate them anyway, from flesh to rind to the fibrous stub that had been the vine. He tried to hold back, to press one yielding yellow chunk at a time between his teeth. No good to try to stash some for later, although some of the men did, gray floss of rot spreading across the surface of the meat. John might have saved a seed or two, his little audacity, to plant once he returned home. A wager he made on himself though he wouldn't have called it that. He'd have called it faith.

2. THE BEST-LOOKING POSSUM IN THE WORLD

American Museum of Natural History, Manhattan

Just look at that full coat of white-tipped fur. Body solid and shapely through haunch and rump, clever paws curled around the perch. On his face, an expression of thoughtful interest; in his eyes, a lively gleam. Two teeth snaggle out from his mouth, giving him a mischievous smile, and even his naked, ratlike tail looks pink and healthy. No flaking skin, no sores. Must be rubber.

He's nothing like the possums I've seen in real life, and I've seen my share. Flattened ones on the roadside, matted with old blood, or worse, the newly dead, bellies tight with trapped gas, paws held beseechingly to the sky. Live ones are hardly better, nosing through bowls of cat food in city backyards, mangy coats swarmed by bluebottle flies. (And hard as I try, I can't bring myself to call them "opossums." The "o" is wrong to my ear, vestigial, branching off from the true name "possum" as does—follow me here—the forked penis of the male, built to suit the female possum's forked vagina, entirely appropriate in that case but so beyond my own ken that I cannot fathom it.)

The best-looking possum in the world resides in this diorama, Gray Fox and Opossum, in the Hall of North American Mammals. Behind the glass, it's October in the Smokies, the sky a hard blue, wrinkled mountains painted with crimsons and golds. For the first time ever, the star of the show is a possum. He looks down from his branch at a clueless fox frozen in the act of poking through bushes in search of persimmons. A hearts-a-bustin' plant frames the scene, nubby pods splitting open to reveal bright orange seeds. Real or fabricated? Museum artists replicated anything that could shrivel, so these sourwood leaves—red, as sourwood always is in October—must be very good fakes.

I've always been fascinated by dioramas, and these are the best in the world. For decades, a deep bench of artists poured their lives into recreating specific scenes from near and far in the niches that line the Museum's vast halls. And the best of them all was James Perry Wilson, whose double-grid system for transferring paintings to walls became the gold standard of the discipline. His backgrounds shoehorn vast stretches of land into spaces no bigger than a closet; he was a magician, an engineer, a figure of mystery. I think of him with awe.

As I lean up against the wall, taking notes, other visitors stream past. "Awesome! It's a possum!" a little boy says. "Okay, gray fox," says another, not breaking stride. And why would you when there's so much else competing for your attention? The other dioramas feature lions and okapi, musk oxen and timber wolves, and if that's not your speed, you can examine meteorites, gemstones, or enormous dinosaur skeletons. The walls of the fabulous Hall of Biodiversity are covered with jars full of rare worms and soft-bodied anemones, glass cases of brightly colored beetles, shark skeletons suspended from hooks, and a double helix of seashells that runs from the floor to the ceiling. A giant clam rests on its very own stand. Its sign reads: DO NOT SIT IN THE CLAM SHELL.

But the longer I stand here, the more I like this diorama, one so quiet that even the curators seem to have forgotten it. Inside are animals and plants I recognize, rooted in a rumpled landscape that looks like home. As I walk away, an old man says, "Hey! Look at that fox!" to nobody in particular. Chewing his lip, he stops a spell before moving on to the next attraction.

3. HUNTING THE CHIMNEYS

I stood with my sister on the side of the road, sucking down the sticky air. July in the Smokies—halfway to noon and already the air shivered with heat. We'd grown up just south of here, but this was the first time we'd ever visited the Great Smoky Mountains National Park. Never felt the need. The mountains we had at home were just as good, probably better, because they weren't as crowded. At the trailhead, where a college kid rubbed sunscreen on his girlfriend's thighs, I spotted a pile of recent bear scat, studded with seeds that looked like plastic but proved to be Solomon's seal. Someone threw a Coke bottle into the varmint-proof trash can and slammed it shut with a clang.

Just then, a mother and son staggered up the trail. "Don't hike it!" the boy said. "It's a death trap!" His T-shirt read, NOBODY IS PERFECT, and then, in smaller print, I AM NOBODY.

"We only went, like, a mile," his mother said. "Don't be dramatic."

"Light, beautiful light!" the boy cried. "I haven't seen you in so long!"

But we weren't there to hike. I was hunting the painted background I'd seen in the Museum. In 1952, a team of artists and scientists traveled from Manhattan to Tennessee to research the park for a new diorama. The result of that work, the Gray Fox and Opossum display, was the twenty-ninth and final scene installed in the Hall of North American Mammals. I wanted to compare that time-capsule image of the Smokies to the actual site on which the diorama had been based.

Even in the Museum pictures I'd saved to my camera, the mountains were hard to make out. But standing here on the side of the road, I couldn't find the horizon line at all—too many tulip poplars and beeches in the way. And then, turning around one last time, I saw it. The Chimneys! The bump on the mountain ridge matched up exactly with the background I'd seen. It only worked if you leaned against the stone wall at the trailhead; James Perry Wilson must have set up his easel right here.

I could see why he'd chosen this scene. The hillside drops off sharply—"It's a death trap!"—and that steep slope is the perfect way to hide the tie-in, the seam where the three-dimensional foreground shades into the two-dimensional painted background.

To match this scene with the diorama, eliminate the routed wood sign reading CHIMNEYS 1.9 MILES; erase the trees in the foreground, none of them as old as the college kids with the sunscreen. People skip the Gray Fox and Opossum diorama in part because it's messy; if you're not careful, you can miss the fox for the greenbriers. But this real scene is even more of a jumble. Sun in my eyes, sweat crawling down my back, fumes of bug dope and diesel. We have to go; the family's waiting. But it feels good to rest here, leaning against the low granite wall where the artist worked.

4. PHOTOGRAPH, WALKER SISTERS (1909)

All seven of them wear the serious expressions that most people held in photos taken then, but there's something more to it. Could be the stoic cast of mouth and chin, inherited from their father, or the cool stare Margaret Jane gives the camera. Suggesting compromise to her would be a waste of breath; don't embarrass yourself. Dangerous to draw too many conclusions from the expressions of a single photograph, but I love this one, the severe, witchlike quality of her gaze staring me down from a hundred years ago. She looks like she could get the better of pretty much anyone or anything who crossed her—bear, rattlesnake, park service. They say Franklin D. Roosevelt visited the sisters in their cabin to try and convince them to sell out. I don't believe it; it sounds too perfect to be true, and FDR's legendary charm would have fallen short with Margaret Jane. Smooth-talking city man. You can treat with Churchill and Stalin but not with me. Clamp the ivory cigarette holder between your polished teeth. "If you smoke it will only make two people ill," she used to say, "you and me."

"It is said that the oldest sister, Margaret Jane, never courted with any man," the National Park Service booklet reads. "She apparently selected spinsterhood early in her life and through reasoning and ridicule attempted to influence her sisters in like manner." Yet something about this, too, feels overly simple.

5. FIELD WORK (JAMES PERRY WILSON)

Wilson was an architect by training, and when he lost that job during the Depression, he brought his draftsman's discipline to his work at the Museum. Other painters fudged the background perspectives, but Wilson worked out a meticulous grid system to account for the diorama's curved back wall. He couldn't leave the system alone until he got it right.

As I page through the Museum's archives, I come across photographs of the field models the artists made. I wonder if Wilson savored the clash between the wide world in which he painted and the boot-box scene in which he recreated the same place, compressed by a hundred. How much sharper and crisper the box seemed than life. The road behind him and its noise of passing cars, smell of diesel from the truck groaning upgrade on its way to town, bits of broken glass from a beer bottle, thumbsmear gout of old blood bristling with squirrel fur. Pea gravel under his feet, and mica in small bright shelves. None of this made it into the box. He kept what mattered most—geologic features, time of day, quality of light—and left the rest behind.

6. DIORAMA-CRAFT (VOL. 1)

Start with a landmark that patrons will recognize. The foreground man collects samples of dirt, stones, grasses, and bushes to carry back to New York. But the animal provides the story. Paint hot wax on the lips of the stuffed raccoon. Make leaves of limped acetate, stems of hot wire. The diorama artist must understand the ways in which light behaves.

I read article after article about various methods of fabricating leaves. Suddenly I can't take for granted the magnolia tree outside my window. The leaves are thick, leathery ovals with undersides coated by brown velvet, which can be imitated by dusting the fake leaf with cotton flocking, "applied when the paint is still tacky," then spraying it with fine coats of varnish. This leaf would look like the real thing, but wouldn't sound like it, blowing along the sidewalk with a clatter.

I remember. In the woods behind our house, green onions poked up through rotted leaves. Knobs of algae grew along the bottom of the brook and a sycamore stood beside a gully. Not widely recognizable by a roadside landmark; not known to anyone, really, except me. But made up of smaller, stranger things. Home.

There was a swampy place under the white oak, dark mud in tussocks where straw stood, emerald fronds of groundsel smelling strongly of evergreen. In February, ladyslippers: jade stems lifting little pink lungs. If you crossed the barbed-wire fence you could hike back to the blackberry thicket, the tallest pines, and the trash dump. Soda bottles, shards of plastic, rusted bedsprings. Just looking at that glittering apron of junk felt dangerous. Never any cobalt milk-of-magnesia bottles, just old mayonnaise jars half-full of congealed slime, thick moss clouding the glass. Never ink bottles or arrowheads, or buttons with an eagle pressed on the top. Never a tortoiseshell comb incised with scrolls, or pottery shards washed white and streaked gray, scraped smooth on the inside or raked while still wet with a blunt tool.

I remember a childhood afternoon. The scrawls under the loose bark on the fallen pine looked like hieroglyphs. We sloughed off the bark and ran our fingertips over the loops, some of them still packed with sawdust. Pick them clean with your nail and uncover the inscrutable message you yearn to read. Bore holes, perfectly round. Cul-de-sacs just like the ants make in the old jelly jar. Make sure you put a queen in there; she's the one with wings. Put it in a shady spot and watch them make rooms, just beyond your finger, on the other side of the glass. What wouldn't I save if I could?

7. MARGARET JANE IN THE GARDEN

Crawled slowly down the corn rows, picking stones. Some people said the devil sowed them every winter, a thing she knew to be untrue. In point of fact they floated up through the soil like beans set to boil. She let them lie until spring equinox so they could feed the soil with their minerals. Summer storms fed the garden, too, every time the lightning hit. Manure from the sheepfold she raked into rows and plowed under with the mule. Shed feathers, too; bits of broken clay pots; even her own water, collected in a jug and set in the shade: nitrogen would push the corn to bear. Knew to save butchering blood for the roses—thirty different kinds. Some Mother had planted, others Grandmother, still others she herself.

She saved seeds in twists of newsprint, labeled in her neat hand. Suffer the lilies to come up on their own, year after year, but the garden for herb doctoring she liked to set out as close to last frost as she could, end of April, start of May. Pieplant, catnip, boneset. Horseradish looked after itself. Couldn't help a friendly feeling toward something like that.

She was the oldest, a responsibility she hadn't chosen

but took to heart just the same. Her sisters said she was the fastest at shearing a sheep; reporters (busybodies!) said she was stern. There was a part of herself she kept instinctively close. Hard to feel easy about all these strangers coming down the path. Better the old times, when people wanted what she knew how to provide: horehound syrup for cough, blue cohosh for female trouble, Uncle Charley's liniment for everything from burns to muscle aches to snakebite. It burned like the hinges of hell and she rubbed it on everything that hurt.

That was summertime. In the winter they lived off the food they'd stored: cured pork, blue Hubbard squash, preserves in glass jars held tight with ceramic seal lids, apples from Daddy's trees. Dried cherries. They had never wanted and now, in their later years, Louisa even ran a little to the fat. And here, in winter, Margaret Jane pulled the loom from the loft and tied a skein of wool to its frame. This one would be Double Bowknot. She read the pattern written on plain paper. Slanting numbers penciled in space.

Could be as simple as this: she did not care to leave. Would spend her earthly life here, where first the mountain laurel bloomed and then the rhododendron, where hemlock rooted by the river. In summer, heat baked a sweet hay smell from the grass; persimmons fell, and ants swarmed the skins to suck clear juice. The preserves she made would last all winter. Frost furring the nail heads, ice slick on the springhouse steps. She knew that hollow in a way nobody ever would again. Could still surprise her—the ice storm that turned to thunder, bobcat showing up in the corncrib with a litter of kits. But sang the songs she dreamed of.

Few people can be as faithful to a place as she was, and I haven't been. But I see something in Margaret Jane I recognize. She would not be moved.

8. DIORAMA-CRAFT (VOL. 2)

"Artistic Work Demands Good Tools," says the old taxi-
dermy supply catalog, listing Brain Spoons, Hooks and
Chains, and Bone Snips ("No. 3. HEAVY"). The mam-
malogist for Gray Fox and Opossum would have needed
a Bone Saw like this "keyhole type," with "metal handle,
pistol grip, removable blade. Will cut metal, wood, bones.
A tool you will use every day. A dandy." Surely he had
a Bone Scraper, which he would have "used for scraping
flesh from the skull and other bones" and "taking out eyes,
scraping fat from skins and plugging holes with cotton."
After he'd cured the skin and flensed the bones, sculpted a
form with the caliper's measurements, and made a papier-
mâché model over which he stretched the skin, he would
have needed to sew the skin together with Neck or Hide
Needles, "real he-man needles." Last, he would have tacked
lips and lids in place with Taxidermists' Nails, "extremely
useful . . . where a nail is desired which will not show." But
where did he source the possum's eyes? At the time, the
best glass eyes were made in France and Germany, so he
might have sent away for them, or hired a glassblower to do
some piecework. He would have needed scores of eyes for
the collections tucked away in these halls. For the Bongo
display, tiny mirrors force light to reflect off the deer's eyes,
creating the illusion of life.

9. SOME MEMORY OF DAYLIGHT

Here every detail matters. Plant specialists knew how to
prepare the grasses shipped back from the field, placing
them in deep freeze and then warmth, mimicking spring

to draw out any stowaway bugs. They burned their finger-tips on wires heated to glowing, which they sanded down into ribs for a just-unfolded maple leaf. Poured cool, musty-smelling clay over a green persimmon, broke the mold care-fully apart, and filled it with wax to make a perfect double. They painted and overpainted it to replicate the whitish bloom, partially rubbed off, that the fruit has in life.

"Some memory of daylight we carry with us in daytime, even in halls where no daylight enters," wrote diorama art-ist F. L. Jaques in 1931, "for who has not marveled at how much better the groups look at night when it is impossible for daylight to influence us?" Sometimes I think he had it all, James Perry Wilson, painting the mountains in the sunshine, then bringing his sketches back to the hulking old museum. The "memory of daylight" he pushed from his mind, turning toward the windowless room he would fill with a vista that stretched to the horizon, set at five feet two inches high, the eye-height of the average Museum viewer.

Standing in front of the beautifully worked glass-and-wood frame, you feel in your bones, *I am here*, and, *That is there*. The three-dimensional work between viewer and background—animals, trees and shrubs, ground—is tanta-lizingly close, but untouchable. (The wooden rails, placed shin high, speak of the collective desire to lean in.) There is a great gulf fixed between the viewer and the scene, and the artist is the only one who can bridge the chasm.

The artist wants to deceive, and we want to be deceived. It's an innocent cheat, or is it? The real danger in creat-ing a closed environment lies in the change that your work imposes on its viewers. Done right, you'll prevent them from seeing the real thing on its own terms. When I walked through the Museum with Stephen Quinn, cura-tor and historian, one of the first things he told me about was his trip to the Lake Kivu volcanoes in the Democratic Republic of the Congo, where Carl Akeley, famous taxidermist, had sited the Mountain Gorilla diorama and later died. Stephen had been on an expedition charged with the difficult task of locating the clearing portrayed in the diorama. "Then there we were," he said, "and I looked back, and there was the background." What he said struck me; not "Mount Mikeno," but "the painting of it." But if the artist decides not to recreate the place at all, we lose even a shadow version of reality and are left with nothing.

I stare at archival photographs of Wilson painting the prairie in the Museum. The scale is all wrong; Wilson is a giant next to the flat-topped mesas in the background. But it's not just that. From sky to ground, he's creating a world, God with nine tubes of paint. "His dark shades contained no black," I read. From three tubes of blue, he made shades of sky that melt into each other so well that you can't tell where one color begins and the next ends. To stipple the margins, he used a brush made of badger hair.

*

When Wilson made the trip to Tennessee in 1952, the Museum's exhibits department was at high tide. Expeditions set out constantly. Scientists and artists flew overseas, booked passage on ships, or packed the Museum station wagon with gear: barrels and shovels, palettes and paint, calipers, hacksaws, tape measures, razor knives, pulp paper for pressing flowers and leaves, jars of formaldehyde.

But things were changing. With the advent of motion pictures and television, dioramas felt old-fashioned. Frank Chapman's famous Pelican Island display that helped convince Theodore Roosevelt to set aside the first federal bird reserve in 1903 was scrapped in 1959. It grieves me to imagine it in the trash, or headed for the city dump on an open scow under a shrieking cloud of gulls. Making this diorama was either an act of faith that what they were doing could still matter, or else a memory under glass. Possibly both.

Back in the Museum archives, I found a photo titled *Buffalo in Cellophane*. The stuffed animal stands on a pallet, head bent down to where grass should be. Sticks hold the sheets of cellophane away from his shoulder and haunch. He's positioned in the niche that will become the finished diorama; a penciled grid marks the wall behind him with low hills and plateaus. Another photo shows Wilson's visit to the Overland Trail for the diorama's field studies. He's set up his easel on the flat ground beside the Museum's truck, a '37 Ford. Not a tree in sight. The foreground man, George Petersen, holds a large cardboard box, ready to be filled with shrubs and grasses; a box on the ground holds a big clump of sagebrush. No animals visible in the photograph, no other people; these could be the last two men on Earth, taking careful notes to record what they have seen.

10. AGAINST COLD FEET

In this late picture, Louisa and Caroline pose near their cabin with a sturdy little dog. Neither of them great beauties, nor ever had been, and even in their own time people thought them backward and strange. But under their hands the bee balm thrived, and the hives and the honey, and the bachelor's buttons.

When their nephews enlisted, the women sheared their sheep, carded the wool, knitted socks from the yarn, and mailed the socks overseas. Said Louisa, "We don't aim for any of our folks to have cold feet, no matter where they are." Those socks must have contained bits of grass from the yard behind the cabin. They removed what they could but surely some specks remained, snared in the knots.

They knew where all their things came from. They papered their cabin with magazine pictures they liked and "scalded the walls" once a year. The only wood that's cleaner is what still grows in the ground, and what with worm and rot even that's no sure thing. Except for persimmon, kin to ebony, that grows hard and strong and slow.

In 1952, the year Museum artists visited the Smokies, reporter John O'Reilly wrote, "More visitors come here than to any other national park. Last year there were 2,300,000 visitors. . . . At times the roads were as jammed as the West Side Highway in Manhattan." Not long after that, Margaret Jane and Louisa wrote a letter to the park superintendent, asking him to take down the sign to their house. "We are not able to do our Work and receive so many visitors," Louisa said, "and can't make our souvenirs to sell like we once did and people will be expecting us to have them." Apple cakes, dolls, handwritten copies of Louisa's poetry. "I write poems to sell but can't write very well," she said. "I used to write of winter but I haven't been able to do much for the two last ones."

✳

By now, sixty years later, annual visitation to the Great Smoky Mountains National Park has nearly quadrupled; this is still the most visited of all the national parks. So as you drive along the Parkway, you have plenty of time to notice things: an upside-down mansion with upside-down palm trees hanging from its porch; a life-sized *Titanic,* chopped in half, with a fiberglass iceberg; go-kart tracks, wedding chapels, a nameless store that can be entered only by walking through a giant shark's mouth. Ease on up to the next red light, trying not to rear-end the truck in front of you. You have to turn on the AC. You have to wait for a table. Because some of the neon letters are burned out, the restaurant sign reads, R UESDAY, which is appropriate, because you are beginning to regret the day you ever decided to visit.

MORE OUTDOORS FOR YOUR MONEY, say the signs at the camping store, where you can play a shooting game for fifty cents. When you hit the moonshine still, it pings, and when you hit the outhouse door, it flies open and a canned voice hollers. A glossy photograph of Ramsey Cascades, a pretty waterfall on the Little Pigeon, covers the lobby Coke machine.

What would Margaret Jane think of the billboard advertising HATFIELD AND MCCOY dinner theater? MAKE EATIN' FUN! it demands. The patriarch wears a battered folding hat and a long white beard. Next to him, a frowning granny raises her rolling pin in a threatening pose. Hardly does justice to the kind of woman who could dispose of any weasel foolish enough to try to steal a hen from her henhouse, as the Walker matriarch once did: "She calmly walked to the wash tub and thrust her hand, weasel and all, under water. It drowned in water stained by [her] blood. She commented that she knew 'sooner or later, it would turn loose.'" What would Hairy John, Union soldier, make of these ball caps with REBEL stitched across the front? Stacked in the gift shop like cordwood, they say, REBEL REBEL REBEL.

"We enjoyed meeting so many nice people from different places from every state in the union and many outside," wrote Louisa in 1953, "but we want to rest a while it is too much work for us now."

Too easy to look back and call those the good old days. The Walker sisters never even had an outhouse; Margaret Jane said other people would see it and know what it was for, and that would have embarrassed her. But she never scrubbed a floor for anyone other than herself, and at the end, I'm glad she took down the sign that read VISITORS WELCOME.

11. DIORAMA-CRAFT (SOME CHALLENGES)

To make a diorama is to try to make a memory physical, to embody the sense impressions and emotions of a single caught moment. You'll never pass this way again.

Viewed in this light, the dioramas start to seem almost desperate in their dogged determination to save something of a world that must always be under siege. Here's a desert, a swamp, a forest: I saved this. But without the living place on which it's based, the diorama is a useless totem. Is this all we have left, scenes salted away in a dark hall?

Something of the Gray Fox and Opossum diorama died with James Perry Wilson in 1976. When he looked at the finished scene, did he feel hot wind pulling sweat from his pores, the tight waistband of his dark puttees? The pure, surprising pain of a wasp sting, the crackle in the grass as locusts leapt out of his way?

12. YOUR OWN PARTICULAR SOIL

To find the Walker Sisters Home, follow the trail from their childhood schoolhouse. Hairy John helped build it, and families from all over the mountain used to come here for church on Sunday and schooling during the week. Something of the two uses remains. There's something unyielding about the building, in a poplar kind of way, a wood that ages well and won't rot, not as soft as pine nor as hard as locust. Good choice for the big square beams overhead. Looking up at the lintel, I can see the adze scars where the men stripped the log.

We hike the trail to the cabin, passing crested irises and Little Brier Creek. Crows yell in the trees and wood-peckers drum, but we can't see them. When the trail hooks right, I think of the girls: this had been their path home. Sometimes they hardly noticed, engaged in thought or conversation, but from childhood to old age, this was the scene that welcomed them back.

Not exactly like this, of course. The sheep are long gone, but you can see where the chickens roosted in the cool springhouse. The gardens have run to grass, but along the edge of the field lilies grow, likely from bulbs the Walkers would have set out, multiplied in the years the house has sat idle. Up on a rise sits the toolshed, a strap from some extinct machine still hanging from a rusty nail. Red clay stains the fieldstones Hairy John stacked to make the chimney. A lilac bush grows on a knoll. When it bloomed, its pale smell would have drifted sweetly into the house through that living-room window.

I step inside the cabin to stand in the living room, and I'm stunned to find scraps of old newspapers still pasted to the puncheon walls. I didn't think there would be any-thing left by now. I lean close, reading the papers in the dim light. Just scraps, so trying to make sense of them is like listening to a fading radio signal. "The route we took was the . . . garden of Eden," one fragment says. "Cold springs of water . . . crystals hanging from the sides . . . truly marvelous."

Most of the clippings seem to come from a magazine called *Successful Farming*. Headlines include "Value of Fish Meal," "Pistons Have Stuck," and "Fighting an Invisible Foe: The Last Days of Bovine Tuberculosis." Reading these feels like sifting through a stranger's mail. "This saves the work," I read. "Brighten up your home," says another piece, "lighten your work. No more hard rubbing and scrub." Did the girls ever shake their heads and laugh? "Your own particular soil," I read. "If your home happens to be situated on sand, why waste time, money and patience trying to raise the same kind of shrubs as does your friend?" On the wall beside the window, where Father and Mother's bed used to sit, there's an article titled "Meredith Jersey Farm Produces Silver Medal Cow: Tycoon's Fixy Maid a Show Cow As Well As a Producer." Fresh bird droppings streak the crumbling newsprint.

I'm strangely moved by these little scraps, even though I doubt they had much significance for the sisters. Their eyes must have been tired, and probably they didn't scald their walls each and every spring like before. The newspapers on the wall became the container in which their hours were held. List of faraway cities, diagrams for how to put chains on a tire. Decorative knowledge they were too wealthy to fool with.

Sometimes, back in the Museum, artists left newspapers in the habitat displays to document the date they finished construction. You can't see them, looking in, but the people who work there sometimes discover these secret gifts. No matter where you find it, an old crumpled newspaper gives off a whiff of time's passage. And once, one of the curators found a homemade measuring stick that

James Perry Wilson had used to mark the curved backgrounds. He had tucked it in the diorama where visitors
couldn't see, the key to his secret, a relic, a tick-marked
walking stick. With it he translated miles of sight lines
into tiny closets. He slipped a world into a bottle, where it
expanded against the glass but couldn't escape. Sealed the
door behind him and stuffed steel wool in the breathing
tube to keep out mice.

✳

Think how it might have been on a day like today. The
sisters sitting in the wide-planked living room on a damp
afternoon in late spring, fireplace lit to take off the chill.
Lick of green flame hovering close to the hickory and a
pop and a hiss when the wood releases old rain.

A ladder stands in the back corner and I climb up it
to look around the loft, where sun shines down through
chinks in the shingles. The ladder is plenty sturdy, not a
bit of wobble to it, and its wood is as smooth as the inside
of your neck from all the palms that have gripped it over
the years.

And as I stand there, suspended between loft and floor,
I realize that for me, this ladder is the tie-in, the place where
the three-dimensional sculpture touches, and becomes
part of, the two-dimensional painted background. This is
the border where the illusion works, these polished rungs
of the ladder. The cabin feels not haunted, but alive.

In one photograph taken of her, Margaret Jane smiles
broadly, and her eyes are bright, hopeful, even friendly.
Maybe she mellowed near the end. She died in 1962, aged
eighty-two. Louisa, the last of the sisters, followed in 1964.
I wonder what it must have been like for her, living those
last months alone in a house that had always been shared.

After Louisa died, the National Park Service took possession of the cabin and all its furnishings. I paged through the list. Among many other things, the Walker sisters had owned a "rifle," a "trunk," and a "chair (rocker), split bottom," made by their father. A "yoke for roguish cow," a "shoe repair 'chisel,'" glass pharmacy bottles, and a pair of crutches. The men's brogans they'd worn. In the loft over the main rooms, "when asked what was stored there, one source said, 'Lord, everything.'"

*

After we leave the cabin and drive home, I'm researching the Walker sisters when I discover an awful document: architect's blueprints for restoration and stabilization of the cabin, circa 1969. Remember, at that point the house had been empty for only five years. But the Smokies have a moist climate with snowy winters and hot summers, and the rain only needs a toehold to pull down a house.

I knew something bad was coming when I read, under the heading WORKMANSHIP, "The restored structure shall retain the primitive character of the original building." When replacement wood was needed, the workers were to use a special saw to recreate the adze marks that Hairy John had made. New nails had to be fabricated the old-fashioned way, one at a time, with flatter shafts than the round wire-cut nails of the present day. I was afraid to read on. Of the newspapers on the walls, the document recommended, "Salvage as much of the original covering material as possible for reuse and reference. Recover the walls in accordance with the photographs with similar material of the same historic period." This was getting complicated. And the final insult, "All new covering shall be stained to match in color the reused existing material."

There was a subheading just for "LADDER: Repair and refasten." My mouth was agape, my heart crushed—I had been living a lie! "If the public is to be allowed access to the garret," I read, "replace the existing ladder with a stronger and safer reproduction."

I called my sister, who took the long view. "Clearly the park wants the visitor to have the experience of seeing the cabin and believing in it," she said. "They value that experience, and they value the cabin. They want to preserve them." I knew she was right, and my argument wasn't with preservation, but with the idea that I had been lied to. I thought I was really seeing these newspaper scraps, little archaeological moments that the archivists hadn't cataloged. I didn't know what to feel anymore. How could I trust my senses?

The cabin had become like a habitat display for me. I knew there was an element of fakery to it, yet it drew me in. What's real, and what's not? Newspapers left inside displays for curators to find. A clue, a bit of non-canonical "trash." Yet I value it.

What moment do we privilege as the real one? Think of the photo of Dad before he shipped out to Vietnam. So skinny, so young. He does not look as fully himself, to my eyes, as when I remember him from growing up. So, too, the cabin is privileging, say, 1936. Why then and not 1962, with its roll of roofing that Louisa tacked up to keep the rain out? Which hen nest should we recreate? Yet consider the swallow's nest in the kitchen. The droppings that streak the wall in the living-bedroom. Fresh, real, of this very moment.

Later, when I asked the park archivist about the cabins, she told me that the newspaper bits likely are original after all. Thanks to budget constraints, most of the recommendations the architect made were never implemented. We think; we can't know for sure.

I don't want to know. Draw me in; dazzle me with detail, so I can imagine myself inhabiting life after life. We live in the tie-in, the eye-fooling line between past and future. The tie-in looks like home.

13. *THE SACRED HARP* (1844)

The singers sit in an open square and take turns to lead. The music responds to the plain wood walls and presses against them, rolls up to the roof. Four-part harmony, and if I call it "otherworldly" don't mistake it for satin robes beyond a crystal sea. Sinew and scar, old blood. Sore feet and bowed limbs, a hard debt put to paid.

They're singing "Nearer, My God, to Thee," and it's one I know. But I like it best when they aren't singing the words. At the very beginning of a song, they sing with *fa so la* syllables, to get a feel for the song and for each other. The banks of the river channel the current that shifts them. Today began as an arbitrary date on a calendar: second Sunday in July, first weekend in August. But by the time they make it to the chorus, we're not in this country anymore, nor this age.

Don't think Margaret Jane didn't know what she was giving up by claiming her one inimitable life. Sister Caroline married; her husband took the family photographs, and joked to a reporter from the *Saturday Evening Post,* "Reckon I'm about the only man that had courage to bust into that family, or else the rest of them girls got discouraged when they couldn't get me and just quit." Margaret Jane traveled to church conventions around the state, ordered needles and nails from catalogs. She knew something of the world beyond but chose to root here, to know her sisters' bodies as she knew her own, binding and plastering sore joints;

plucking barbs from stung palms; washing and combing long hair after it dried in the sun. Together they wove cloth for each other's dresses from sheep that shied if they saw anyone wearing pants.

No piano or organ, no pitch pipe or tuning fork. No cushions, stained glass, or wall hangings. *I've felt that music so strong,* I heard one boy say, *it was like you could almost stand up and walk on it.* Some nights they sang the old songs together at home. Spot of light glowing in a knothole. Poplar planks their daddy had planed and pegged. No matter how raw the night, the roof he'd raised sheltered them, and the apple cakes Mother had taught them to bake were still the pride of Little Greenbrier. It wasn't that Margaret Jane valued some earlier day more than the blessed present in which she now found herself. More that the homemade tools the antique dealers badgered her to sell were things she still used. "We'd have the money," sister Martha said, "but what would we work with?"

After the last sister passed, the Park Service had the notion to have a ranger live on-site in the cabin, as the sisters themselves had lived. This idea seems never to have come to fruition, and I'm glad of it. Playacting someone else's life, too bound by its scores of dicta. Impossible to capture the slow breathing of a sister asleep, huckleberry crumble made from wild warm August fruit, the poke bonnet Margaret Jane pieced and stitched and hung on its peg, linsey-woolsey chin straps hanging free.

14. WHAT KIND OF MOMENT

By the time I left the Museum, the afternoon was broiling, and I made for the subway. The walls at that stop were inlaid with mosaic creatures in bright thumbnails of glass: grasshopper, frog, turtle, giant cockroach. "Stand clear of the closing doors, please!" said the voice, and we were off, passing through interesting country, dark walls and red lights, train cars swinging right and left. The connecting springs clipped to their loops jounced, and I caught flashes of other people in other trains, then the cold white lights of the platform.

I got off the train, pushed through the turnstile, and was on my way toward the street when the girls in front of me stopped so short I almost banged into them. What was the holdup? Then we all looked up toward the sky, where rain poured down. "This never happens!" the woman behind me said, dropping her wheeled suitcase with a click. I leaned against the wall, just out of the weather, and within a few minutes a crowd had gathered. Wet people rushing down the steps threaded their way through the crush. "This weather is *atro*cious," a kid behind me said. "If you go out now, you'll be *soaked* to the *skin*." A German-speaking family debated what to do, mother tidily pregnant, father holding a foldout map, boys in matching red shirts. The hallway grew moist and warm. A young guy carrying a new broom and a multipack of paper towels slid past me and headed up into the storm. A woman in a purple burnout-velvet scarf sighed and leaned against the wall under faded graffiti that said TEEZ. A woman holding a bouquet of yellow irises in a plastic cone made for the staircase and I watched her go, the muscles in her calves flexing, step by careful step.

"It's just water," said a soaked man hustling down from Fourth Street, the crowd stretching further back now than I could see. "Ha! All backed up!" A grinning boy followed him, wearing a clear plastic garbage bag as a poncho with a slit over his face so he could breathe. He peeled it off, looking satisfied. "This is the worst *possible* thing for my service," said the girl beside me, tapping on her phone as filthy puddles collected on the floor. A man wearing a helmet leaned in close, trying to keep his bicycle out of the way of the people hurrying down the stairs. One of the boys in back, he of the *atro*cious weather, yelled, "Do you *know* what kind of moment this is? Do you KNOW what kind of moment this is?" Then he tore off his T-shirt, vaulted up the steps, and shouted, "It's the kind of moment where you run out in the rain and get all wet!"

Later, walking up Bleecker, I'll hear a fight explode behind me, a cabbie yelling at a bus driver: "What the fuck, why you hit me? Why you do that, asshole?" Stormwater swirls along the curb and my face burns with blood and I, hoof it, wet-footed, past expertly parked cars and tagged light boxes on my way toward my friends, waiting for me by the Astor Place Cube somewhere in the future, along with the Gideon Bible in the nightstand with a torn-to-scraps dollar bill tucked between Psalms 34 and 35 ("The poor man cried, and the Lord heard him"); toward the airport security line and television monitors that read WHY WHY WHY; and later still toward the slow drive down a Tennessee gravel road, where we'll stop to ease our feet in the cold, clear current of the Little Pigeon, next to a still life of wilted daisies and ferns and toadstools, spread out on a flat stone like an offering.

But here, now, do you know what kind of moment this is? "Good thing we don't have any place to be," the girl says, staring at her phone, crammed together with a bunch of strangers in a little space not really large enough for all it has to hold. Once the rain lets up, we'll climb the steps into the open air under a sky that's higher than I remembered, and if you walked down those stairs today there'd be nothing to show how it used to be. A receipt for a package of paper towels, a torn MetroCard, an apple core. Lord, everything.

NOTES AND ACKNOWLEDGMENTS

After the years it has taken me to complete this book, it is a real joy for me to be able to thank some of the many people and sources who have helped me with this material.

OVERTURE

What Looks Like Mad Disorder: I wrote this essay while serving as the Kenan Visiting Writer at the University of North Carolina at Chapel Hill. I thank the creative writing program there for its support. Thanks, too, to Jeff Bernard and Julie Chisholm for their hospitality on the California junket.

Thanks to Anna Lena Phillips and Emily Louise Smith for their thoughtful editing of the piece for *Ecotone*.

An important natural-history source, intertwined with biblical quotations, was *The Medieval Book of Birds: Hugh of Fouilloy's Aviarium*, translated by Willene B. Clark (Binghamton: Medieval and Renaissance Texts and Studies, 1992).

For more about earthquakes, specifically the strange actions of animals right before an event, see Motoji Ikeya's *Earthquakes and Animals: From Folk Legends to Science*. See also Gladys Hansen and Emmet Condon's *Denial of Disaster: The Untold Story and Photographs of the San Francisco Earthquake of 1906* for more about governmental response to the quake. This book also includes stunning newspaper photos from the time.

For more about spiders, refer to Jean-Henri Fabre's *The Life of the Spider*, translated by Alexander Teixeira de Mattos. (Fabre's *The Life of the Fly*, *The Mason-Bees*, and *Hunting Wasps* also make for lively reading.)

One of my favorite sources was Amos J. Loveday Jr.'s *The Rise and Decline of the American Cut Nail Industry: A Study of the Interrelationships of Technology, Business Organization, and Management Techniques*. Pick up a nail and see the world reflected there.

"What will it profit a man if he gain the whole world, and lose his own soul?": see Mark 8:36.

ACT ONE

Damn Cold in February: Thanks to Ander Monson, who chose this essay for *DIAGRAM*. The Nevada Test Site Oral History Project, administered by the University of Nevada, Las Vegas, was invaluable to me for this piece. Words don't do justice to the debt we owe to the atomic veterans and the historians who interviewed them. Thank you.

I relied on John Goldrosen and John Beecher's excellent *Remembering Buddy: The Definitive Biography of Buddy Holly* (New York: Da Capo, 2001) for details and quotations. The Crickets appeared on *The Arthur Murray Party* on December 29, 1957.

Special thanks to Tess; our long walks at St. George helped me work out the connections. I miss you.

Beautiful Beyond Belief: Thanks to Tara Rae Miner, who ably edited this essay before it appeared in *Orion*. Her help was instrumental in making the piece what it became. Thanks to my parents, Earl and Margie Tevis, for taking me to Rock City the first time, and to Richard and Sue Bernardy for taking me back.

For a useful history of grottoes and other follies, see

Hazelle Jackson's *Shell Houses and Grottoes* (Buckinghamshire: Shire, 2001). I also relied on Naomi Miller's *Heavenly Caves: Reflections on the Garden Grotto* (New York: George Braziller, 1982).

My thanks to Karen Baker, of Lookout Mountain, for more information about the gardens and about Clark Byers, barn painter. Anita Armstrong Capps's *See Rock City Barns: A Tennessee Tradition* (Lookout Mountain: See Rock City, 1996) provided particulars about individual barns.

A visit to the National Museum of Nuclear Science and History in Albuquerque, New Mexico, provided key historical context for this piece. I am indebted to Ferenc Morton Szasz's *The Day the Sun Rose Twice: The Story of the Trinity Site Nuclear Explosion, July 16, 1945* (Albuquerque: University of New Mexico Press, 1984) for its clear explanation of the Trinity project. See also "New Mexico's Atomic Bomb Crater," *Life*, September 24, 1945. See also *The Manhattan Project: A Secret Wartime Mission* (Carlisle: Discovery Enterprises, 1995) edited by Kenneth M. Deitch—concise and helpful.

No need to watch a horror movie when you can read *Survival Under Atomic Attack: The Official U.S. Government Booklet* (Washington, DC: US Government Printing Office, 1950).

For more about the Battle Above the Clouds, refer to B. F. Taylor's *Mission Ridge and Lookout Mountain with Pictures of Life in Camp and Field* (New York: Appleton & Company, 1872). This book provides a real sense of Taylor's time embedded with the Union army. Dedication page: "To The Boys in Blue this little package of letters is respectfully inscribed."

To learn more about tobacco farming, visit the Duke Homestead in Durham, North Carolina.

"You will beg the mountains to cover you, and the rocks

to hide you": see Hosea 10:8, Luke 23:30, and Revelation 6:16.

Ten Years You Own It: Thanks to Adam Kullberg, who chose this essay for *Terrain*. Thanks to David and Diantha LaVine for taking me to the Salton Sea, and circling back to make sure I got the details exactly right, despite a massive tilapia die-off.

Backstage with John the Beloved Disciple: Thanks to Darren Lawson for taking the time to explain *tableau vivant* to me, and for allowing me to go backstage and see the work as it happened. Thanks to Alison Gray for demonstrating her wigmaking skills.

Something Like the Fire: Thank you to my students in Atomic Literature, Spring 2011. Your discoveries fueled my own. A trip to the National Atomic Testing Museum, in Las Vegas, Nevada, provided particulars and inspiration. I also referred to *Atmospheric Nuclear Weapons Testing: 1951-1993* (Washington, DC: US Department of Energy, 2006).

The Measure of My Days (Buddy Holly Reprise): Thank you to Jenny Willoughby and Kurt Gegenhuber, boon companions, adventurers, and wonderful writers, for driving me to Clear Lake and points beyond (Manly; Forest City). Thank you to Phyllis Willis, fairy godmother of Fertile, Iowa, for leading us to the crash site.

To learn more about pianomaking, see Steinway and sons "The Making of a Steinway."

ACT TWO

Warp and Weft: Thank you to Steve Gailey and Rená Welzbacher for sharing their mill stories with me. Steve Richardson at the Furman University Library helped with sources and shared his encyclopedic knowledge about this part of our state's history. Bill Ranson let me tag along on his tour of the Greenville Crescent. Thanks to Tom and Popie Whitted for taking the time to show me around the Easley Mill. Special thanks to Brad Raines, true friend and knower of every back road in the upstate.

I relied on *Easley Mill Memories: 1900-1991*, edited by Tony Owens (Easley: Easley Mills Reunion Committee, 1991) for particulars about the mill I visited. Wilt Browning's *Linthead: Growing Up in a Carolina Cotton Mill Village* (Asheboro: Down Home Press, 1990) focuses on life in Easley during the 1940s and 1950s. *Like a Family: The Making of a Southern Cotton Mill World* (Chapel Hill: University of North Carolina Press, 1987) edited by Hall, Leloudis, Korstad, et al. was a foundational piece of scholarship for me. The oral histories and context collected there provide an overall picture of what life on the mill hill was like. The excellent *Textile Town: Spartanburg County, South Carolina*, edited by Betsy Wakefield Teter (Spartanburg: Hub City Writers Project, 2002) provided invaluable context for upstate textile mill communities.

For more about mill smokestacks, refer to the fascinating Alphons Custodis Chimney Construction Company's *Radial Brick Chimneys* booklet (New York: 1924). I am in awe of what these masons created—and the integrity that many of these chimneys still display.

"The Lord can raise up these stones to give praise": see Luke 19:40.

Coathook in an Empty Schoolhouse: Thanks to Furman University for supporting the research travel to fading railroad towns in North Dakota. Thanks to Lauren Cobb and Sean Hill for risking trespassing charges with us.

The Scissorman: Thanks to Ralph E. Lee, the Scissorman, who let me tag along on two separate occasions and graciously answered scores of questions about his job. Thanks to Mary Alice Kirkpatrick, research companion, who rode shotgun and helped me keep pace with the Scissorman's van.

Hammer Price (Song of the Auctioneer): Thanks to Mike Hendrix for taking the time to explain the finer points of auctioneering to me. Our conversation was a real pleasure.

Reader, do yourself a favor and listen to Flatt & Scruggs play "Foggy Mountain Breakdown."

Pacing the Siege Floor: Thanks to Bev Hogue of Marietta College, Ohio, for making it possible for me to visit Fenton while it was still open. Thanks to Jolene Powell, artist at Marietta College, for visiting the Marble King factory with me, and sharing her amazing photographs of the cullet piles there. For more glass history see E. William Fairfield's *Fire and Sand: The History of the Libbey-Owens Sheet Glass Company* (Cleveland: Lezius-Hiles, 1960).

ACT THREE

What the Body Knows: Thanks to Furman University for supporting the research travel for this essay. Thanks to Terrell Dixon of Houston, Texas, for giving me the idea to visit the Arctic National Wildlife Refuge in the first place. Thanks to Amy Leland, gifted midwife. Thanks to Dirk Nickisch and Danielle Tirrell of Coyote Air, Coldfoot, Alaska. Thanks to Jennifer Sahn for her thoughtful editing of this piece before it appeared in *Orion*.

Special thanks to Carl Donohue of Expeditions Alaska, best damn guide in the land.

For more about the plants and mosses of Alaska, refer to *Plants of the Western Boreal Forest and Aspen Parkland,* by Derek Johnson, Linda Kershaw, Andy MacKinnon, and Jim Pojar (Edmonton, AB: Lone Pine Publishing, 1995). Trevor Goward, lichenologist, delighted me at every turn.

The World Is On Fire: The Cave of the Apocalypse:
Section 6: see Revelation 1:9, 10.

Section 7: Johnny Cash, "The Man Comes Around."

Section 8: see Psalms 90:12.

Section 10: see Revelation 10:9. The Melville quote is from Chapter 132 of *Moby-Dick*, "The Symphony" (New York: Norton, 1999).

Section 11: see Revelation 21:4 and Revelation 1:11.

For more about the lives of the saints, refer to Voraigne's *The Golden Legend* (Hammersmith: Kelmscott Press, 1892).

Touch the Bones: For more about La Specola, refer to *Encyclopaedia Anatomica: Museo La Specola Florence* by Monika von Düring and Marta Poggesi (Cologne: Taschen, 2006).

I am also indebted to *The Anatomical Waxes of La Specola*, by Rumy Hilloowala, translated and edited by Joseph Renahan (Florence: Arnaud, 1995).

For more about the Capuchin Monastery in Rome, refer to *The Cemetery Crypt*, by Father Rinaldo Cordovani (Rome: Gangemi Editore, 2012). My thanks to Bill Aarnes for bringing a copy back from Italy for me.

For more about hair jewelry, refer to Helen Sheumaker's excellent *Love Entwined: The Curious History of Hairwork in America* (Philadelphia: University of Pennsylvania Press, 2007).

Special thanks to Renée Zitkloff.

Somebody to Love: Thanks to Kendall Driscoll for explaining the music theory behind the song. Her help was invaluable.

Lorrie Moore's "People Like That Are the Only People Here: Canonical Babbling in Peed Onk" appeared in *Birds of America* (New York: Picador, 1999).

For the full text of Jonh Ingham's delicious profile on Queen, see "A Riot at the Opera: Queen Triumphant,"

Sounds, November 29, 1975. I referred to Phil Sutcliffe's compendium, *Queen: The Ultimate Illustrated History of the Crown Kings of Rock* (Minneapolis: Voyageur Press, 2009) for details about Brian May's "Red Special" guitar, as well as the band's early years.

Kahlil Gibran, from *The Prophet* (New York: Knopf, 1952): "The deeper that sorrow carves into your being the more joy you can contain. Is not the cup that holds your wine the very cup that was burned in the potter's oven?"

FINALE

Some Memory of Daylight: Thanks to Stephen Quinn, former curator at the American Museum of Natural History, for showing me around backstage and answering my many questions. His excellent *Windows on Nature: The Great Habitat Dioramas of the American Museum of Natural History* (New York: Abrams, 2006) gave me the idea for this essay. I also referred to Karen Wonders's fine *Habitat Dioramas: Illusions of Wilderness in Museums of Natural History* (Uppsala: Almqvist & Wiksell, 1993). Thanks to Mai Qaraman for her help in the museum archives.

Thanks to the Andrew W. Mellon Foundation, via Furman University's Shi Center for Sustainability, for the funding that allowed this research travel to take place. Thanks to Julie Goolsby for leading us around town like a boss. Thanks to Diantha LaVine for helping me find the sites in the Smokies. Thanks to Annette Hartigan, formerly of the National Park Service, for answering so many of my questions about the Walker sisters.

For more about the Walker sisters, see John Maloney's "Time Stood Still in the Smokies," *Saturday Evening Post,* April 27, 1946. See also Rose Houk's *The Walker Sisters of Little Greenbrier* (Gatlingburg: Great Smoky Mountains Association, 2005). I also referred to Robert R. Madden and T. Russell Jones's *Mountain Home: The Walker Family Farmstead* (Washington, DC: National Park Service, US Department of Interior, 1977).

Some of these essays have appeared previously in the following magazines:

"Beautiful Beyond Belief: Rock City and Other Fairy Tales of the Atomic Age" and "What the Body Knows" appeared in *Orion*.

"Damn Cold in February: Buddy Holly, View-Master, and the A-Bomb" appeared in *DIAGRAM*.

"Brain Sweat and Blueprints," "The Scissorman," and "Girl Power: Ode to the Demolition Derby" appeared in *Oxford American*.

"Ten Years You Own It" appeared in *Terrain*.

"What Looks Like Mad Disorder: The Sarah Winchester House" appeared in *Ecotone*.

Thanks to everyone who sustained, encouraged, read, and wandered with me during the writing of this book. Gilbert Allen, keen of eye and generous of heart. Hannah Auringer. Charles Baxter. Jim Cihlar. Lisa Colby. Valerie Jean Conner and Stan Makielski. All my Furman compatriots. Caroline Goforth. Julie Goolsby. Laura Flynn. Renata Golden. Braden Kerwin. Sarah Lageman. Amy Leach. Kim Meyer. Rachel Moritz. Juliet Patterson. Steve Gailey, Durham Hunt, and Rulinda Price, research librarians at the South Carolina Room, Greenville County Library. Mike Rollin. Lynne Shackelford.

Special thanks to Earl Tevis, automotive consultant and guru, for identifying all of the cars in this book—of which there are a fair number. Special thanks to Margie

Tevis, founder of Camp Grandma Margie, which allowed me extra time to write.

Particular thanks to everyone at Milkweed Editions, especially Daniel Slager and Patrick Thomas. Your love for books heartens me and gives me hope. Thanks to Casey O'Neil and Connor Lane for tirelessly spreading the good word.

Thank you, Caroline. You are a true road warrior with the spirit of adventure and a thousand-yard stare. Research travel—and, come to think of it, pretty much everything else—is so much better with you along for the ride.

Thank you, David, for reading everything first and often, for shouldering the load at home so I could finish, for being ready for anything, for staying strong. From Apalach to Brownlow Point, Bombay Beach to Weeki Wachee, from Florence to Rome and all the way home, this is for you most of all.

Formerly a park ranger, factory worker, and seller of cemetery plots, JONI TEVIS is author of the acclaimed book of essays, The Wet Collection. Her nonfiction has been published in *Oxford American*, the *Bellingham Review*, *Shenandoah*, *Gulf Coast*, and *Orion*. She currently teaches literature and creative writing at Furman University in Greenville, SC, where she also lives.

Interior design by Mary Austin Speaker
Typeset in Baskerville

English type founder, stonecutter, and letter designer John Baskerville (1706-1775) began his career as a headstone engraver, snuff-box japanner and writing master before starting his printing business. The first book Baskerville printed took seven years to produce, during which time he was responsible for major innovations in press construction, ink, papermaking and letter design. His work was admired by Fournier, Bodoni and Benjamin Franklin, among others, and revived in the 1920s by Bruce Rogers.